D0908707

ANNALS OF COMMUNISM

Each volume in the series Annals of Communism will publish selected and previously inaccessible documents from former Soviet state and party archives in the framework of a narrative text that focuses on a particular topic in the history of Soviet and international communism. Separate English and Russian editions will be prepared. Russian and American scholars work together to prepare the documents for each volume. Documents are chosen not for their support of any single interpretation but for their particular historical importance or their general value in deepening understanding and facilitating discussion. The volumes are designed to be useful to students, scholars, and interested general readers.

The Unknown Lenin

From the Secret Archive

Edited by Richard Pipes

With the assistance of David Brandenberger

Basic translation of Russian documents by
Catherine A. Fitzpatrick

Yale University Press

New Haven and London

This volume has been prepared with the active support of the Russian Center for the Preservation and Study of Documents of Recent History (RTsKhIDNI) of the State Archival Service of Russia in the framework of an agreement concluded between RTsKhIDNI and Yale University Press. Yury A. Buranov of RTsKhIDNI provided valuable assistance in the preparation of this volume. I. N. Seleznyova aided in the research.

Copyright © 1996 by Yale University.
All rights reserved.

Documents that are held by RTsKhIDNI are used by permission.

Basic translation by Catherine A. Fitzpatrick.
Designed by James J. Johnson and set in Sabon and Melior types by The Composing Room of Michigan, Inc., Grand Rapids, Michigan.
Printed in the United States of America by Vail-Ballou Press, Binghamton, New York.

Library of Congress Cataloging-in-Publication Data

Lenin, Vladimir Il'ich, 1870–1924.
    The unknown Lenin: From the secret archive / edited by Richard Pipes, with the assistance of David Brandenberger; Russian documents translated by Catherine A. Fitzpatrick.
        p.   cm. — (Annals of communism)
    Includes index.
    ISBN 0-300-06919-7 (alk. paper)

    1. Lenin, Vladimir Il'ich, 1870–1924—Archives.   2. Heads of state—Soviet Union—Archives.   3. Soviet Union—Politics and government—1917–1936—Sources.   I. Pipes, Richard.   II. Brandenberger, David.   III. Catherine A. Fitzpatrick.   IV. Title.   V. Series.
DK254.L3A254   1996
947.084′1—dc20   96-8415

A catalogue record for this book is available from the British Library.

The paper in this book meets the guidelines for permanence and durability of the Committee on Production Guidelines for Book Longevity of the Council on Library Resources.

10   9   8   7   6   5   4   3   2   1

Yale University Press gratefully acknowledges the financial support given for this publication by the

Lynde and Harry Bradley Foundation
Historical Research Foundation
William T. Morris Foundation
John M. Olin Foundation
Open Society Institute

Contents

List of Illustrations   xi

Acknowledgments   xiii

Acknowledgments by Yury A. Buranov   xv

Works Frequently Cited   xvii

Political and Governmental Organizations   xviii

Note on the Documents   xix

Introduction   1

Lenin: A Biographical Sketch   14

From the Secret Archive

  1. Patent of Nobility   12 December 1886   19

  2. Transfer of Shmit Funds   21 February 1909   20

  3. Draft Resolution   November 1909   22

  4. Shmit Legacy Receipt   13 November 1909   24

  5. Telegram to Badaev   23 or 24 May 1914   25

  6. Letter to Armand   7 June 1914   26

  7. Letter to Armand   Before 6 July 1914   27

  8. Letter to Armand   16 July 1914   27

  9. Letter to Armand   Before 25 July 1914   27

 10. Letter to Malinovsky   13 November 1915   31

 11. Letter to Malinovsky   22 December 1915   31

 12. Letter to Malinovsky   14 November 1916   32

13. Letter to Armand   26 November 1916   33
14. Letter to Armand   12 January 1917   33
15. Letter to Armand   19 January 1917   34
16. Letter to Armand   22 January 1917   34
17. Deposition About Malinovsky   8 June 1917   35
18. Remarks at Central Committee Meeting   15 November 1917   41
19. Message to Yuriev   26 March 1918   43
20. Exchange with Yuriev   9–10 April 1918   44
21. Exchange with Unidentified Person   5 June 1918   46
22. Cable About Ex-Tsar   16 July 1918   47
23. Conversation with Krasin   11 August 1918   47
24. Letter to Penza Communists   11 August 1918   50
25. Letter to Berzin   14 August 1918   53
26. Exchange with Chicherin   19 August 1918   54
27. Letter to Vorovsky   21 August 1918   55
28. Memo to Krestinsky   3 or 4 September 1918   56
29. Letter to Berzin   15–20 October 1918   58
30. Letter to Berzin   18 October 1918   59
31. Exchange with Kursky   26 November 1918   60
32. Telegram to Zinoviev   7 January 1919   61
33. Letter to Rozhkov   29 January 1919   62
34. Minutes of Eighth Congress   23 March 1919   63
35. Draft re Printers' Strike   Before 28 April 1919   66
36. Trotsky's Exchange with Central Committee   5 July 1919   67
37. Note to Klinger   9 August 1919   69
38. Telegram to Frunze   30 August 1919   69
39. Memo from Trotsky   1 October 1919   70
40. Letter to Eliava   16 October 1919   74
41. Telegram to Zinoviev and Others   17 October 1919   75
42. Policy in the Ukraine   Before 21 November 1919   76
43. Telegram to Stalin   14 February 1920   78
44. Telegram to Stalin   17 March 1920   78
45. Exchange with Chicherin   6 April 1920   79
46. Telegram to Atkarsk   20 April 1920   81
47. Note to Trotsky   7 May 1920   82
48. Notes on Finnish Communists   18 June 1920   83
49. Note to Politburo   24 June 1920   84
50. Telegram to Terek   25–30 June 1920   84
51. Letter from Chicherin   10 July 1920   85
52. Telegram to Unshlikht   15 July 1920   88
53. Draft Resolution of RKP(b) Plenum   Before 17 July 1920   89
54. Telegram to Stalin   23 July 1920   90
55. Telegram to Smilga   4 August 1920   92

56. Exchange on Armenia   Before 9 August 1920   92
57. Note to Chicherin   21 August 1920   93
58. Draft of Politburo Resolution   21 August 1920   94
59. Report on Polish War   20 September 1920   95
60. Directives to Ioffe and Berzin   2 October 1920   116
61. Report on Pogroms   17–18 October 1920   116
62. Telegram to Stalin   18 November 1920   119
63. Dzerzhinsky's Report on POWs   November 1920   119
64. Resolution on Turkey   Before 4 December 1920   121
65. Draft of Politburo Resolution   26 January 1921   122
66. Remarks at Tenth Congress   13 March 1921   123
67. Telegram to Tsaritsyn   25 March 1921   125
68. Exchange on Weapons Purchases   18 May 1921   125
69. Exchange with Litvinov   29 June 1921   126
70. Telegram to Siberia   2 July 1921   127
71. Report on Pogroms   6 July 1921   128
72. Note to Chicherin   25 July 1921   129
73. Telegram on Food Supply   30 July 1921   130
74. Letter to Chicherin   6 August 1921   132
75. Note to Molotov   23 August 1921   133
76. Letter to Berzin   8 September 1921   134
77. Note to Unshlikht   21 September 1921   135
78. Note from Trotsky   4 October 1921   136
79. Telegram to Tsaritsyn   4 October 1921   136
80. Remarks on Weapons Purchases   21 October 1921   137
81. Remarks About Kamenev   1 December 1921   138
82. Letter to Krestinsky   28 January 1922   138
83. Letter to Molotov   30 January 1922   140
84. Letter to Molotov   31 January 1922   141
85. Letter to Sokolnikov   4 February 1922   142
86. Letter to Stalin and Kamenev   4 February 1922   142
87. Note to Sokolnikov   After 4 February 1922   144
88. Letter to Chicherin   10 February 1922   144
89. Request to Pharmacy   13 February 1922   146
90. Note to Kamenev   20 February 1922   146
91. Exchange with Molotov   6–7 March 1922   147
92. Trotsky's Memorandum   10 March 1922   148
93. Exchange with Trotsky   11 and 12 March 1922   150
94. Letter on Events in Shuia   19 March 1922   152
95. Note to Gorbunov   21 March 1922   156
96. Exchange with Kamenev   After 4 April 1922   157
97. Request to Pharmacy   6 April 1922   158
98. Telegram to Chicherin   17 April 1922   159

99. Telegram from Politburo   17 April 1922   160
100. Telegram to Chicherin   25 April 1922   161
101. Letter from Trotsky   28 April 1922   162
102. Letter to Stalin   19 May 1922   163
103. Note to Politburo   22 May 1922   164
104. Letter to Stalin   15 June 1922   165
105. Note to Stalin   7 July 1922   165
106. Note to Kamenev   mid-July 1922   166
107. Letter to Stalin   17 July 1922   168
108. Letter to Stalin and Kamenev   28 August 1922   170
109. Letter to Stalin   11 September 1922   171
110. Note to Unshlikht   17 September 1922   174
111. Letter to Radek   28 October 1922   174
112. Note to Zinoviev   October–December 1922   175
113. Letter to Stalin   13 December 1922   176

Appendix

1A. Memo from Marchlewski   26 October 1919   179
2A. Telegram from Frunze   24 August 1920   181
3A. Telegram from Artuzov   November 1920   182
4A. Telegrams from Trotsky   4 October 1921   183
5A. Message from Chicherin   30 January 1922   184
6A. Chicherin's First Telegram   15 April 1922   185
7A. Chicherin's Second Telegram   15 April 1922   186
8A. Resolution About Lenin   18 December 1922   188
9A. Instructions After Lenin's Death   22 January 1924   188

List of Document and Illustration Credits   191
Index   197

Illustrations

Facsimiles of Documents

DOCUMENT 9. Letter to Armand, Before 12 (25) July 1914

DOCUMENT 22. Cable to Danish Newspaper About the Fate of the Ex-Tsar, 16 July 1918

DOCUMENT 24. Letter About Suppressing Peasant Uprising in Penza, 11 August 1918

DOCUMENT 28. Memorandum to N. N. Krestinsky, 3 or 4 September 1918

DOCUMENT 54. Telegram to Stalin, 23 July 1920

DOCUMENT 61. Cover Memo to Report on Red Army Pogroms, 18 November 1920

DOCUMENT 106. Note to Kamenev Opposing Trotsky's Expulsion, mid-July 1922

DOCUMENT 109. Letter to Stalin, 11 September 1922

Photographs

1. Lenin in Paris, 1910
2. Lenin in Stockholm, 30–31 March 1917 (OS), En Route to Russia (*Lenin in the middle, carrying an umbrella*)
3. Lenin Speaking on His Return to Russia, April 1917

4. Trotsky at Brest-Litovsk, December 1917 or January 1918
5. Lenin Confers with Bukharin and Zinoviev During a Break Between
   Sessions of the Second Comintern Congress at the Kremlin,
   July or August 1920
6. Kamenev and Lenin in Gorki, September 1922
7. The Paralyzed Lenin in Gorki, Summer 1923
8. Lenin's Funeral Cortege, January 1924 (*Dzerzhinsky in front*)

Acknowledgments

In preparing these documents for publication, I was assisted by several members of the RTsKhIDNI staff in Moscow, under the direction of Yury A. Buranov; they supplied me with the documents and provided typewritten texts of manuscripts. On a number of occasions they also deciphered obscure passages.

I greatly benefited at all stages in the preparation of this book from the help of David Brandenberger. My research assistant, Lynn Garth, helped edit the manuscript. Jonathan Brent and Susan Abel of Yale University Press were most helpful in their capacities, respectively, as editor of the Annals of Communism series and manuscript editor.

Acknowledgments by Yury A. Buranov

We thank Yale University Press for publishing these previously un-published works by V. I. Lenin. Let it be noted that the Russian Center for the Preservation and Study of Documents of Recent History (RTsKhIDNI) assisted Richard Pipes's work on this volume in every possible way, furnishing him with the documents and transcriptions of certain illegible passages in Lenin's manuscripts as well as with informa-tion on some obscure facts.

The interpretation of the materials is a matter of the creative and scholarly assessment on the part of the American editor.

Though concurring with many of the positions that Richard Pipes has advanced in the Introduction to the volume, as well as in his com-mentaries on Lenin's texts, we reserve the right to maintain our own perspective on them.

Readers of this volume should bear in mind that there are to this day in contemporary Russia a considerable number of "mysteries" and enigmas in connection with Lenin's documentary legacy. It cannot be ruled out that a portion of Lenin's documents was destroyed at one time or another. Other documents that might illuminate their essence are not yet available in full to researchers. It cannot be ruled out, moreover, that certain documents may have been falsified. (See Yury Buranov, *Lenin's Will: Falsified and Forbidden* [Prometheus, 1995].)

That such mysteries remain unsolved is, of course, not the fault of Richard Pipes or of the Russian researchers. Work on unpublished Lenin materials should be continued, in our view, by both Russian and American scholars, working in collaboration. The publication of the present volume is a first step in that direction.

Works Frequently Cited

BKh V. I. Lenin, *Biograficheskaia khronika, 1870–1924* [Biographical chronicle], 13 vols. (Moscow, 1970–85)

Dekrety *Dekrety sovetskoi vlasti* [Decrees of the Soviet government], 13 vols. (Moscow, 1957–89)

LS *Leninskii sbornik* [The Lenin collection], 40 vols. (Moscow, 1924–85)

PSS V. I. Lenin, *Polnoe sobranie sochinenii* [Complete collection of works], 5th ed., 55 vols. (Moscow, 1958–65)

RR Richard Pipes, *The Russian Revolution* (New York, 1990)

RUBR Richard Pipes, *Russia Under the Bolshevik Regime* (New York, 1994)

TP Jan M. Meijer, ed., *The Trotsky Papers, 1917–1922*, 2 vols. (The Hague, 1964–71)

Political and Governmental Organizations

Cheka (VCheka)	Secret police (1917–22)
Duma	Lower house of the Russian parliament, 1906–17
Gosplan	State Planning Commission
GPU	Successor to the Cheka
OGPU	GPU renamed (1924)
Okhrana (Okhranka)	Tsarist secret police
RKP(b)	Russian Communist Party (Bolshevik)
RSDLP	Russian Social Democratic Labor Party
Soviet	In the Communist state, the formal source of popular sovereignty
Sovnarkom (SNK)	Council of People's Commissars
VSNKh	Supreme Council of the National Economy
VTsIK (TsIK)	All-Russian Central Executive Committee of the Soviets

Note on the Documents

The documents included in this collection present unusual problems of translation. They consist, for the major part, of memos and interoffice messages, written in a telegraphic style and often alluding to people or events whose identity and significance are far from clear today. Lenin tended to write and speak hurriedly, repeating or omitting words, without paying attention to stylistic niceties. In rendering the texts into English, the translators and the editor made every effort to fill in the gaps (interpolations are always in brackets) and otherwise clarify the meaning. But no attempt was made to improve the style of the original. If the English translation is occasionally dense and muddled, it is because the corresponding Russian text is dense and muddled.

Most documents are complete. When material has been omitted, such omissions are marked by ellipses in brackets. The ellipses without brackets appeared in the original documents.

Words or passages that were underscored for emphasis in the original are set in bold type. Italics are used to reproduce anything originally written in English; in these passages, the original spelling and punctuation have been retained. Where a sentence is clearly meant as a question but no question mark was supplied in the original, a question mark is placed in brackets in the translation. When no date appears in the document itself, the document date is enclosed in brackets. Detailed information on the documents is provided in the Document and Illustration Credits at the end.

The basic translation was done by Catherine Fitzpatrick. I went over it, as did a second professional translator. I also wish to thank Genrik Deych for his assistance with the text.

RICHARD PIPES

Introduction

THE WRITTEN LEGACY OF LENIN, the leader of the Bolshevik Party and head of the Soviet state, enjoyed the status of Holy Scripture in the Soviet Union: his every opinion was cited to justify one policy or another and treated as gospel. The difficulty with that procedure was that Lenin frequently changed his mind, because he was first and foremost a tactician who modified his opinions to fit the situation at hand. Thus it was possible to cite him both as favoring the boycott of the elections to the Russian prerevolutionary parliament and as favoring participation in them, as favoring collaboration with the "bourgeoisie" and as favoring conflict with it, and so on. Claiming his authority for divergent and even contradictory policies required "dialectical" juggling, a skill which professional Communist ideologists developed to a high degree.

Even more problematic were statements by Lenin that were not intended for publication; they often contradicted his public pronouncements and clashed with his official image as an idealist who resorted to deception and violence only out of necessity. Statements that revealed him as a heartless cynic, who in many ways provided a model for Stalin, it was thought best to conceal.

There have been five Russian editions of Lenin's works. The first, which began to appear in 1920 while Lenin was still alive and was completed in 1926, consisted of twenty volumes in twenty-six books. It

1

reproduced some 1,500 documents, all of them previously published. The second and third editions, identical except for the format and price, contained more than 2,700 items and appeared in thirty volumes between 1925 and 1932, accompanied by an extensive scholarly apparatus. The editors, who included N. Bukharin, did not claim completeness: "The present edition," they wrote in the introduction, "as a rule, does not include the manuscripts of works which have not been published at the time of its compilation."[1] Stalin disliked the scholarly apparatus of the second and third editions and ordered the preparation of yet another edition. The fourth, in forty-five volumes (1941–67), reproduced nearly 3,000 documents. Textually it was superior to the previous editions, but the scholarly apparatus was reduced to the barest minimum. Finally, after the era of de-Stalinization, the fifth edition appeared, titled *Polnoe sobranie sochinenii* [Complete collection of works], in fifty-five volumes (1958–65). Unlike its predecessors it introduced many previously unpublished works; it also included some items formerly scattered in specialized periodicals such as *Leninskii sbornik* [The Lenin collection]. The latter had reproduced over the years thousands of minor Lenin items. In theory, all Lenin manuscripts were deposited in the Central Party Archive (Tsentral'nyi Partiinyi Arkhiv) of the Marx-Engels-Lenin Institute (IMEL) in Moscow—an affiliate of the party's Central Committee—which enjoyed a monopoly on Leniniana. In practice, this rule seems not always to have been observed.

It has long been known to scholars that the fifth, the "complete" edition was in fact far from complete. The two-volume *Trotsky Papers*, based on the Trotsky Archive at the Harvard Houghton Library, brought to light a number of previously unpublished documents by Lenin.[2] It was also apparent to Western scholars that in addition to omitting entire documents, the editors of the fifth edition had occasionally tampered with Lenin's texts, censoring passages which for one reason or another they judged unfit for public consumption. But just how incomplete the fifth edition was did not become known until the breakup of the Soviet Union in late 1991, when President Boris Yeltsin ordered Russian archives to be removed from the control of the Communist Party and placed under the authority of state organs. It then transpired that the Central Party Ar-

1. V. I. Lenin, *Sochineniia* [Works], vol. 1 (Moscow, 1925), viii. Nikolai I. Bukharin (1888–1938): Old Bolshevik, writer on economics. Helped Stalin defeat Trotsky, Kamenev, and Zinoviev but was then accused of "Trotskyism" and shot.

2. Jan M. Meijer, ed., *The Trotsky Papers, 1917–1922*, 2 vols. (The Hague, 1964–71).

chive, now renamed the Russian Center for the Preservation and Study of Documents of Recent History, or RTsKhIDNI, held no fewer than 6,724 unpublished Lenin manuscripts[3]—that is, twice the number included in the so-called complete collection! It also became known that the Lenin Deposit (*Fond*) at the Central Party Archive had been divided in two sections: Fond 2, Opis (Index) 1, contained manuscripts of the published works, while Fond 2, Opis 2s (the *s* stood for *secret*), held the classified items. Subsequently, it was announced that 3,714 of the previously secreted Lenin papers had been declassified.[4] The only reason the remaining 3,010 are in the archive is that they bear Lenin's signature.[5]

All Lenin documents in the old Central Party Archive are said now to have been declassified and made available to scholars. But it is by no means certain that this is the case. First of all, declassification is an ongoing process that will take some time to complete: on each of my several visits to RTsKhIDNI, I have been shown new materials; still others have appeared in Russian journals and newspapers. Second, it has emerged that the Central Party Archive did not, in fact, enjoy a monopoly on documents written by Lenin, for some of them are stored at the so-called Presidential Archive (APRF). The Presidential Archive is meant to contain materials of current political importance, such as minutes of the Politburo and the cabinet. From recent publications, however, it can be established that the archive also holds unpublished manuscripts by Lenin. Thus the journal *Istochnik*[6] has published a previously unknown exchange between Lenin and Stalin from March 1922, and *Istoricheskii arkhiv*[7] has reproduced five manuscripts of Lenin's from the archive of the tsarist police, including three letters to Roman Malinovsky; all of them came from the Presidential Archive. The late Dmitri Volkogonov, one of the few scholars to have enjoyed access to the Presidential Archive, asserted that all the Lenin documents in it were copies. Even so, some of them are copies of originals that are either lost or still concealed. Hence, I can give no assurance of having seen all or even the bulk of previously unpublished Lenin documents.

Finally, it must be borne in mind that even as dictator of Russia, Lenin did not shed the habits acquired in the prerevolutionary underground, to judge by the frequency with which the words *secret, conspir-*

3. Rudolf Pikhoia, in *Rodina* [Motherland], 1 (1992): 81.
4. Dmitri Volkogonov, in *Izvestiia* [News], 19 July 1994, p. 5.
5. Dmitri Volkogonov, *Lenin: A New Biography* (New York, 1994), xxix.
6. *Istochnik* [Source], 2 (1993): 60.
7. *Istoricheskii arkhiv* [Historical archive], 3 (1994): 4–12.

atorial, and *clandestine* appear in his confidential communications. When a message was particularly sensitive and likely to cause acute embarrassment if leaked, Lenin insisted that no copies be made and that the original be either returned to him for destruction or destroyed by the recipient. In some cases (Document 88, for example) Lenin's injunction fortunately was not heeded. But it must be assumed that in most cases it was: it is certain that an indeterminate number of Lenin's communications were destroyed by either the author or the recipient. Thus even if every single Lenin document in all the archives were made public, we still would not know some of the deepest secrets of his life and regime.

It is not quite clear what criteria the Soviet authorities used in secreting Lenin's manuscripts. We have a hint from a confidential communication by G. L. Smirnov, the director of the Central Party Archive, sent in December 1990 to the deputy general secretary of the Central Committee.[8] In connection with the projected sixth edition of the works of Lenin, Smirnov wrote, the staff of his institute had inspected the unpublished Lenin documents in its files. As of 1 October 1990, he advised, IMEL had 30,820 original manuscripts by Lenin. Of this number, 24,096 have been published in one form or another. Smirnov expressed concern that the publication of some of the unpublished material could cause serious harm:

> There are documents the contents of which can only be interpreted as encouraging violence against sovereign states—India, Korea, Afghanistan, England, Persia, Turkey, etc. (offering help with weapons and money to units waging revolutionary war in one country or another; providing weapons to Afghan rebels; assisting Persian rebels; making appropriations for revolutionary activity in Mongolia; financing, e.g., [assigning] 10 million rubles to Finnish Communists, etc.).
>
> In specific documents certain secret working methods of the state organizations of the Soviet republic are revealed (about concentration camps for foreign subjects, about surveillance of foreign delegations, campaigns to have them discredited, as happened, for instance, with the English trade union delegation).
>
> There are Lenin's notations on materials sent to him which depict the Red Army in an unfavorable light (for instance, the participation

8. *Istoricheskii arkhiv,* 1 (1992): 216–17.

of units of the First Cavalry Army in Jewish pogroms, etc.). A number of documents deal with the exploitation by state organs of national animosities (in Transcaucasia; attempts to "sovietize" Lithuania, Hungary, Czechia, Romania; the struggle against separatism by means of executions in Karelia, etc.).

A large number of documents are connected with the most sensitive diplomatic problems of that period.

It would be inexpedient to publish documents of this kind at the present time.

As these words indicate, the Communist regime concealed first and foremost everything that implicated Lenin personally, as the head of the Soviet state, in subversive activities abroad, for the authorities were extremely eager to depict foreign Communist parties as independent in their operations and finances, and revolutionary turbulence abroad as indigenous in origin. To reveal the Soviet source of communist subversion would have endangered diplomatic relations with foreign countries and jeopardized loans and economic aid on which Moscow heavily counted. *The Unknown Lenin* reproduces several of the manuscripts that Smirnov alludes to concerning the delivery of money to foreign parties, as well as some that provided directives for subversive action abroad.

In selecting documents for this volume, I have excluded everything published in the *Polnoe sobranie sochinenii* (*PSS*) and *Leninskii sbornik (LS)*. I have, however, included passages censored from the documents in the complete collection. I have also omitted writings of Lenin's which appeared in *The Trotsky Papers*. Included are several documents published in Russian newspapers and other ephemeral sources after 1991, since they are, for all practical purposes, beyond the reach of foreign scholars. In a few cases I have made an exception to my rules, translating items that have appeared in regular Russian scholarly publications: for example, Lenin's speech from September 1920 on the Red Army's debacle in Poland,[9] and his ultrasecret letter to the Politburo outlining the campaign against the Orthodox Church at the time of the famine.[10] These documents are so revealing of the man that a reader unfamiliar with Russian should be given a chance to become acquainted with them.

9. First published in *Istoricheskii arkhiv*, 1 (1992): 14–29.
10. Published in *Izvestiia TsK* [News of the Central Committee], April 1990: 190–93.

What do these newly released documents add up to?

It would be naive, of course, to expect them to alter in some fundamental way our perception of Lenin's personality or his policies. What is known of both from previously published sources is not subverted by these newly released materials. They do, however, cast fresh light on Lenin's motives, attitudes, and expectations, as well as on the personal relationships among Communist leaders. They reinforce the familiar image of Lenin, minus the retoucher's distortions. His policies, concealed behind a smoke screen of self-righteousness and defensiveness in his public pronouncements, appear, in his private communications, cynical and aggressive.

For example: it was long known that the Allied landings in Murmansk in the spring of 1918, which marked the beginning of Allied involvement in the Russian civil war, had the approval of the local soviet. But now we know, from their own words, that Lenin and Stalin had also given their explicit consent (Documents 19 and 20). Similarly, it comes as no surprise that the July 1920 Red Army invasion of Poland had broader objectives than the sovietization of that country; but just how broad these objectives were we learn only now (Document 59). That the Communists torpedoed the Genoa Conference by signing a separate, bilateral treaty with Germany is alluded to in every history of the period; that Lenin deliberately set himself to "wreck" Genoa before the conference had even convened is new (Document 88).

I will discuss the contribution made by the documents published in this volume under two rubrics: Lenin's politics and Lenin's personality.

One of the most interesting documents in this collection is the stenographic record of a secret speech that Lenin delivered in September 1920 to a closed meeting of party officials to explain the disaster that had befallen the Red Army in Poland the preceding month (Document 59). His remarks leave no doubt that in the summer of 1920 Lenin believed western Europe to be on the brink of social revolution; this revolution he was determined to promote and consummate with the help of the Red Army. We now learn from his coded telegram to Stalin (Document 43) that Moscow was preparing a "striking force" against Galicia (southeastern Poland) even before the Poles invaded the Soviet Ukraine; and Galicia, in Lenin's words, was "a base against all the contemporary states" (Document 59). The Polish attack in April 1920 gave the Kremlin the pretext to set in motion military operations that quickly shifted from the defensive to the offensive mode. The purpose of invading ethnic

Poland, it now transpires, was not merely to sovietize that country but to use it as a springboard for the invasion of Germany and England. As Lenin spelled it out in his speech, after the defeat of the White armies, which in his eyes were nothing but pawns of the Allies, the time had come to take the offensive against the West. Lenin grotesquely overrated the revolutionary ardor of the English workers—indeed, he compared the England of 1920 with the Russia of 1917!—and conceived in his imagination phantom armies of hundreds of thousands of German Communists marching to join the Red Army. It thus emerges that the "miracle on the Vistula"—Pilsudski's counteroffensive launched on 16 August 1920, which lifted the siege of Warsaw and sent the invaders reeling in retreat—was indeed one of the decisive battles in world history, as the British diplomat Viscount d'Abernon contended.[11]

Lenin's telegram to Stalin (Document 54) adds intriguing details to these events, suggesting that Lenin intended to send the southern army, commanded by A. I. Yegorov, with Stalin as political commissar, into Czechoslovakia, Hungary, and Romania, and ultimately, Italy. It helps explain why Stalin did not move the southern army toward Warsaw to join in the siege, inaction that Trotsky later attributed to insubordination and blamed for the Red Army's defeat. Stalin almost certainly acted on Lenin's orders.

From the documents presented here, valuable insights can be gained into Soviet tactics at the Genoa Conference, which was convened by the Great Powers in early 1922 for the purpose of settling certain problems left unresolved by the Versailles treaty—and specifically of bringing Russia and Germany back into the international community. Lenin decided to have his country participate in the conference mainly because he was desperate to secure large loans for the reconstruction of the Soviet economy, ruined by the civil war and the experiments of War Communism. But he also feared a rapprochement between Germany and the Allies. Hence his instructions to Georgy Chicherin, the commissar of foreign affairs and head of the Soviet delegation, to arrange that the Genoa Conference be "wrecked," though not by Russia; he believed that this might even make it easier for his country to secure loans (Document 88). This objective was achieved through a separate treaty with Germany signed during the Genoa Conference at Rapallo. But Lenin

---

11. Viscount d'Abernon, *The Eighteenth Decisive Battle of the World: Warsaw, 1920* (London, 1931). Lenin, for his part, called it "a turning point for the world" (Document 59).

outsmarted himself, because in wrecking the conference, he failed to obtain foreign credits.

It comes as something of a surprise that despite repeated fiascoes with attempts at sedition abroad, Lenin's faith in the imminence of a social revolution in the West, especially in England, remained unabated as late as February 1922, when he wrote Chicherin: "Everything is flying apart for 'them.' It is total bankruptcy (India and so on). We have to push the falling one unexpectedly, not with our hands" (Document 88).

The various documents dealing with Soviet subversion in foreign countries—Finland, Turkey, and so on—speak for themselves. Especially revealing are Lenin's plans to communize Lithuania during the Polish campaign of 1920, namely his instruction to Moscow's agents there, "first sovietize Lithuania and then give it back to the Lithuanians" (Document 51, note 8). Lenin made no pretense in this private communication that the projected creation of Soviet Lithuania would be of indigenous origin.

As far as Lenin's personality is concerned, we note, first and foremost, his utter disregard for human life, except where his own family and closest associates were concerned. Of them he was very solicitous, making certain they did not overwork—to such an extent that he would order Stalin and Kamenev to take compulsory rests three days every week (Document 91). He made sure that they scrupulously followed doctors' orders (Document 30). He found them comfortable living quarters in Moscow and quiet dachas in the country (Documents 91 and 102). They were his soldiers—but only as long as they obeyed him. When Chicherin, an Old Bolshevik, had the temerity in early 1922 to suggest a minor change in the Soviet constitution to please the Americans and coax them to come up with a generous loan, Lenin decided that his minister was insane—not metaphorically, but in the clinical sense of the word—and that he should be required by the Politburo to be forcibly confined in a medical facility.[12] This is an early instance of resorting to medical treatment as a means of dealing with dissent, a method that was to flourish in the Brezhnev era.

As time went on, Lenin began to lose confidence in his other lieutenants as well. Documents from the year 1922, when illness forced him to

---

12. *PSS*, vol. 54, pp. 36–37, 596. For some inexplicable reason, this embarrassing communication was published in Lenin's works.

be a passive—and increasingly frustrated—observer of events much of the time, indicate that he found all save Stalin wanting; and at the very end of the year, he lost confidence even in Stalin. He saw Kamenev, a member of the triumvirate which ruled during his absences, as a pitiful weakling (Document 81). Trotsky, he declared, understood nothing of politics (Document 66). Rykov was a nuisance (Document 96). Lenin must have doubted their mental balance, because he ordered the lot of them to be subjected to examination by a visiting German specialist in "nervous diseases" (Document 95).

Of special interest are Lenin's relations with Trotsky and Stalin. In exploiting Lenin's rift with Stalin in the winter of 1922–23 to depict himself as Lenin's closest and most trusted associate, Trotsky entirely misrepresented his relationship with the Bolshevik leader. Lenin valued Trotsky's talents as organizer and orator highly; for that reason he angrily rejected the suggestion conveyed by Kamenev that Trotsky be expelled from the Central Committee (Document 106). But Lenin had little regard for Trotsky's judgment on any matter of substance and generally kept him at arm's length. Several documents in the present collection attest to this fact. Lenin dismissed as a case of "bad nerves" an urgent appeal by Trotsky, his commissar of war, to redeploy the Red Army at the critical juncture in the civil war (Document 39). He similarly ignored Trotsky's advice to keep the party from interfering in the econ-omy: "Into the Archive" (Document 92). It is known from other sources that he was appalled and annoyed by Trotsky's "categorical refusal" to accept the post of one of four "deputies" (zamy) in the state apparatus during Lenin's illness (Document 109).[13] It was only in the winter of 1922–23, when he had but a short time left before a stroke would leave him permanently paralyzed and speechless, that, feeling totally isolated, Lenin tried to form a tactical alliance with Trotsky against Stalin, Ka-menev, and Zinoviev—an offer Trotsky tacitly rejected.

By contrast, there is much evidence of Lenin's reliance on Stalin, not only in running day-to-day government operations but also in setting major policy goals. We have his notes to Stalin asking for advice on numerous issues. The notes acquire additional importance in the light of recent information that it was Lenin personally who in April 1922 desig-nated Stalin to occupy the newly created post of the party's general

13. *RUBR*, 464, 466–47.

secretary.[14] Trotsky lied in claiming that this appointment, soon to become the most important in Soviet Russia, was made against Lenin's wishes.[15]

So much for Lenin's relations with the inner circle.

For humankind at large Lenin had nothing but scorn: the documents confirm Gorky's assertion that individual human beings held for Lenin "almost no interest" and that he treated the working class much as a metalworker treated iron ore.[16] In early September 1918 he decided to launch mass terror. The curt note to the then secretary of the Central Committee, Krestinsky (Document 28), probably dating from that month, marks the birth of a campaign that in time would claim tens of thousands of victims.

Documents 61 and 71 reproduce alarmed reports from Jewish Communists informing Lenin of pogroms perpetrated by the Red Army on its retreat from Poland, and requesting prompt intervention. "Into the Archive," Lenin scribbled, meaning that no action was to be taken. Dzerzhinsky, the head of the Cheka (an institution not known for its sensitivity to suffering), reported that one hundred thousand prisoners of war from the defeated White armies were held in internment camps under inhuman conditions. "Into the Archive" was Lenin's reaction (Document 63). Less than a year after he had seized power, he was prepared to "burn Baku to the ground" in the event of an external attack (Document 21). The following year, he ordered Frunze, the commander of the Turkestan front, to threaten "to exterminate every Cossack to a man if they set fire to the oil in Guriev" (Document 38). Such calls for the burning of cities and the extermination of their inhabitants are reminiscent of the age of Genghis Khan and Tamerlane. Nor are those directives unique. In a notorious directive to the Communist authorities in the province of Penza, where the peasantry had rebelled to protest confiscations of grain, Lenin ordered one hundred "kulaks" to be publicly hanged so that the peasants would take fright and submit (Document 24). Even more shocking are his instructions to launch an offensive against the Orthodox Church by exploiting the unprecedented

14. Feliks Chuev, *Sto sorok besed s Molotovym (Iz dnevnika F. Chueva)* [One hundred forty conversations with Molotov (From the diary of F. Chuev)] (Moscow, 1991), 181.

15. L. Trotskii, *Moia zhizn'* [My life], vol. 2 (Berlin, 1930), 202–3; and *The Suppressed Testament of Lenin* (New York, 1935), 22.

16. M. Gor'kii, *Vladimir Il'ich Lenin* (Leningrad, 1924), 9; and *Novaia zhizn'* [New life], 10 November 1917, cited in Maxim Gorky, *Untimely Thoughts*, ed. H. Ermolaev (New York, 1968), 89.

famine stalking Russia and the Ukraine in 1921–22: here cannibalism provided an opportunity for a political offensive against the clergy (Document 94). Priests resisting seizures of church property were to be shot: the more the better.[17] In light of these barbarous orders, one is no longer surprised to learn that when Molotov, the only Communist official to serve both Lenin and Stalin throughout their political careers, was asked to compare the two, he declared without hesitation that Lenin had been the "more severe" or "harsher" (*bolee surovyi*).[18] Those who still idealize Lenin and contrast him favorably with Stalin will find little comfort in the Lenin documents which are now coming to light.

His contempt for Russians, known also from other sources, is corroborated. He thought them slovenly and unreliable as well as "soft." He wished them to acquire the work habits of Germans, although he had no particular sympathy for that nation either.

Lenin is revealed in these documents as a thoroughgoing misanthrope. They corroborate what Gorky wrote of him on the basis of long and close acquaintance: that Lenin "in general" loved people but "with abnegation. His love looked far ahead, through the mists of hatred."[19] That is, he "loved" humankind not as it really was but as he believed it would become when the revolution triumphed and produced a new breed of human beings. Curiously, his writings to the one person toward whom he displayed warm human feelings—his mistress, Inessa Armand—were also censored from the *PSS*. The collected works reproduced only those of his letters to her which dealt strictly with party affairs: all intimate communications, especially if they hinted at a sexual relationship, were either omitted or expurgated. It was apparently thought unseemly for the godlike leader of the world revolution to indulge in extramarital love.

In dealing with non-Bolsheviks, he either played on fear or appealed to greed. To dominate the human beings under his control, he had resort to unbridled violence. To win over those whom he needed for his own purposes, he dangled money. Angelica Balabanoff, who had served as the first secretary of the Communist International, recalled in her memoirs her surprise at the frequency with which Lenin would encourage her

17. Volkogonov reported having seen a document by Lenin requesting that he be informed on a daily basis how many priests had been executed: *Literator* [Literateur], August 31, 1990, p. 4.

18. Chuev, *Sto sorok besed*, 184.

19. Gor'kii, *Vladimir Il'ich Lenin*, 10.

to be generous with money: "I beg you, don't economize. Spend millions, many, many millions."[20] This is confirmed by some of the declassified documents. He instructs his envoy in Switzerland to be lavish in spreading communist propaganda: "Don't spare money!!" (Document 25). He consents to subsidize the Finnish Communists (Document 48). The French Communists, who liked to boast that they alone did not take money from Moscow, are exposed as having accepted funding as well (Document 37). The one sentiment Lenin never appealed to was idealism: apparently he had no faith in it.

Lenin scattered money about but he also showed no compunction about taking it. Documents 2–4 spell out in pedantic detail the arrangements Lenin made to appropriate for his Bolshevik faction the legacy of a rich industrialist, N. P. Shmit, which the deceased had bequeathed to the entire Social Democratic Party. It has been long known that Lenin accepted subsidies from the Germans in 1917–18, but ever the conspirator, he was careful to leave no paper trail that would implicate him in such financial dealings. We now learn that as late as August 1918, three months before Germany's surrender, he badgered Berlin for money to carry out anti-French and anti-British—that is, pro-German—propaganda in western Europe through his representative in neutral Switzerland (Document 25). This surely qualified him as a German agent in the strict meaning of the word.

Another trait of Lenin's which emerges with stark clarity from these documents is his policeman's mentality. No head of the tsarist Okhrana ever tracked dissident intellectuals so closely as he did, classifying them according to their attitude toward his regime and turning the information over to the Cheka or GPU for repressive action. He had lists drawn up of those he wanted expelled from Soviet Russia: he ordered the GPU to prepare a roster of "several hundred [intellectuals] who must be deported abroad without mercy" (Document 107). The case of a minor Menshevik historian with a Bolshevik past, N. A. Rozhkov, bothered him so much that he brought it up on several occasions before the Politburo, unable to decide whether to send him into exile inside Russia or to deport him abroad (Documents 107, 112, and 113). The British Trade Union delegation which visited Soviet Russia on Moscow's invitation was to be infiltrated with English-speaking agents and subjected to well-orchestrated political harassment (Document 45). The same ap-

20. Angelica Balabanoff, *Impressions of Lenin* (Ann Arbor, Mich., 1964), 29.

plied to Hoover's American Relief Administration, which came to dispense free food to tens of millions of starving Russians and Ukrainians (Document 75). From this evidence one can only conclude that he lived in constant dread that Russian socialists and foreign powers would do unto him as he had done and was doing unto them; and as no conspiracy unfolded, his suspicions and anxieties intensified to the point where they became impervious to rational argument. In fact, the Russian intellectuals whom he persecuted so savagely—academics, current and past; economists; journalists—were harmless creatures who, for all their grumbling about the Soviet regime, felt too happy to have escaped with their lives from the Revolution and the Red Terror, as well as the famine and the typhus epidemic, to entertain any thoughts of sedition.

Lenin treated his vast realm like a private estate, ordering remote provinces on one day to ship logs, specified to a fraction of an inch (Document 79), and on another, to deliver sheep and pigs (Document 46). Nothing escaped him, except the causes of the boundless corruption of the communist apparatus which he had placed above the law, and the reason the world did not follow the Soviet example.

We cannot tell, of course, what the Lenin documents that are still secreted will disclose when they are finally made public. The chances are that they will reinforce still more emphatically the features of Lenin the man and Lenin the politician that are laid bare by the materials currently available.

Lenin
A Biographical Sketch

VLADIMIR ILICH ULIANOV (Lenin) was born in 1870 in Simbirsk, the son of a school inspector. His brothers and sisters participated in the radical movement; his elder brother, Aleksandr, was executed in 1887 for membership in an organization that planned to assassinate the tsar. Lenin, however, showed no interest in politics until after he had been arrested and expelled from the University of Kazan in the fall of 1887 for joining in a student demonstration against university regulations. Prevented from resuming his studies, he spent the next four years in enforced idleness, absorbing radical literature. In 1891 the authorities finally relented and allowed him to take external examinations for a law degree at the University of St. Petersburg. By this time he was a confirmed revolutionary—though a non-Marxist—sympathetic to the People's Will, which favored terrorism.

In the 1890s, under the influence of more mature and better-read radical intellectuals (G. V. Plekhanov, P. B. Struve), Lenin moved toward Marxism and, thanks to his organizational abilities, quickly gained a prominent place in the ranks of the clandestine Russian Social Democratic Labor Party. He was arrested in 1897 and sentenced to three years' exile in Siberia for agitating among St. Petersburg workers. While in exile (1897–1900), he learned of reformist trends in the movement and decided to create a splinter group within it dedicated to orthodox

Marxism. By this time he had lost faith in the commitment of the working class to revolution.

After his release from exile, Lenin moved to Germany, where with several colleagues he put out the journal *Iskra* [Spark]. At the Second Congress of the Russian Social Democratic Labor Party, held in London in 1903, he broke with those socialists who wanted the party to be democratically organized and closely affiliated with the labor movement. He himself favored an underground organization modeled on the People's Will and staffed with full-time professional revolutionaries. Lenin named his faction Bolshevik (the Majority) and his opponents Mensheviks (the Minority), although in reality the Mensheviks had a somewhat larger following. Over the next ten years, he gradually formed his adherents into a separate organization, called the Russian Social Democratic Labor Party (Bolshevik). In 1918 it would be renamed the Russian Communist Party. He directed the activities of his Russian supporters from abroad, where he spent nearly all the pre-revolutionary years.

At the outbreak of World War I, Lenin immediately came out against the hostilities, urging international labor to transform the war between nations into a civil war between classes. He also called for the defeat of Russia. This program attracted the attention of the Germans and Austrians, the latter of whom subsidized his activities.

At the outbreak of the February Revolution of 1917, Lenin ordered his followers in Russia not to support the Provisional Government but to prepare for an immediate socialist revolution. He returned to his homeland in April 1917 with the assistance of the German government, which, aware of his antiwar and anti-Allied stand, hoped to use him to remove Russia from the war. Henceforth, and until Germany's surrender in November 1918, the imperial German government supplied Lenin and his party with generous financial subsidies.

These subsidies helped Lenin to create a party press and a network of Bolshevik cells in Russia, as well as his private army (the Red Guards). As the ineffective Provisional Government lurched from one crisis to another, Lenin kept his forces in readiness for a strike. In July 1917, however, when the government had amassed enough evidence linking him with the Germans to bring him to trial for treason, Lenin thought it prudent to seek refuge in Finland.

He returned secretly to Petrograd in October and, overcoming the hesitations of his lieutenants, persuaded the Central Committee to authorize the party's military organization to stage a coup d'état. The Bolsheviks seized power in the capital city of Petrograd on 25–26 October, ostensibly on behalf of the Petrograd Soviet, but in fact for themselves. They quickly made peace with the Germans and proceeded to establish a novel one-party regime, the prototype of all twentieth-century totalitarian states.

From then on, Lenin's life is indissolubly linked with the history of the Soviet Union. Resort to terror eliminated all overt opposition groups in areas under Bolshevik control and cowed the rest of the population. But the principal objectives of the new regime—spreading the revolution abroad and creating a communist economy at home—failed. By 1921 Lenin realized that ahead lay a long and arduous period of consolidation. In May 1922 he suffered the first of several debilitating strokes, which curtailed his ability to serve as leader of the Communist Party and head of the Soviet state and compelled him to entrust authority to his lieutenants, none of whom he judged fully capable of shouldering his responsibilities. By the time he suffered yet another stroke in March 1923, which deprived him of speech and left him partly paralyzed, he was quite isolated. Power had devolved into the hands of a triumvirate consisting of Stalin, Kamenev, and Zinoviev.

Lenin died in January 1924.

From the Secret Archive

The text of Document 1 was written on a certificate (dated 29 November 1886) attesting to the enrollment of M. A. Ulianova and her children, including Vladimir, the future Lenin, in the genealogical register of the nobility of Simbirsk (17 June 1886). It confirms a fact well known to historians but embarrassing to the Soviet authorities—namely, that Lenin was a hereditary noble.

Document 1
Excerpt from a Transcript of the Proceedings of the Assembly of Deputies of the Simbirsk Nobility

29 November (12 December) 1886[1]

1886. On 29 November, this copy of its ruling was issued by the Assembly of Deputies of the Simbirsk Nobility to the son of the actual councillor of state, Vladimir Ilin Ulianov, with the proper signature and stamp, as proof of his rights to hereditary nobility. This ruling of the Assembly of Deputies was ratified by Ukase No. 4566 of the Governing Senate on 6 November 1886, confirmed in this certificate.

> The Province's Marshal of the Nobility,
> Chamberlain of the Court of His
> Imperial Majesty [signature illegible]
> Secretary of the Nobility [signature illegible]

1. Dates for the earlier documents in this collection are given first in Old Style (OS)—that is, according to the Julian calendar, which was used in Russia until February 1918, and then in New Style (NS)—that is, according to the Western, or Gregorian, calendar. In the twentieth century, the Julian calendar was thirteen days behind the Gregorian calendar.

An episode in the history of the Bolshevik Party connected with the legacy of a wealthy Social Democratic sympathizer, Nikolai Pavlovich Shmit, is related in Documents 2 through 4. Shmit was arrested in the winter of 1905–06 on the charge of having assisted in the Bolshevik uprising in Moscow in December 1905. While under arrest he died, apparently by his own hand. He had told Maksim Gorky that he wanted his fortune, amounting to some 500,000 rubles ($250,000), to be turned over to the Social Democratic Party. Because the party lacked legal status, however, it could not inherit the money. The legacy, therefore, was given to Shmit's minor brother. The Bolsheviks, anxious to get hold of the money before it was turned over to the common Social Democratic treasury (administered jointly by the Mensheviks and the Bolsheviks), persuaded the teenage boy to consign his inheritance to his two sisters. As soon as this was done, the girls were married to Bolsheviks, with the view of having them transfer the legacy to the Bolshevik treasury. Once the hesitation of one of these husbands to part with the money had been overcome with threats of force, the Shmit legacy passed into the Bolshevik treasury. The Mensheviks considered this action a theft of funds belonging to the Social Democratic Party as a whole. Under pressure from them, the Bolsheviks agreed to pay 750 to 1,000 rubles each month to the common treasury, provided the party adhered to the "revolutionary" course (Document 3).[1]

1. See *RR*, 370–71; Bertram D. Wolfe, *Three Who Made a Revolution* (New York, 1948), 379; S. Shesterenin in *Staryi Bol'shevik* [Old Bolshevik], 5, no. 8 (1933): 155–56; N. K. Krupskaia, *Vospominaniia o Lenine* [Recollections of Lenin] (Moscow, 1932), 141–42; and Dietrich Geyer, *Kautskys russisches Dossier* [Kautsky's Russian File] (Frankfurt, 1981), 18–25.

Document 2
Protocols of the Transfer of the Yelizaveta P. Shmit Funds to the Bolshevik Center

8 (21) February 1909

Protocols

In January 1908 Yelizaveta X. [Yelizaveta Pavlovna Shmit] informed the Bolshevik Center (the expanded editorial board of *Proletarii*)[1] that in fulfilling punctiliously the wish of her late brother N. [Nikolai Pavlovich Shmit] she considers herself morally obligated to transfer to the Bolshevik Center one-half of her brother's property, consisting of eighty-three (83) shares of the N. N. joint-stock company and approximately forty-seven (47) thousand rubles in cash, which she has legally inherited.

Ye. X. has further stated that she is prepared to undertake all formal and practical steps connected with the receipt, sale, and transfer of the property to the illegal organization and also to compensate the Bolshevik Center from her personal means for the expenses related to the inheritance probate. The Bolshevik Center has resolved: 1) to accept this property; 2) to accept the compensation for the expenses connected with the probate; 3) after receipt of these sums, to refuse any further contributions from Ye. X.; 4) to discuss with Ye. X. all the practical measures necessary for the successful completion of this transaction.

In the course of the past year, Ye. X., upon consultation with the Bolshevik Center and under its direct guidance and through attorneys designated by it, undertook a series of actions required by the state of affairs and at present, at the suggestion of the Bolshevik Center and through its attorney, has transferred abroad all the available cash in the estate. Upon review of all the official documents (copies of the district court's probate ruling, official statements from the N. N. office on the status of the property, a bank receipt for the funds received, and others), it has been established that the entire amount in cash comes to the sum of forty-seven thousand one hundred and twenty (47,120) rubles or 124,915 (one hundred and twenty-four thousand nine hundred and fifteen) francs, calculated at the exchange rate at which the money was transferred from Russia here to Paris (2.651). The capital has been turned over in its entirety to the Bolshevik Center (the expanded editorial board of *Proletarii*), and thus the Bolshevik Center considers all its claims to the portion of the above property consisting of cash to be fully satisfied. As concerns the remainder of the property, consisting of eighty-three (83) shares of the N. N. joint-stock company, the method of their receipt, sale, and transfer to the Bolshevik Center is being discussed and implemented as previously by the Bolshevik Center in conjunction with Ye. X.

N.B.: There is a discrepancy of approximately one thousand (1,000) rubles between the district court's probate ruling and the official statement of the N. N. joint-stock company office regarding the amount of the cash. The Bolshevik Center has assigned its attorney to clear up this misunderstanding through private discussions with the N. N. office.

With our signatures we attest to the authenticity of all of the above, and also to the receipt of cash listed above by the Bolshevik Center.

Paris, 21 February 1909 [NS]

> Members of the Bolshevik Center (the expanded editorial board of *Proletarii*):
>
> | | |
> |---|---|
> | Grigory[2] | N. Lenin |
> | Marat[3] | Maksimov[4] |
> | V. Sergeev[5] | Yu. Kamenev[6] |

1. The Bolshevik Center consisted of people chosen by the Bolshevik delegates to the Fifth (London) Congress of the Russian Social Democratic Labor Party (RSDLP) in 1907. The members of the center also served as the editorial board of *Proletarii* [Proletarian].

2. Grigory Yevseevich Zinoviev (1883–1936): Old Bolshevik (*Old Bolsheviks* is the term applied to those who joined the party before 1917), close associate of Lenin's in emigration and after the establishment of the Soviet regime. Communist boss of Petrograd and first head of the Communist International. In the 1920s, member of the "troika" (triumvirate) that ran the country during Lenin's illness and following his death. Subsequently purged, arrested in 1935 and again in 1936, charged with complicity in the assassination of Kirov, and executed.

3. Virgily Leonovich Shantser (1867–1911): in his younger years an adherent of the People's Will, later a pro-Bolshevik Social Democrat, member of the Bolshevik Central Committee.

4. K. G. Maksimov (1894–1939): carpenter by trade. Participated in the civil war.

5. Vladimir A. Korenev (1887–1919): Old Bolshevik.

6. Lev Borisovich Kamenev (1883–1936): Old Bolshevik, one of Lenin's closest associates. In October 1917, along with Zinoviev, disagreed with Lenin's strategy of immediate power seizure. After the October coup, chaired the Moscow Soviet, served as Lenin's deputy chairman in the Sovnarkom, and during Lenin's illness, formed, together with Stalin and Zinoviev, the "triumvirate" that hounded Trotsky. Subsequently, a victim of Stalin's repression. Shot.

Document 3
Draft Resolution of the Executive Commission

[November 1909]

1. From the total assets of the Bolshevik Center (about 300 thousand francs), 60 thousand francs is allocated as follows: for the history of the Revolution (20 thousand), to the congress (20 thousand), and for emergency expenses and repayment of debts (20 thousand).

2. The remainder (240 thousand francs) is allocated for the maintenance of the [Bolshevik] faction and party centers for approximately four years, for which the Economic Commission is assigned to draft a budget with a reduction of expenses (if not immediately, then in stages, but no later than in half a year) to the sum of 5 thousand francs per month.

3. The property of the [Bolshevik] faction is legally justified to the party in a statement, submitted to the Central Committee, about the finalization of the matter of inheritance (received for the needs of the Bolshevik faction, according to the wishes of the contributor), without a declaration of the total sum and the monthly budget, at which time a calculation is to be made of previous contributions to the Central Committee from the faction that more than cover the 10-percent contributions rightfully due to the party.

4. The [Bolshevik] faction officially declares to the [Social Democratic] Party's Central Committee that it will provide the sum of 750 to 1,000 rubles monthly to its treasury.

5. The [Bolshevik] faction reserves for itself the right to cease these contributions to the Central Committee if it becomes convinced that the Central Committee is not maintaining the party line or measures or is straying from the line of revolutionary Social Democracy and the like. This statement is, of course, not to be submitted to the Central Committee [of the Social Democratic Party].

6. The Bolshevik Central Committee members (Grigory, Innokenty,[1] Viktor,[2] Lenin) are immediately to submit to the Central Committee a written statement about speeding up the convocation of the Central Committee, and to facilitate in every way its most rapid convocation.

7. Regarding Trotsky,[3] the faction acknowledges the maximum concession to *Pravda* to be an agreement to leave *Pravda* in Vienna, with the appointment of an editorial board on the basis of equality (i.e., one editor from *Pravda*, one Bolshevik from the Central Committee) and the conversion of *Pravda* into the organ of the Central Committee. The faction will not give any special financial aid to *Pravda*, except for general contributions to the Central Committee.

8. Regarding two points of view within the Central Committee on the question of internal party organizational policy in the near future (Grigory, Innokenty, and Kamenev on one side and Lenin on the other), it is acknowledged that either articles on this question should be set aside, or two articles expounding each viewpoint or one article developing a middle line should be printed. The last is considered to be the most desirable. What applies to the articles also applies to speeches to organizations, the Central Committee, the central organ, and so on.

9. The Russian members of the Bolshevik Center are to be informed of these two viewpoints in no other way than by one common letter expounding both points of view, and it is acknowledged that it is impermissible to air further disagreements, and it is [further] acknowledged that the disagreements are reconcilable.

1. Iosif Fyodorovich Dubrovinsky (1877–1913): an old Social Democrat, member of the Bolshevik Center.

2. Viktor Konstantinovich Taratuta (1881–1926): Old Bolshevik. Helped Lenin secure the Shmit legacy by marrying one of the two heiresses. Emigrated in 1909; returned to Soviet Russia in 1919 and worked for the government.

3. Lev Davidovich Trotsky (1879–1940): Russian revolutionary leader. Until 1917, acted either independently or alternately with the Mensheviks and the Bolsheviks. In July 1917, joined the Bolsheviks; played a prominent role in the October 1917 coup. Subsequently commissar of foreign affairs and commissar of war. In 1923, fell out with Lenin's successors (Stalin, Kamenev, and Zinoviev). Demoted and exiled, first to Central Asia and then abroad. Murdered in Mexico by an agent of Stalin.

Document 4
Acknowledgment of Receipt of the Shmit Legacy

[31 October (13 November) 1909]

In accordance with the decision and the accounting of the Executive Commission of the Bolshevik Center (the expanded editorial board of *Proletarii*) at the meeting of 11 November 1909, I have received from Ye. X. two hundred seventy-five thousand nine hundred eighty-four (275,984) francs.

Signature: N. Lenin

R oman Malinovsky, a Pole by origin and an occasional thief, was the only industrial worker to rise high in the Bolshevik hierarchy. Lenin was greatly impressed with his organizational and agitational abilities and appointed him to the Russian Bureau of his Central Committee. He became in a short time the Bolshevik spokesman in the Duma and played a critical role in the founding of *Pravda*. Rumors abounded, however, that he was a police agent. Lenin stuck to him through thick and thin, charging the accusers, prominent Mensheviks among them, with slander. Malinovsky suddenly resigned from the Duma in May 1914, under pressure from a new head of the police anxious to avoid a political scandal. Even though Malinovsky's resignation seemed to confirm the rumors of treachery, Lenin continued throughout the war, during which Malinovsky was taken prisoner by the Germans, to believe in his innocence and to carry on a friendly correspondence with him. It cannot be determined to this day whether Lenin simply refused to believe that Malinovsky was an agent provocateur or allowed for this possibility but thought that even if Malinovsky was an agent, the Bolsheviks benefited more than the police from his duplicity. Lenin's testimony to the commission of the Provisional Government (Document 17) does not completely clear up the matter.

Malinovsky returned to Russia in November 1918, apparently counting on Lenin to exonerate him. But Lenin refused to have any further dealings with him, and Malinovsky was executed.[1]

Lenin pretended in 1917 that he had had no contact with Malinovsky after he resigned from the Duma. The letters below clearly belie Lenin's version of events; that is why they were omitted from every edition of Lenin's works.

1. See *RR*, 372–75; R. C. Elwood, *Roman Malinovsky: A Life Without a Cause* (Newtonville, Mass., 1977); *Delo provokatora Malinovskogo* [The case of the provocateur Mal-

inovsky] (Moscow, 1992); I. S. Rozental, *Provokator: Kar'era Romana Malinovskogo* [Provocateur: The career of Roman Malinovsky] (Moscow, 1994).

Document 5
Telegram to A. E. Badaev[1] in St. Petersburg

[10 or 11 (23 or 24) May 1914]

To Badaev, Shpalernaia 44B, Petersburg

Russian newspapers are wiring Burtsev[2] that Malinovsky has been accused of provocation. Burtsev has not heard anything. A deputy who has collected information from seven Poles should be coming. Do not worry, there is a possibility of slander.

Elect a chairman [of the faction] and declare that the Muscovites will elect a worthy person.[3]

1. Aleksei Yegorovich Badaev (1883–1951): Old Bolshevik, metalworker, Bolshevik deputy to Fourth State Duma. Arrested and exiled to Siberia in 1914. Worked, after the Bolsheviks had taken power, in various Soviet organizations, mainly those concerned with supply matters.

2. Vladimir Burtsev (1862–1936): Socialist-Revolutionary (SR). Exposed Yevno Azef, the police agent heading the SR Combat Organization. After 1917, in emigration, vigorously criticized the Bolshevik regime.

3. In mid-May, Malinovsky was replaced as Bolshevik Duma spokesman by G. I. Petrovsky.

I nessa Armand (1874–1920), the daughter of French actors and the wife of a well-to-do Russian, broke with her husband and joined the Bolsheviks. She met Lenin in Paris in 1910 and soon became, under Krupskaia's tolerant eye,[1] both his mistress and his faithful follower. She took part in the Zimmerwald and Kiental conferences. Judging by Lenin's request (Document 7) that she bring "all our letters," it may be assumed that he later had many of them destroyed. The surviving exchanges between the two, however, no longer leave any doubt of an intimate relationship. For one, she is the only correspondent whom Lenin addresses in the second person singular (*ty*) as his "dear and dearest friend." Armand writes that she "could get by without the kisses" if she could only be near him.[2] He reciprocates (Document 8). The more personal letters from Lenin to her were either omitted from his collected works or edited to delete the intimate passages, reproduced here. Armand traveled with Lenin and Krupskaia by way of Germany to

Russia in March–April 1917. She worked in 1919 and 1920 for the Comintern and died of cholera in September 1920.[3]

1. Nadezhda Konstantinovna Krupskaia (1869–1939): Lenin's wife and close collaborator.

2. Letter from December 1913 in *Svobodnaia mysl'* [Free thought], 3 (1992): 81.

3. See Ralph Carter Elwood, *Inessa Armand: Revolutionary and Feminist* (Cambridge, England, 1992); Jean Freville, *Une grande figure de la révolution russe: Inessa Armand* [A great figure of the Russian Revolution: Inessa Armand] (Paris, 1957).

Document 6
Letter to Armand

25 May (7 June) 1914

7 June 1914[1]
Dear friend!

I am always very busy now & worried with the same story of Malinowsky. He is here & it is very hard to see him—so useless & helpless now. And the liquidators[2] continue their infamous compagn of slander & chantage. Wiring [sic] with brother[3] & small misunderstandings with him do not cease. Generalle he is very good, excellent—but exceptionally in such crisis he is from time to time a little too weak. The liquidators have published (if we understood rightly the wire (news)) that we knew oui dire (rumors) about political improbity (dishonesty) of Malinovsky!

In fact, we heard it from the Viennese (the liquidators), who blabbed—but we, of course, rejected the rumors, **submitting** [them] to a collegium of three members of the Central Committee.[4] As for the liquidators!! To whom have they submitted [the rumors]??

Well, the workers have already given and will continue to give these filthy slanderers what for!

We are sending you the new newspaper.[5]

If possible, do not be angry against me. I have caused you a great pain, I know it . . .

Yours truly W. L[enin]

After your depart from Paris—you will not accomplish anything there! What can you do with people like that!

1. The date is recorded in the hand of Armand.

2. A term of opprobrium coined by Lenin for Mensheviks who wanted the movement to adapt itself to the workers' desires and needs and thereby to "liquidate" the revolution.

3. L. B. Kamenev.

4. The reference is to a Central Committee commission of inquiry made up of Lenin, G. Ye. Zinoviev, and Ya. S. Ganetsky, established to investigate the charges of provocation against Malinovsky.

5. Reference to the newspaper *Rabochii* [The worker], the first issue of which was published on 22 April (5 May) 1914.

Document 7
Excerpt of a Letter to Armand

[Prior to 23 June (6 July) 1914]

*Never, never have I written that I esteem only three women. Never!! I've written that **fullest friendship, absolute** esteem and confiance of mine are confined to only 2–3 women. That is quite another quite, quite another thing. I hope we will see each other here after the congress and speak about it. Please bring when You will come (that is, bring with you) all our letters (sending them by registered mail here is **not** convenient: the registered paket **can very easily** be opened by **friends**. And so on . . .) Please, bring all letters, Yourself and we shall speak about it.*

Document 8
Excerpt of a Letter to Armand

[3 (16) July 1914]

My dear & dearest friend! [. . .][1]

> *Oh, I would like to kiss you thousand times greeting you & wishing you but success: I am fully sure you will be victorious.*

1. The *PSS* version has it, "My dear friend!"

T he importance of Document 9 lies in the opening sentence, which reveals that Lenin saw the outbreak of the First World War as inevitably leading to a revolution in Russia.

Document 9
Letter to Armand

[Before 12 (25) July 1914]

My dear & dearest friend!

> *Best greetings for the commencing revolution in Russia. We are here without news. Extremely eager to know what is hap-*

My dear & darling friend! Best greetings
for the [commencing] revolution in Russia. We are here
without news. Extremely eager to know what is happening — but no telegrammes! Now the great town would
be better that a village in Galicia. This evening at six
o'clock the question of war between Austria & [Serbia]
will be answered... The idiot Brussels conference can
be forgotten in real time. (I understand that the [Liqui?]
+ Plek. & other canailles are preparing a communiqué
forth. The traitors Poles, opposition, will not sign it!!
Already the decomposition of the new "third-July block"(!)

To-morrow I expect here the comrade You
have seen in Brussels from the "Lettow party."

This summer is extremely unhappy: at
first "affair" of Mal., then the conf. at Brux. & now
totally unknown if the great meeting of our
party will be possible after the events in S.P.B.

Here extremely unpleasant "stories" with
the stupid wife of the army. She is here with
army & two her new friends :) young men with

DOCUMENT 9. Letter to Armand, Before 12 (25) July 1914

grey hair, whom you have seen at first after
having left Krakow in summer 1912, — And
the former editor of our scientific review.
Both are friends of wife of the army. Both hate
Malinowsky & repeat: the wife ... is "convinced", that he "is an agent - provocateur".

We in our quality as a committee of
investigation, have lost many, many tours
to hear the "evidence" of the wife of the
army. Stupid talks, hystery, — nothing serious. She accuses us to be partial (in relation
to Mal.)!! Confrontation of her with Mal.
She is blamed — she has mixed personal affairs
& intimities with the politics. Mal. reveals
her intime discourses. Now comes the "three"
(army & both friends) & will have "almost" a
duel with Mal. & so on & so on.... Oh, quelle
misère! These hysterical stupid creatures, I
am so angry, so angry "losing of time for such
stupid stories"! Yours very truly, I hope you are not
angry against me, my dear friend? Yours W. I.

pening—but no telegramms!! Now the great town would be better than a village in Galicia. This evening at . . . o'clock the question of war between Austria & Serbia will be answered . . . The idiot Brussels conference can be forgotten in such time.[1] (I understand that the liquidators + Plekhanov[2] & other canailles are preparing a common manifesto. The traitors Poles, opposition, **will not** sign it!! Already the decomposition of the new "third-july block"!!)

To-morrow I expect here the comrade You have seen in Brussels from the letton [Latvian] party.[3]

This summer is extremely unhappy: at first "affair" of Malinovsky, then the conference at Brussels. And now totally unknown if the great meeting of our party will be possible after the events in SPB [St. Petersburg].[4]

Here extremely unpleasant "stories" with the stupid wife of the army.[5] She is here with army & two her new friends: 1) young man with grey hair, whom You have seen **at first** in Russia after having left Krakow in summer 1912,—and the former editor of our scientific review. Both are friends of wife of the army. Both hate Malinowsky & repeat: the wife . . . is "convinced", that he **is** an agent-provocateur!!

We in our quality as a committee of investigation, have lost many many hours to hear the "evidence" of the wife of the army. Stupid talks, hystery,—nothing serious. She accuses us to be partial (in relation to Malinovsky)!! Confrontation of her with Malinovsky. She is blamed—she has mixed personal affairs & intimities with the politics. Malinovsky reveals her intime discourses. Now come "the three" (army & both friends) & will have almost a duel with Malinovsky & so on & so on . . . Oh, quelle misère! These hysterical stupid creatures, I am so angry, so angry!! Losing of time for such stupid stories!!!

> Yours very truly, I hope You are not
> angry against me, my dear friend?
> Your W. L.

In our capital "état de siège." Both [Bolshevik] papers must be closed. Arrests innombrable. The brother[6] must be safe, because I've got a despatch from Finland with allusion that the brother is there & safe. But this is only a supposition. Nothing is certain.

1. Reference to conference in Brussels of the International Socialist Bureau, 16–18 July 1914 (NS).

2. Georgy Valentinovich Plekhanov (1856–1918): founding father of Russian Social Democracy. Before the 1917 Revolution, lived mainly in Switzerland; vacillated between the Bolsheviks and the Mensheviks. During World War I, adopted a "defensist" position. On his return to Russia, opposed Lenin's dictatorship.

3. Ya. A. Berzin (1881–1938): Old Bolshevik of Latvian origin. On 8 April 1918, was appointed the Soviet "political representative" in Bern, Switzerland. After Bern, posted in London (1921–25) and in Vienna (1925–27). Perished in Stalin's terror.

4. Reference to major industrial strike in St. Petersburg on 12–14 July 1914 (NS).

5. Possibly A. A. Troianovsky (1881–?): Russian writer and economist. Vacillated between the Bolsheviks and the Mensheviks. In the 1920s, emigrated to the United States.

6. L. B. Kamenev.

Document 10
Letter to Malinovsky

31 October (13 November), 1915

13 November 1915
My dear friend!

The other day I happened to get your address, and hasten to dash off a few words. I hope that you will receive this letter without much delay and reply to me as to how you are—are you safe and sound? Don't you need anything? Can anything be sent to you, and what would you need? Do you read Russian newspapers and books? How should they be sent?

I am living here in Bern for the second year with my wife[1] (my mother-in-law died half a year ago). My wife asks [me] to send you her warm regards, as do the acquaintances. I got some news recently from friends who ended up in Siberia; it was not bad. So, I await a prompt reply, and heartily wish you health and courage.

Yours, V. Ulianov

1. Krupskaia.

Document 11
Letter to Malinovsky

9 (22) December 1915

22 December 1915
My dear friend Roman Vatslavovich!

I received your letter and passed on to the committee here your request for the shipment of some things. I have received from them—through a comrade of my acquaintance—a report that everything has been sent.

Drop me a line about whether you have received [it].

We were very glad to hear that you have a library there and the opportunity to study and give lectures. If you have the chance, it would be good to try, if it is permitted, to organize a survey of the prisoners concerning their political views and sympathies in relation to their social status. Most likely you have a lot of interesting materials and observations.

I hope you are well and keeping up your courage. Write me about yourself and give my regards to all the friends you certainly have, even in your new setting.

N. K.[1] sends her warm regards.

Yours, V. Ulianov
Seidenweg, 4a, Bern, Switzerland

1. Krupskaia.

Document 12
Letter to Malinovsky

[1 (14) November 1916]

Dear Roman Vatslavovich!

For some reason there is still no news from you. Nadia[1] and I wrote you in the fall to clear up the misunderstanding into which you (and we) have fallen. We had thought (on the basis of your spring letter) that you had gone away to work, and kept waiting for your new address. It turned out—we learned this only toward the fall—that you had not left.

We are at present living again in Zurich; the libraries are better here. Furthermore, Nadia has found a modest-paying job here, which we badly needed. She still suffers from her Basedow's disease.[2] We put out one issue of Sbornik "Sotsial-Demokrata" [An anthology from the "Social Democrat"] and one issue of the newspaper. I hope you have already received them.

I am very sorry that you did not manage to go away to work—either on a farm or at a factory—most likely that would have been both useful and agreeable. Well, even so, don't let your spirits fall! Take it in stride! I think that studies, lectures, and so on, in any event ease your difficult circumstances.

Times are hard everywhere. And things are so damned expensive!
Greetings to all our friends! Try to write anyway, at least once in a while.

Yours, V. Ulianov

Nadia sends warm greetings.

Wl. Ulianow
Spiegelgasse 14 (bei Kammerer)
Zurich, Switzerland

1. Krupskaia.
2. A form of goiter.

Document 13
Letter to Armand

[13 (26) November 1916]

Dear friend,

I have just sent you a business letter, so to speak, in reply to your comments and thoughts regarding your letter on women's organizations. But apart from the business letter, I felt like saying a few friendly words to you and pressing your hand very tightly. You write that even your hands and feet are swollen from the cold. That's just terrible. Even without this your hands were always chilly. Why bring it to that? You write yourself that you will be leaving soon (I am not going into this because you asked that I not write to you about my requests concerning how it would be better for you to go where there are people around). I am very glad that you are getting ready to leave, and from the depth of my soul I hope that things will be easier for you elsewhere.

Once again I press your hand tightly and send best regards.

Yours, Lenin

Document 14
Excerpt of a Letter to Armand

30 December 1916 (12 January 1917)

12 January 1917[1]
Dear friend!

Your last letters were so full of sadness, and these aroused such sorrowful thoughts and stirred up such pangs of conscience in me that I simply cannot compose myself. I would like to say at least something friendly and urgently beg you not to sit in virtual solitude in a little town where there is no social life, but to go somewhere where you can find old and new friends, and shake yourself out of it.

1. Date in the hand of Armand.

Document 15
Excerpt of a Letter to Armand

6 (19) January 1917

19 January 1917[1]
Dear friend!

Regarding the "German captivity" and so on, **all** your appre-
hensions are excessive and baseless.[2] There is no danger at all. We are
staying here for the time being. I urge you, when choosing your place of
residence, **not** to take into account whether I will come there. It would be
quite absurd, reckless, and ridiculous if I were to restrict you in your choice
of a city by the notion that it "may" turn out in the **future** that I, too, will
come there!!!

I ordered the addresses of the youth organizations. They promised
[them to] me.

Thus, in terms of the publishing strategy: **move** the matters forward.
And what about the paper on pacifism?

1. Date in the hand of Armand.
2. This reference is unclear. It may allude to Lenin's contacts with the Germans
through the Estonian nationalist Alexander Kesküla, who, in exchange for Lenin's intelligence about conditions in wartime Russia, helped finance the publication of Lenin's
and Bukharin's writings in Sweden. See RR, 381–82.

Document 16
Excerpt of a Letter to Armand

9 (22) January 1917

22 January 1917[1]
[. . .] Apparently your failure to reply to several of my last letters
reveals on your part—in connection with some other matters—a somewhat changed mood, decision, or state of affairs. Your last letter contained
a word repeated twice at the end—I understood and dealt with it. Never
mind. I don't know what to think, whether you took offense at something or
were too preoccupied with the move or something else . . . I'm afraid to ask,
because I suppose such queries are unpleasant for you, and therefore I'll
agree to interpret your silence on this point in precisely this sense, that
queries are unpleasant for you, period. Therefore, I beg your pardon for all
[the queries] and, of course, will not repeat [them].

1. Date in the hand of Armand.

Document 17
Deposition in the Case of R. V. Malinovsky

26 May (8 June) 1917

Protocols of 26 May 1917, N. A.

Kolokolov,[1] sent to the Extraordinary Commission of Inquiry, questioned the below-mentioned with observance of Article 443 of the Criminal Code, and the latter testified[:] [I am] Vladimir Ilich Ulianov, forty-seven years old, a resident and member of the editorial board of the paper *Pravda*, 32 Moika.

I first saw Malinovsky at the Prague Conference of our party (the Russian Social Democratic Labor Party, "Bolsheviks") in January 1912. Malinovsky came to the conference with the reputation of being one of the most prominent [party] workers of the legal labor movement, much talked about in Menshevik circles, which considered him one of theirs. I heard that the Menshevik Sher[2] even called Malinovsky the Russian Bebel.

Malinovsky enjoyed especial popularity—not only among the leaders of the Social Democratic Party but among the broad working masses—because he was secretary of one of the largest trade unions, the Union of Metalworkers. It was not easy to advance in this trade, which included many fully mature workers, and to acquire popularity in a position requiring constant contacts with the masses. For this reason, all of us, the participants in the Prague Conference, came to view Malinovsky's authority as indisputable. When Malinovsky also told us that he had only gradually, after the most serious reflections and observations, converted from Menshevism to Bolshevism, and that in the spring of 1911, owing to his conversion, he had had a very sharp conflict with the most prominent Menshevik workers, who had invited him to an important and high-level Menshevik meeting, Malinovsky's authority rose even higher in the eyes of all the delegates. Incidentally, it would be particularly instructive for the history of Malinovsky's provocation to study and analyze this spring 1911 Menshevik meeting, which we described in an issue of our foreign publication, *Sotsial-Demokrat* [Social Democrat]. I recall that Malinovsky named Chirkin,[3] a fierce Menshevik, as one of those who attended the meeting. I had personally clashed with Chirkin once or twice in 1905–06.

Malinovsky was elected to the Central Committee [of the Bolshevik Party] at the Prague Conference, and we immediately nominated him a candidate to the State Duma. In the interests of ensuring his election, we in the Central Committee gave him a direct order to behave with extreme caution before the elections, to stay at his factory, not travel to Moscow, and so on.

As for our party's line, this line, which had led directly and inevitably to a split with the opportunistic Mensheviks, it had emerged on its own from the history of the party beginning in 1903, and especially from the 1908–10 struggle with the "liquidators" and the extreme exacerbation of this struggle after the disruption of the January 1910 "plenum" decisions by the liquidator leaders in Russia. Malinovsky could not have gotten into the Central Committee or the State Duma from our party if he had not depicted himself as a fervent and dedicated Bolshevik who had come to know the meaning of the whole danger of liquidatorism "through his own experience" during his long legal work.

Malinovsky told me in Prague, supposedly as a great secret, supposedly "only" for me (although later it turned out it was **not** only for me), that he had been forced to live under a false passport because of the events of 1905. After the revolution and the Japanese war, this was not at all unusual among the Social Democrats, and the trust that many thousands of metal-workers placed in Malinovsky, [after] observing every step of their secretary's life and actions, removed any shadow of doubt from my mind.

I saw Malinovsky for the second time in Kraków, where I had gone from Paris in the spring of 1912 to work full-time for *Pravda*, founded in April 1912, which immediately became our chief organ of influence over the masses. When he came to Kraków, Malinovsky, like Muranov,[4] was already a member of the State Duma. Later—I recall it was in December—came Petrovsky[5] and Badaev.

Malinovsky is a spirited man, unquestionably very capable. We were assured that he enjoyed great success at workers' meetings. I heard only one of his major speeches (in January 1912 at the congress of the Latvian Social Democratic Party in Brussels) and it seemed to me to confirm Malinovsky's popularity as an agitator. We valued Malinovsky as a Central Committee member particularly for his activity as an agitator and Duma member; as an organizer, he seemed to us too nervous and rough with people. Malinovsky was somewhat irritated by the inclusion of **other** [Duma] deputies in the Central Committee, not objecting but apparently not enthusiastic (we quickly began regularly to co-opt, one after another, **all** of our [Duma] deputies into the Central Committee). We attributed this to his extreme vanity and love of power, which even local [party] workers had sometimes complained about and which was evident at meetings as well. Following the unfortunate experience with several deputies from the First and Second State Dumas, we were not surprised that the "high title" of State Duma member turned people's heads and sometimes "ruined" them.

It is clear to me now that Malinovsky was nervous when he saw other deputies brought into the Central Committee, because it completely undermined his "omnipotence" (alone, he would have held all the connections in Russia in his hands, given that we were compelled to live abroad).

Malinovsky came to Kraków more frequently than the others, explaining this, on the one hand, by extreme exhaustion and by the desire to visit Warsaw (where he supposedly had Polish friends and relatives), and so on. As a Pole, Malinovsky became acquainted in Kraków with Daszyński[6] (I was not acquainted with him) and with the leaders of the Polish Social Democrats, with whom we were very friendly and in whom he also inspired complete confidence.

My wife, a Central Committee secretary for many years, followed Malinovsky's organizational ties and affairs more than I did. I was most interested in the Duma's work, and I spoke frequently with Malinovsky about it and, as I did for the other [Bolshevik] deputies, wrote drafts of speeches; and next I was interested in Pravda. Knowing how much Poletaev[7] had done for Pravda, we demanded from Malinovsky as well more attention to Pravda, its distribution and its consolidation. Since we took legal work extremely seriously, as long as it was undertaken in the spirit of uncompromising struggle with liquidatorism and in unwavering loyalty to revolutionary principles, we demanded that Pravda comply strictly with the law. It would be instructive to check with other workers and employees of Pravda about the extent to which Malinovsky complied with our demands.

Malinovsky quite often had friction and conflicts with the other deputies, especially after all of them had become members of the Central Committee—all because of his pride and love of power. We repeatedly reprimanded Malinovsky for this and demanded that he treat his colleagues in a more comradely fashion.

Regarding Pravda's line and the split of the Social Democratic faction, Malinovsky completely followed the policy indicated by us (myself, Zinoviev, and others) at meetings abroad, [the policy] which, as I have said, was preordained by the history of Bolshevism.

I heard that in Moscow around 1911 there arose suspicions regarding Malinovsky's political integrity, and we were informed of these suspicions in a particularly definite form after his sudden resignation from the State Duma in the spring of 1914. As for the Moscow rumors, they came at a time when the "spy mania" was reaching its climax, and not a single fact was reported that could be verified to any extent.

After Malinovsky's resignation, we appointed a commission to investigate the suspicions (Zinoviev, Ganetsky,[8] and myself). We interrogated quite a few witnesses, arranged personal confrontations with Malinovsky, wrote up hundreds of pages of transcripts of these testimonies (unfortunately, because of the war, much was destroyed or left behind in

Kraków). Definitely, not one member of the commission was able to find any proof. Malinovsky explained to us that he had resigned [from the Duma] because he could no longer hide his personal history, which had forced him to change his name, a story that supposedly involved a woman's honor and had taken place long before his marriage. He named for us a number of witnesses in Warsaw and Kazan, one of whom, I recall, was a professor at Kazan University. The story seemed plausible to us; Malinovsky's passionate nature gave it the appearance of probability, and we considered it to be none of our business to publicize an affair of this sort. We decided to summon witnesses to Kraków or to send the commission's agents to them in Russia, but the war prevented this.

But the general conviction of all three members of the commission was that Malinovsky was not a provocateur, and we stated so in the press.[9]

I have personally concluded on many occasions that after the Azef affair,[10] nothing could surprise me. But I do not believe in the alleged provocation in this case, not only because I saw no proof or evidence but also because if Malinovsky were a provocateur, the Okhranka[11] would not have gained from that as much as our party gained from Pravda and the whole legal apparatus.

It is clear that in putting a provocateur into the Duma and for that purpose removing the rivals of Bolshevism, etc., the Okhranka was led by a crude image of Bolshevism—I would say a cartoon caricature of it: the Bolsheviks will "stage an armed insurrection." To have in hand all the threads of this insurrection-in-the-making—from the point of view of the Okhranka—it was worth anything to get Malinovsky into the State Duma and the [Bolshevik] Central Committee.

When the Okhranka achieved both these ends, it turned out that Malinovsky became one of those links in a long and solid chain connecting (from various sides) our illegal base with the two major organs of the party's influence **over the masses**—that is, Pravda and the Duma's Social Democratic faction. The provocateur was supposed to protect both these organs in order to justify himself to us.

We directly controlled both these organs, since Zinoviev and I wrote **daily** for Pravda and the resolutions of the party completely determined its line. Influence over forty thousand to sixty thousand workers was thus guaranteed. The same was true of the Duma faction, in which Muranov, Petrovsky, and Badaev in particular worked increasingly independently of Malinovsky, expanding **their** ties, influencing [by] **themselves** the broad strata of workers.

Malinovsky could have destroyed a number of individuals, and in fact did so. [But] he could neither arrest nor control nor "direct" the growth of party work in terms of the development of its significance and influence **over the masses,** on tens and hundreds of thousands (through the strikes, which increased after April 1912). I would not be surprised if among the [Okhrana's] arguments in favor of removing Malinovsky from the Duma was that in reality he was involved with the legal *Pravda* and the legal faction of the deputies who were conducting **revolutionary** work among the masses to a greater extent than was tolerable to "them," the Okhranka.

I have written this deposition in my own hand.

Vladimir Ulianov

I continue my testimony on individual questions put to me.

There were not many members of the Central Committee in Russia; after all, Zinoviev and I lived abroad. Of the local men, Stalin (Dzhugashvili)[12] was in prison or exile for the most part. Malinovsky, of course, stood out here. It is possible that we did give him instructions from abroad on ties with the Finnish Social Democrats, or about setting up a printing press in Helsingfors. I do not recall this, however. Malinovsky had the right and the opportunity to act along these lines on his own. Thus Malinovsky could have set up the printing press on his own initiative. I can say that Malinovsky was, in my opinion, outstanding as an active [party] worker. He and I were together in Brussels in January 1914, and we traveled together from Kraków to the Latvian congress as representatives of the Central Committee. From Brussels we traveled together to Paris, where he delivered a major public report about the Duma's activity to an audience of several hundred. I must have been busy at the time and, it seems, did not attend Malinovsky's lecture.

As for Malinovsky's relationship to us, I can also clarify the following. He came to see us a total of six or seven times—in any event, more frequently than any of the other deputies. He wanted to play a leading role among the Russian Central Committee members and was apparently displeased whenever we gave a responsible assignment to someone else, and not him. In general, we had a rule whereby we did not allow those to the left of us to make speeches; if a speech was somewhat to the right, it was still possible to correct it, but more leftist statements could cause great harm. Apparently Malinovsky did not always like this line of conduct; he preferred bolder illegal work, and we often had conversations about this in Kraków. We merely chalked this up to Malinovsky's hotheadedness, however. I can now say, in recalling all of Malinovsky's activity, that undoubtedly a commission of intelligent people stood behind him, directing his every political step, because on his own he could not have pursued such a line so subtly. I am not able to recall at present any other details concerning Malinovsky that could be of interest. We could not consider him a provocateur after Malinovsky had left the Duma, because of insufficient evidence. He left the village of Poronin (near Kraków), and I did not see him again. News reached me, however, that Malinovsky had been captured by the Germans. He initiated party activity among our prisoners of war, gave lectures, explained the Erfurt program.[13] I know this from the letters of several other prisoners of war who gave enthusiastic reviews of Malinovsky and his lectures.[14] In general, he is a clever fellow and very adaptable to circumstances. I can add nothing more to this.

Signature: Vladimir Ulianov

1. This individual could not be identified.

2. Vasily V. Sher (1883–1940): a Menshevik. In 1905, served as secretary of the Moscow Soviet; occupied a similar post in 1917. In 1931, was jailed and tortured on charges of counterrevolutionary activity and sentenced to ten years' imprisonment. Perished in Stalin's terror.

3. Vasily Gavrilovich Chirkin (1877–1954): a Menshevik who in 1920 went over to the Bolsheviks. Worked in various capacities, mainly in the Ukraine.

4. Matvei Konstantinovich Muranov (1873–1959): Old Bolshevik, deputy to Fourth State Duma. Arrested and exiled in 1914. After the Revolution, elected to the Communist Central Committee.

5. Grigory Ivanovich Petrovsky (1878–1958): Old Bolshevik of worker origin. Served in the Fourth State Duma; arrested and exiled in 1914. From 1919 to 1930, served as chairman of the Ukrainian Central Executive Committee.

6. Ignacy Daszyński (1866–1936): prominent Polish Socialist, later leader of the right wing of the PPS (Polska Partia Socialistyczna, the Polish Socialist Party). In independent Poland, served as marshal of the parliament (Sejm).

7. Nikolai Gorevich Poletaev (1872–1930): Old Bolshevik of worker origin. Elected to the Third Duma. Involved in publishing *Pravda*. In the 1920s, served in various economic institutions.

8. Yakov Stanislavovich Ganetsky (Fürstenberg) (1879–1937): a Pole closely associated, while residing in Sweden during World War I, with Lenin. Served as a conduit to Lenin for German money. Held various positions in the Soviet government. Perished in Stalin's terror.

9. *PSS*, vol. 32, pp. 511–12.

10. Yevno Fishelevich Azef (1869–1918): head of the SR Combat Organization, which carried out terrorist acts against high government officials. Revealed in 1909 to have been a police agent.

11. Okhrana, popularly known as Okhranka, the tsarist secret police, part of the Department of Police.

12. Iosif Vissarionovich Stalin (1879–1953): Lenin's close collaborator, whom he appointed general secretary of the Communist Party in 1922. After Lenin's death, formed coalitions with various Old Bolsheviks until he eliminated virtually all of them, mostly by torture and execution. In the 1930s, carried out massive expropriations of peasants (collectivization), a program of industrialization, and an unprecedented nationwide bloodbath. His nonaggression pact with Hitler in August 1939 unleashed World War II.

13. The program of the German Social Democratic Party adopted in 1891 and in force until 1921. Based on the draft prepared by Karl Kautsky. Served as the model for the programs of other socialist parties in Europe.

14. The reader will note that Lenin is highly disingenuous here, implying that he has heard thirdhand about Malinovsky's capture. In fact, as Documents 10, 11, and 12 indicate, he had corresponded with him directly.

E ven after they had successfully carried out their October coup, the Bolsheviks continued to disagree on what course to follow and especially whether to form a coalition government with the other socialist parties. The hurried notes that follow are from a meeting of the Central Committee at which Zinoviev and Kamenev criticized Lenin for his refusal to share power.[1]

1. See *BKh*, vol. 5, p. 27; *PSS*, vol. 35, pp. 44–47, and vol. 50, p. 2.

Document 18
Notes on Remarks Made at the Meeting of the Central Committee RSDLP(b)

[2 (15) November 1917]

"We don't dare win"—that's the main conclusion of all the speeches.

———————————

Zinoviev: "The exhaustion of the masses is unquestionable" (Zinoviev)
On 10 October all were in favor of this program of agreement . . .

1. You have replaced the civil war with a war against the SRs.

2. [You have] replaced the power of the soviets with that of the Central Committee of the RSDLP [Russian Social Democratic Labor Party].

We are quarreling over **fifty peasants from the provinces!**

———————————

Kamenev: The revolution is not all-Russian.
Nogin[1] on the Military-Revolutionary Committees
. . . "We must seek a way out through political means, not military ones . . ."

———————————

Bourgeois revolution (Kamenev)[2]

1. Viktor Pavlovich Nogin (1878–1924): Old Bolshevik active in Moscow. Opposed the October coup and Lenin's one-party government.

2. A note from an unknown person, underlined by Lenin, reads: "The sailors are organizing a group of one hundred agitators in the southern grain provinces; I have just met them."

I n the spring of 1918, the British and French landed small expedition- ary forces in Murmansk. Their principal mission was to serve as the advance guard of a large Allied force that was to reactivate the eastern front against Germany, following Soviet Russia's conclusion of the Brest-Litovsk peace treaty with the Central Powers. They were also to prevent the Germans and pro-German Finns from capturing this ice-free port and constructing a submarine base there. As Documents 19 and 20 make clear, the landings, which communist propaganda has for decades exploited as alleged proof of the Allied intention to overthrow the Soviet government, were in fact carried out with the explicit approval of both the Soviet government and the Murmansk Soviet, to repel a threatened German-Finnish capture of the port, Russia's only remaining year- round naval outlet to Europe. The exchanges by direct wire reveal the ways in which the Soviet government sought to conceal its collaboration in the foreign intervention on its soil. On 18 April 1918 Lenin requested F. F. Raskolnikov[1] to demand that Murmansk publicly deny newspaper reports that the local authorities had authorized Allied landings.[2] An- other reason to conceal the exchange was that Trotsky had separately advised Murmansk to accept any and all Allied help—advice which Stalin subsequently used to charge Trotsky with treason. A falsified version of this conversation, published in 1935, contrived to suggest that Stalin also opposed Allied intervention.[3]

A. M. Yuriev,[4] who in 1918 chaired the Murmansk Soviet domi- nated by Mensheviks and SRs, concluded a verbal agreement with En- glish and French representatives authorizing them to land troops in Murmansk. After approving the landings in March, in June Moscow reversed itself, declaring them to be a hostile act, and on 1 July 1918 denounced Yuriev as an "enemy of the people" and "outside the law."[5]

1. F. F. Raskolnikov (1892–1939): Old Bolshevik. Served in the Kronshtadt Soviet in 1917; was active in the civil war. In the 1930s, held various diplomatic posts abroad. When recalled to Moscow, refused to return and attacked Stalin in an open letter. Died in southern France, apparently at the hands of Stalin's agents.

2. See f. 5, op. 1, d. 2,993.

3. *Pravda*, 21 February 1935, p. 1. See George F. Kennan, *Soviet-American Relations, 1917–1920*, vol. 2, *The Decision to Intervene* (Princeton, N.J., 1958), 39–57; Richard H. Ullman, *Intervention and the War* (Princeton, N.J., 1961), 116–18.

4. Aleksei Mikhailovich Yuriev (Alekseev): after joining the Bolsheviks in 1917, was in charge of Murmansk during its occupation by Allied forces in early 1918. Denounced as a renegade in 1918; arrested in February 1920 and sentenced to a prison term, which was subsequently commuted.

5. *Dekrety*, vol. 2 (Moscow, 1959), 20–21.

Document 19
Message from Lenin and Stalin by Direct Wire to A. M. Yuriev

[26 March 1918]

Please receive our reply: it seems to us that you have gotten yourself into something of a fix. Now you have to extricate yourself. As the international situation grows more complicated, the English might use the presence of their forces in the Murmansk region and their actual support of Murmansk, a military act of a certain character, as grounds for occupation. We advise you to draft an official document in the form of a report to the central government—that is, to the Sovnarkom [Council of People's Commissars]—on conditions in your region. In this report you should mention the agreement as if in passing, citing its text according to the transcript and stressing the statements of the British and French denying a possible occupation of the region, also according to the transcript of your discussion with them. Furthermore, you should propose to the British and the French in a very polite manner that they acknowledge these statements regarding an occupation as in accordance with existing circumstances. In doing so, you may refer to the fact that under the constitution of the Russian Republic, you, as the representative of the government in the region, are obligated to provide the central government with a completely accurate account, with statements for the record concerning such an important event as the organization of regional defense against an advance by the Germans and the Finnish agents toward the sea. If you accomplish this, it will be a serious step toward the rapid liquidation of this complicated situation that in our opinion you find yourself in against your will. Your report to the government should be entirely official, but secret—that is, not subject to publication. Meanwhile, in the next few days we will send you detachments of armed Red Guards and one person who will serve as a permanent link between you and Moscow. We strongly urge you to keep the government informed more frequently. Please tell us how you view our proposal.

Lenin, Stalin

Document 20
Exchange by Direct Wire Between A. M. Yuriev and Stalin and Lenin

9–10 April 1918

Urgent

To Comrade Yuriev, Murmansk

Although Podvoisky[1] is not here and your note is addressed to Podvoisky, nevertheless Lenin asked me to reply to you and I am doing so:

We advise you to accept the help of the English without as yet giving them an agreement on the minesweepers and, no matter what, to chase away the White Guards. Our agreement with the Finnish government calls for the transfer to the [Finnish] socialist government of the zone known to you, on the condition that the principle of self-determination will be observed.

But now the situation is such (I mean the indisputable victory of the [Finnish] Senate) that there will not be a socialist government in Finland; furthermore, the population of this zone, as you state, is protesting the zone's transfer to the Finns.[2]

Thus you have both formal and material grounds for declaring the agreement null and void and occupying the old frontier with border guards.

You understand, of course, that preliminary work is required regarding self-determination.

Podvoisky will be there this evening and will speak to you about the project. I believe that the creation of a regional Soviet of Deputies would only make the Moscow comrades happy.

Stalin

Murmansk,[3] 9 April

Message from A. M. Yuriev to Lenin

13:00 hours, 10 April 1918
To Comrade Lenin

First. Yesterday morning's entirely official telegram was addressed to the Sovnarkom, with only a copy to Podvoisky.

Second. Your phrases "we advise you to accept the help of the English" and "no matter what, to chase away the White Guards"—does this mean accepting English and French military aid in the form of the dispatch of an insignificant detachment to aid our Red Army[?].

Third. Can it be officially declared, according to point two, that aid is accepted in the name of the Sovnarkom, to defend the middle and northern sectors of the Murmansk road from the Finnish White Guard[?].

We understand that perhaps you cannot say this officially. In that case we will take the responsibility upon ourselves and act on our own. But it is essential for us to be certain here that our actions do not conflict with your plans. The exact expression of your approval will be kept secret.

Fourth. Regarding the minesweepers: we are sending a special report to the Naval Commissariat, the Arkhangelsk Central Navy, and the Soviet of Deputies, without which, of course, we will not resolve the issue.

13:30 hours
Comrade Stalin speaking. Receive reply:
Accept aid.

Regarding the minesweepers, inquire at the institutions you have mentioned; there are no obstacles on our part. The scheme should be absolutely unofficial. We will treat this matter as if it were a military secret; safeguarding it is your responsibility as well as ours.

It seems clear; if you are satisfied, I consider the conversation closed.
Lenin, Stalin

[YURIEV:] I consider that we are acting not against your wishes, but independently.

[STALIN:] Besides, act absolutely in secret and more or less autonomously.

[YURIEV:] Meaning we will ask the English and French in our name to help defend with armed force the middle section of the Murmansk road.

[STALIN:] Besides, do not forget to move the border guards to the old frontier in the west, on the grounds that given the changed circumstances, the zone ceded under the agreement remains ours.

[YURIEV:] What to do about the Russo-Finnish Commission?

[STALIN:] Refer the commission to the Sovnarkom, stating that you did not receive instructions from the latter on ceding the zone.

[YURIEV:] Thank you for the agreeable communication. Don't delay Podvoisky, send him quickly.

[STALIN:] Good-bye, comrade. All the best.
Murmansk,[4] 10 April

1. Nikolai Ilich Podvoisky (1880–1948): Old Bolshevik. In 1917, directed the Bolshevik Military Organization and the forces that seized power in October.

2. In late January 1918 (NS), Finnish Communists, with the assistance of the local Russian garrison, staged a coup that gave them control of Helsinki and much of southern Finland. The purpose of the coup was to proclaim a Finnish Soviet Republic. Finnish

nationalists, however, headed by General Karl Mannerheim, initiated a counteroffensive, which was assisted by a German expeditionary force. On 12 April, the Communists were expelled from Helsinki. This outcome meant that Moscow Bolsheviks no longer had a motive to transfer certain border territories to the Finns.

3. So in the original.
4. So in the original.

Document 21
Exchange Between an Unidentified Person and Lenin

[5 June 1918]

Note from an Unidentified Person to Lenin

The matter is urgent—Ter-Gabrielian is waiting, and a train is waiting for him.[1]

Note from Lenin to the Unidentified Person

What? He hasn't left yet?
I already signed one certificate for him.
Can you still relay the message to Ter that he should prepare **everything** to **burn** Baku to the ground, in the event of an attack, and that he should announce this in the Baku press.[2]

1. Saak Mirzoevich Ter-Gabrielian (1886–1937): Old Bolshevik, member of the ruling body of the Central Oil Administration. Sent to the Caucasus to take charge of the petroleum industry and to ensure fuel shipments to the center.
2. Baku, Russia's principal oil-producing city, was seized on 1 April 1918 in a joint coup carried out by the Communists and Armenian nationalists. On 28 May Azerbaijan proclaimed its independence and with the aid of Turkish troops moved to capture Baku. Lenin's threat to burn Baku was not carried out.

In late June 1918, rumors began to circulate in Europe that the ex-tsar, incarcerated with his family in Yekaterinburg, had been murdered. It is possible that the rumor was floated by the Soviet government to test Western reactions to the contemplated execution of Nicholas and maybe his family as well. Lenin's denial was cabled hours before the entire imperial family, along with its retainers, was massacred and when preparations for the massacre were well under way. A Danish daily wired Lenin on 16 July 1918 as follows: "Rumour here going that the oxszar [ex-tsar] has been murdered. Kindly wire facts. National Tidende."[1] Lenin responded in English on the same telegraphic blank.[2]

1. F. 2, op. 1, d. 6,601.
2. See *RR*, 765.

Document 22
Cable to Danish Newspaper About the Fate of the Ex-Tsar

[16 July 1918]

National Tidende **Kjobenhavn**
Rumour not true exczar safe all rumours are only lie of capitalist press.
Lenin

A dolf Ioffe,[1] who at the time served as Soviet ambassador in Berlin, together with L. B. Krasin[2] conducted negotiations for the Supplementary Treaty with the Central Powers called for by the Treaty of Brest-Litovsk. The Supplementary Treaty was signed in Berlin on 27 August 1918. Apparently Ioffe wished to come to Moscow to consult on its terms. He had urged Lenin to continue maintaining diplomatic relations with the Allies, even after Russia had been taken out of the Alliance.[3]

1. Adolf Abramovich Ioffe (1883–1927): a Social Democrat from his youth, joined the Bolsheviks in 1917. In 1918, served as Soviet envoy to Germany. A close friend of Trotsky's, he committed suicide when Trotsky was purged from the party.
2. Leonid Borisovich Krasin (1870–1926): Old Bolshevik. Worked before the Revolution for the German engineering firm Siemens-Schukert. After the October coup, served the Soviet government in various business capacities, negotiating trade agreements with Germany, Great Britain, and so on. Commissar of foreign trade.
3. See *PSS*, vol. 50, pp. 134–35.

Document 23
Wire Conversation of Lenin and Chicherin[1] with Krasin

[11 August 1918]

Note from Lenin

Comrade Krasin,

If Ioffe is going to repeat idiotic speeches that we have broken off with the Entente, I will not even listen to him. As concerns the

ТЕЛЕГРАФЪ ВЪ МОСКВѢ

ТЕЛЕГРАММА

LENIN MEMBER OF TE GOVERNEMENT MSK

DE KJOEBENHAVN 354/4/28 19 16 30

RUMOUR HERE GOING THAT THE OXSZAR HAS BEEN MURDERED KINDLY WIRE FACTS NATIONALTIDENDE

National Tidende Kjobenhavn

Rumour not true exczar safe all only lie of capitalist press Lenin rumours are

DOCUMENT 22. Cable to Danish Newspaper About the Fate of the Ex-Tsar, 16 July 1918 treaties, we do not consider this substantive. I don't see the slightest reason for him to come to Moscow.

Lenin

Note from Krasin

At the apparatus, Comrade Krasin:

Please inform Comrade Lenin in reply to his telegram, the harshness of which is incomprehensible to me. I see no reason why you are not authorizing a trip acknowledged by everyone as unquestionably necessary. On my personal behalf, I request that the decision be reversed. I think satisfying this request will do no harm to the work in Berlin and will greatly facilitate my future cooperation with you in Moscow as well. I value your personal authority too highly not to submit to your decision, but I assure you that you are mistaken and later you yourself will regret it if Ioffe's trip does not materialize. I will wait for your decision no later than half an hour from now, since it is time to board the train.

Krasin

Forward to Comrade Chicherin:

I add that in recent days Ioffe himself was also against the trip and I personally, along with the other comrades, am bringing him to Moscow almost by force. I await Lenin's decision.

Krasin

Note from Lenin and Chicherin

To Comrade Krasin:

If you so insist, the matter falls to your responsibility. We agree to Ioffe's trip.

Lenin
Chicherin

1. Georgy Vasilievich Chicherin (1872–1936): Old Bolshevik of aristocratic origin. People's commissar of foreign affairs from 1918 to 1930. Member of the Central Committee.

This is a response to reports from Penza of a "kulak" uprising there.

Document 24
Letter to V. V. Kuraev,[1] Ye. B. Bosh,[2] A. E. Minkin[3]

11 August 1918

11 August 1918

To Penza

To Comrades Kuraev, Bosh, Minkin, and other Penza Communists

Comrades! The uprising of the five kulak districts should be **mercilessly** suppressed. The interests of the **entire** revolution require this, because now "the last decisive battle" with the kulaks is under way **everywhere.** One must give an example.

1. Hang (hang without fail, so **the people see**) **no fewer than one hundred** known kulaks, rich men, bloodsuckers.
2. Publish their names.
3. Take from them **all** the grain.
4. Designate hostages—as per yesterday's telegram.[4]

Do it in such a way that for hundreds of versts[5] around, the people will see, tremble, know, shout: **they are strangling** and will strangle to death the bloodsucker kulaks.

Telegraph receipt and **implementation.**

Yours, Lenin

Find some truly hard people.

1. V. V. Kuraev (1892–1938): joined the Bolsheviks in 1914. Active in Penza.
2. Yevgenia B. Bosh (1879–1925): Old Bolshevik. In 1917, worked in the Military-Revolutionary Committee in Kiev. After October, entered the first Soviet Ukrainian government. Later sided with Trotsky.
3. A. E. Minkin (1887–1955): Old Bolshevik. After October, active in Penza and Perm party and state organs. Later, Soviet envoy to Uruguay and deputy chairman of the Russian Supreme Soviet.
4. The telegram was published in *Proletarskaia revoliutsiia* [Proletarian revolution], no. 3 (1924): 168–69.
5. A verst (*versta*) is approximately one kilometer.

The following is the only known document in which Lenin explicitly refers to the German government's financing of Communist activities in 1918.

...ищите, дес..." с кулаками. Образцу надо дать.

1) Повесить (непременно повесить, дабы народ видел) не меньше 100 заведомых кулаков, богатеев, кровопийц.

2) Опубликовать их имена.

3) Отнять у них весь хлеб.

4) Назначить заложников — согласно вчерашней телеграмме.

Сделать так, чтобы на сотни верст кругом народ видел, трепетал, знал, кричал: душат и задушат кровопийц кулаков.

Телеграфируйте получение и исполнение.

Ваш Ленин.

P.S. Найдите людей потверже.

DOCUMENT 24. *Continued*

Document 25
Letter to Ya. A. Berzin

14 August 1918

14 August 1918
Dear Comrade Berzin!

I am using an opportunity to dash off a few words of greeting. I thank you from the bottom of my heart for the publications: do not spare **money** and effort on publications in three (or four) languages and distribution. The Berliners will send some more money: if the scum delay, complain to me **formally.**

Yours, Lenin

P.S. Send some samples of interesting newspapers (with comments about the Bolsheviks) and any and all new pamphlets: British, French, German, and Italian. Spare no money.

Greetings to Gorter[1] and Guilbeaux!![2] It would be good if people well read in the worldwide socialist literature would send us good quotations appropriate for street displays (to the attention of **Gorter and others, etc.**)

P.S. Give the attached to Platten.[3]
Did you help Itchner?[4] And the **Swiss leftists? Don't spare money!!**

1. Herman Gorter (1864–1927): Dutch Social Democrat. During World War I, associated with the Zimmerwald Left. Later joined the Dutch Communist Party and took part in the Comintern. In 1921, quit the Communist Party over disagreements with Comintern policies and abandoned political activity.

2. André Guilbeaux (1885–1938): French Socialist and journalist. In the 1920s, correspondent for the Communist organ L'Humanité [Humanity] in Germany.

3. Friedrich (Fritz) Platten (1883–1942): Swiss Left Social Democrat and one of the organizers of the Swiss Communist Party. Participated in the Zimmerwald and Kiental conferences. Played a key role in arranging for Lenin's passage through Germany to Russia. Member of the Comintern Executive Committee. In 1923, moved to Soviet Russia. Lenin's letter to him is reproduced in LS, vol. 37, p. 99.

4. Hans Itchner (1887–1962): Swiss radical. Represented the Swiss Communists in the Comintern.

The following document refers to the Supplementary Treaty between Moscow and Berlin signed on 27 August 1918. It contained three secret clauses calling for German intervention in Russia to expel Allied troops from Murmansk and Baku and to crush the White Volunteer Army of the South.[1]

1. See J. Wheeler-Bennett, *Brest-Litovsk: The Forgotten Peace* (New York, 1956), 427–46; W. Baumgart, *Historisches Jahrbuch*, [Historical yearbook] 89 (1969): 146–48; *RR*, 662–66.

Document 26
Exchange Between Chicherin and Lenin

[19 August 1918]

Note from Chicherin to Lenin

Hauschild[1] has received a telegram from Ludendorff saying he is requesting us to send a high-ranking officer to Berlin to work out the details regarding the Murmansk matter. A telegram just received from Ioffe mentions this, only it attributes it to me. The whole telegram is very important. It is odd that my long telegram of yesterday concerning Baku is not mentioned.

Skliansky[2] is awaiting a reply.

A reliable person.

Skliansky proposes sending two people to Berlin: Parsky[3] and Antonov.[4] We must also come to an agreement about the south.

Note from Lenin to Chicherin

Send **only** arch-reliable Bolsheviks, even if they are poor strategists, but **reliable** and **intelligent** people, because it must be done **tactfully: not an agreement, but a coincidence of interests.**[5]

1. Herbert Hauschild: German consul general in Moscow.
2. Yefraim Markovich Skliansky (1892–1925): Old Bolshevik. From September 1918 to 1924, served as deputy to Trotsky in the latter's capacity as commissar of war.
3. D. P. Parsky: tsarist general in Soviet service.
4. Vladimir Aleksandrovich Antonov-Ovseenko (1883–1938): joined the Bolsheviks in 1917 and served in various military capacities during the civil war, especially in the Ukraine. Directed suppression of the peasant rebellion in Tambov in 1921. Perished in Stalin's terror.
5. The meaning here is that German intervention in Russia, requested by the Soviet government, was not a joint action with the Red Army but separate and parallel. See Document 27.

This letter (Document 27) is a response to V. V. Vorovsky,[1] who apparently objected to two (secret) clauses in the Soviet-German Supplementary Treaty—those calling for German military operations against Allied forces in Murmansk and against the Volunteer Army in southern Russia. To assuage Vorovsky's fears, Lenin makes it sound as if the plan to attack Murmansk and Alekseev originated with the Germans.

1. V. V. Vorovsky (1871–1923): Old Bolshevik, served as a Soviet diplomat. Killed in Switzerland by a Russian monarchist.

Document 27
Letter to V. V. Vorovsky

21 August 1918

21 August 1918
Comrade Vorovsky!

Please have the attached letter to American workers translated into German and copied as quickly as possible, and send the original to Balabanova.[1]

As for the hysterics and other "departments," for God's sake, you are nitpicking. There was not a shadow of panic. No one asked for "help" from the Germans, but we agreed on **when and how** they, the Germans, will implement **their** plan to march on Murmansk and Alekseev. This is a coincidence of interests. We would be idiots not to take advantage of this. It is not panic, but sober calculation.

Greetings to you and your wife from all of us.
Yours, Lenin

Why aren't you sending **any** new literature? This isn't good.
Yours, Lenin

1. Angelica Balabanova (Balabanoff) (1878–1965): Italian Socialist of Russian origin. Attended the Zimmerwald and Kiental conferences and subsequently served as the first secretary of the Comintern.

The following important document is unfortunately undated. After a great deal of vacillation, I have decided that its most likely date is 3 or 4 September 1918, a day or two before the Soviet government issued two decrees inaugurating the Red Terror.[1] While it is true that Lenin at that time was recovering from the wounds he had suffered in an attempt made on his life on 30 August, he had made very rapid progress and took an active part in government affairs. Thus, on 5 September he signed a decree dealing with Soviet-German relations.[2] Document 28 seems to mark the critical first step launching the Red Terror.

1. *RR*, 818–19.
2. *Sobranie uzakonenii i rasporiazhenii raboche-krest'ianskogo pravitel'stva* [Collection of statutes and decrees of the worker-peasant government], 1 (1918–19), 777.

Document 28
Memorandum to N. N. Krestinsky[1]

[3 or 4 September 1918]

The Russian Federated Soviet Republic
Chairman of the Council of People's Commissars
Moscow, the Kremlin

To Comrade Krestinsky:

I propose to form a commission immediately (initially this can be done secretly) to work out emergency measures (in the spirit of Larin:[2] Larin is right).

Let us say you + Larin + Vladimirsky[3] (or Dzerzhinsky[4]) + Rykov?[5] or Miliutin?[6]

It is necessary secretly—and **urgently**—to prepare the terror. And on Tuesday we will decide whether it will be through SNK [the Council of People's Commissars] or otherwise.

Lenin

1. Nikolai Nikolaevich Krestinsky (1883–1938): Old Bolshevik. Served as secretary of the party's Central Committee from 1918 to 1921. Subsequently Soviet envoy to Germany and member of the Commissariat of Foreign Affairs. Perished in Stalin's terror.
2. Yury Larin (Lur'e) (1882–1932): Menshevik who joined the Bolsheviks in August 1917; their specialist on the German economy. Served as Lenin's principal economic adviser during the period of War Communism.
3. Mikhail Fyodorovich Vladimirsky (1874–1951): Old Bolshevik. Spent much time in emigration. One of the leaders of the October coup in Moscow. In 1918, elected to the Central Committee. Subsequently occupied various party and government positions in Russia and the Ukraine.
4. Feliks Edmundovich Dzerzhinsky (1877–1926): Polish radical Socialist and Bolshevik. From December 1917 on, head of the secret police: the Cheka and its successors, the GPU (State Political Administration) and OGPU (Unified State Political Administration). Directed the Red Terror. In 1921, was appointed commissar of transportation, and in 1924, chairman of VSNKh (Supreme Council of the National Economy).
5. Aleksei Ivanovich Rykov (1881–1938): Old Bolshevik, member of the Bolshevik Central Committee before the October Revolution. After his appointment as commissar of the interior in October 1917, resigned to protest Lenin's refusal to form a coalition government. In February 1918, was appointed chairman of VSNKh, and the following year, member of the Politburo. One of Lenin's deputy chairmen on the Sovnarkom. Perished in Stalin's terror.
6. Vasily Pavlovich Miliutin (1884–1938): Old Bolshevik. In 1917, member of the Bolshevik Central Committee. In October 1917, was appointed commissar of agriculture,

РОССІЙСКАЯ
ФЕДЕРАТИВНАЯ
СОВѢТСКАЯ РЕСПУБЛИКА.

ПРЕДСѢДАТЕЛЬ
СОВѢТА
НАРОДНЫХЪ КОМИССАРОВЪ.

Москва, Кремль.

_____ 191 г.

№ _____

[Handwritten memorandum in Russian]

Н. Н. Крестин-
скому

Я предлагаю тотчас
образовать (для начала - может
тайно) комиссию для выработки
экстренных мер (в духе Лари-
на. Ларин прав).

Схема: Вы + Ларин +
Владимирский (или Держин-
ский) + Рыков?
или Милютин?

Тайно подготовить террор:
необходимо — и срочно.

А во вторник решим: через
СНК оформить или иначе.

Ленин

DOCUMENT 28. Memorandum to N. N. Krestinsky, 3 or 4 September 1918 but resigned promptly to protest Lenin's refusal to form a coalition government. In 1918–21, deputy chairman of VSNKh; later, deputy chairman of Gosplan (the State Planning Commission). Perished in Stalin's terror.

T he Soviet mission in neutral Switzerland served as the center for spreading defeatist propaganda in France and England with German financial help.

Document 29
Letter to Berzin

[Between 15 and 20 October 1918]

To Comrade Berzin
Dear Comrade Berzin!

Before I forget: give some help to Ilin's wife (he is here).[1] We must, after all, help the families of those coming to work in Russia.

Leiteizen[2] should not be put in the chancery **but [employed] in agitation** (in French Switzerland and **illegally in France**).

Do not stint at spending millions for illegal communications with France and agitation among the French and English.

When will my *State and Revolution* come out?[3]

Send it at once.

I would add about Vandervelde[4] to the French translation (without holding it up). Write or telegraph.

Gorter should give a list of pamphlets and **articles** in all languages that hold **theoretical** interest for me.

Greetings from me to everyone.

Convey my special greetings to Guilbeaux and Hertzog.[5]

Yours, Lenin

P.S. So, stay well and keep **strictly** to the [doctor's] **regimen.**

1. M. V. Ilin: employee of the Publications Bureau of the Soviet embassy in Switzerland.

2. G. D. Leiteizen (G. Lindov) (1874–1919): Social Democrat who vacillated between Menshevism and Bolshevism. Killed on the eastern front during the civil war.

3. Berzin arranged for the publication in Switzerland of Lenin's *State and Revolution* in German translation.

4. Emile Vandervelde (1866–1938): Belgian statesman and prominent member of the Second International. In 1922, served briefly as defense lawyer in the show trial of the SRs in Moscow. Held ministerial posts during the interwar period.

5. Jacob Hertzog (1892–1931): Swiss Socialist, later Communist, one of the founders and leaders of the Swiss Communist Party. Active in the Comintern.

Document 30
Letter to Berzin

18 October 1918

18 October 1918
Dear Comrade Berzin!

I heard Chernykh's[1] report and see that things are going badly with you.

First of all, you must obtain serious medical treatment.

N.B.: Once the doctors have told you to stay in bed, not one step outside the sanatorium.

N.B.: If the doctors said "two hours of work," [then] not a minute more.

Feel free to refuse to receive people, devote one-quarter hour to reports about "business" and talk about "business," and one and three-quarter hours to directing agitation.

Appoint **responsible persons:**

Peluso[2]

+ an Italian

+ a German (didn't Akselrod[3] visit you? He should be beaten up!! Kascher[4] or Shneier[5] should be sent for from Zurich; through them some **leftists** should be found, and one of them should be appointed).

You should demand from them: two to three pages [and][6] pamphlets per **week.**

You should give the **topics** and materials for compilation.

Assign work to the Russian fools:

to send newspaper clippings here, and not occasional issues (as these idiots have been doing up till now). Appoint persons responsible for this by name (Leiteizen and others) and we will take them in hand. As is, you have no **responsible** people.

The articles from *Volksrecht* [People's right] and other newspapers which have written that supposedly the soviets [councils] are not [suitable] for Europe (according to Chernykh) **were not sent here.** Who should be flogged for that? You should appoint **responsible people.**

Two to three times a week you should get to see people like Guilbeaux, Hubacher,[7] and the like, from Geneva, Italians from Lugano, Germans from Zurich (not like Platten, but better: **workers** from among the Zurich leftists). Appoint agents from among them, and pay **extremely generously** for their trips and work.

Pay minimal attention to official formalities.

Pay maximal attention to publications and illegal trips. I am sending pamphlets: immediately order (and urgently) translation into **all** languages.

Publish. Publish. Publish.

Greetings!

Yours, Lenin

1. A. S. Chernykh: Russian representative in Finland.

2. E. P. Peluso (1882–1942): Italian Socialist. In 1918–19, collaborated with the Spartacists in Germany. In 1923, represented Italy on the Executive Committee of the Comintern. In 1927, emigrated to the USSR.

3. Pavel Akselrod (1850–1928): one of the founders of Russian Social Democracy and a leading Menshevik. After 1917, resided in Europe and opposed the Soviet regime.

4. Leonie Kascher (1890–?): Swiss Communist, active in the Comintern.

5. This individual could not be identified.

6. Corrected from or.

7. This individual could not be identified.

T his document indicates the lengths to which Lenin was prepared to go to annihilate private ownership in Russia. It cannot be established whether the measures proposed by Lenin were actually carried out.

Document 31
Correspondence with D. I. Kursky[1]

[26 November 1918]

Note from Lenin

Is it not time to place on the agenda the matter of **destroying** documents on private property

notarized deeds of land ownership[:]
factories
real estate
and so forth, etc.

Prepare this **secretly,** without publicity.

Seize **to start with . . .** [ellipsis in the original]

The papers, I think, should be pulped (study this technically **beforehand**).

Note from Kursky

The measure is not superfluous and can be implemented quickly, since the **notarial archives** are in our hands.

Note from Lenin

So, will you undertake [to do] this **without** a special resolution from the SNK? (and involve in **consultations** the Commissariat of **Internal Affairs** and others). But **in secret.**

1. D. I. Kursky (1874–1932): Communist jurist. From 1918 to 1928, commissar of justice for the Russian Soviet Federative Socialist Republic (RSFSR), following which he served as Soviet envoy to Italy.

Document 32
Telegram to Zinoviev

7 January 1919

7 January 1919
Petrograd. Smolny. To Zinoviev

According to Lunacharsky,[1] Afanasiev,[2] Kormilitsyn,[3] and other members of the Detskoe Selo Cheka have been charged with drunkenness, rape, and other similar crimes. I demand that all the accused be arrested, that no one be released, and that the names of all the special investigators be sent to me, because if those guilty are not exposed and shot in a case of this kind, then unheard-of shame will fall on the Petrograd Council of Commissars. Arrest Afanasiev.

Chairman of the Sovnarkom, Lenin

1. Anatoly V. Lunacharsky (1875–1933): Old Bolshevik. Before World War I, experimented with possibilities of combining socialism and religion. Joined Bolsheviks in 1917 and was appointed first commissar of enlightenment, a post he held until 1929.
2. This individual could not be identified.
3. This individual could not be identified.

L enin responds in Document 33 to N. A. Rozhkov's[1] letter of 11 January 1919, in which Rozhkov urged him to assume dictatorial powers in order to solve the country's desperate economic situation.[2] It emerges from the letter that Lenin thought it impossible to institute a personal dictatorship of the kind that actually came into being several years later, after his death.

1. Nikolai Aleksandrovich Rozhkov (1868–1927): professional historian, specialist on Muscovite Russia, who in his youth joined the Bolsheviks but then went over to the Mensheviks. Lenin maintained a love-hate relationship with him, which in 1922 turned to pure hate and caused him to demand that Rozhkov be expelled from Soviet Russia (see Documents 107, 110, 112, and 113). Rozhkov was not expelled and eventually made peace with the Communists.
2. Rozhkov's letter, deposited in f. 5, op. 1, d. 1,315, l. 1–4, was published in *Neizvestnyi*

Gor'kii (k 125-letiiu so dnia rozhdeniia) [The unknown Gorky (125 years from the date of his birth)], vol. 3 (Moscow, 1994), 27–29.

Document 33
Letter to N. A. Rozhkov

29 January 1919

29 January 1919
Nikolai Aleksandrovich!

I was very glad to get your letter—not because of its contents but because I am hoping for a rapprochement on the general factual basis of soviet work.

The situation is not desperate, only difficult. But now there exists very serious hope of improving the food situation thanks to the victories over the counterrevolution in the south and east.

You should not be thinking of free trade—to an economist, of all people, it should be clear that free trade, given the absolute shortage of essential produce, is equivalent to frenzied, brutal speculation and the triumph of the haves over the have-nots. We should not go backward through free trade but forward through the **improvement** of the state monopoly, toward socialism. It is a difficult transition, but despair is impermissible and unwise. If, instead of serenading free trade, the nonparty intelligentsia or the intelligentsia close to the party would form emergency groups, small groups, and unions for all-around assistance to the food supply, it would seriously help the cause and lessen hunger.

As for "personal dictatorship," excuse the expression, but it is utter nonsense. The apparatus has already become gigantic—in some places **excessively so**—and under such conditions a "personal dictatorship" is **entirely** unrealizable and attempts to realize it would only be harmful.

A turning point has occurred in the intelligentsia. The civil war in Germany and the struggle precisely along the lines of soviet power against "the universal, direct, equal, and secret ballot, that is, against the **counterrevolutionary** Constituent Assembly"—this struggle in **Germany** is breaking through even to the most stubborn intelligentsia minds and will succeed in breaking through. This is more visible from the outside. *Nul n'est prophète en son pays.*[1] At home, in Russia, they regarded this as "merely" the "savagery" of Bolshevism. But now **history has shown** that it is the worldwide collapse of bourgeois democracy and bourgeois parliamentarism, that you cannot get by anywhere without a civil war (*volentem ducunt* *fata, nolentem trahunt*).[2] The intelligentsia will have to arrive at the position of helping the workers precisely on a Soviet platform.

Then, I think, circles, organizations, committees, free unions, groups, small groups, and gatherings of the intelligentsia will grow like mushrooms and offer their selfless labor **in the most difficult** posts in food and transportation work. Then we will shorten and ease the birth pangs by months. Because something amazingly good and viable will be born, no matter how difficult those pangs are.

Greetings, N. Lenin

1. "No one is a prophet in his own country," written in Latin characters.
2. "Fate leads the willing and drags the unwilling," written in Latin.

T he following passage was omitted from both the official records of the Eighth Congress of the Communist Party and Lenin's collected works.[1] Its importance lies in the indication it provides of the relative popularity among Communist Party executives ("responsible workers") of the various party leaders.

1. *Vos'moi s"ezd RKP(b), Protokoly* [Eighth Congress of the Russian Communist Party (Bolshevik), Protocols] (Moscow, 1959), 362–63; *PSS*, vol. 38, pp. 211–15.

Document 34
Minutes of the Eighth Congress of the Russian Communist Party (Bolshevik)

23 March 1919

Meeting of 23 March [1919], Evening
After the break, the meeting resumed under the chairmanship of Comrade Lenin.

LENIN. The presidium requests several minutes for consultation.
⟨Break of four minutes.⟩[1]

LENIN. Comrades. The presidium has decided to turn over to the congress that casuistic question on which it could not reach unanimity. The results of the vote are as follows. List of the members of the Central Committee: Lenin—262, Trotsky—219, Zinoviev—255, Stalin—258, Kamenev—252, Krestinsky—235, Dzerzhinsky—241, Rakovsky[2]—171 ⟨inaudible⟩ Bukharin—258, Stasova[3]—155, Muranov—164, Serebriakov[4]—125, Stuchka[5]—128, Tomsky[6]—226, Beloborodov[7]—218, Smilga[8]—135, Kalinin[9]—152, Yevdokimov[10]—127, and Radek[11]—115. Thus there are nineteen members. In next place was Piatakov[12]—108.

Candidates: Mitskevich[13]—198, Danishevsky[14]—149, Bubnov[15]—148, Shmidt[16]—143, Yaroslavsky[17]—141, Artyom[18]—131, Smirnov, Ivan Nikolaevich[19]—101, Vladimirsky[20]—95. Inspection Commission: Kursky—191, Tsivtsivadze[21]—139, Lunacharsky—129.

And so, comrades, this casuistic question consists of the following. Radek received 115 votes and was elected to membership in the Central Committee. Because the list of members of the Central Committee was separated from the special list of candidates, from that perspective the first candidate on that list [of candidates] replaces Radek, who is absent, and so on. Another opinion holds that given that Radek was elected clearly for show and that Piatakov is the next in line in the number of votes, during Radek's absence, Piatakov will replace him, and only after that has been done, the replacement of members of the Central Committee with candidates will begin. The bureau exchanged brief opinions about this and ruled unanimously to request the congress to resolve this controversial matter by vote and without debate. I ask: Is the congress in favor of accepting the method of resolving this matter proposed to it by the presidium? Is this clear to everyone? ⟨Voice: It is not clear.⟩ It is not clear. Then I will repeat the matter. ⟨Lenin restates the problem.⟩ Is this clear? ⟨Voices: Clear.⟩ I ask for a vote.

⟨Pause for voting.⟩

By a majority of votes the congress has approved the first decision. Consequently, Comrade Radek is considered elected, and while he is absent, he is to be replaced by a comrade from the list of candidates in order of the majority of votes.

KAMENEV. ⟨Reads a statement out of order⟩ The signatories below bring the following to the attention of the congress: Comrade Vladimir Mikhailovich Smirnov,[22] who reported on military policy, has just been removed from all work in the army by order of Comrade Trotsky. The signatories below protest this act. ⟨Inaudible.⟩

LENIN. Comrades, on instructions from the outgoing Central Committee, I am duty-bound to inform the congress that at the meeting held at the beginning of the arrival of the delegates to the congress and at which Comrade Trotsky was present, when we reviewed the statement from Comrade Smirnov regarding the as yet unchanged Central Committee resolution on travel to the front of frontline delegates, responsible [party] workers, Comrade Trotsky spoke up and the Central Committee tacitly approved it to the effect that Comrade Smirnov could remain at the congress, although Comrade Trotsky added that on the basis of all the material that Comrade Trotsky has in his possession, Comrade Smirnov could not remain in the army. Thus we all heard the decision of Comrade Trotsky at the Central

Committee at a time when there could not be a shadow of an idea about the connection of that resolution with the voting at the congress.

Our agenda, comrades, is now exhausted . . .

1. The angle brackets here enclose interpolations that appear in the Russian typescript.

2. Khristian G. Rakovsky (1873–1941): Bulgarian-born Communist. During the Revolution and civil war, served in Soviet organs in the Ukraine; later worked as a diplomat abroad. Victim of Stalin's purges.

3. Yelena Dmitrievna Stasova (1873–1966): Old Bolshevik. From 1917 to 1920, served as secretary of the Central Committee, of which she became a full member.

4. Leonid Petrovich Serebriakov (1888–1937): Old Bolshevik. After October 1917, served in the Moscow Soviet and on the All-Russian Central Executive Committee. Associated with Trotsky; expelled from the party in 1930 and executed seven years later.

5. Pyotr Ivanovich Stuchka (1865–1931): Latvian Social Democrat. After the Bolshevik coup, held various posts in the Soviet government; in 1921, served as deputy commissar of justice and in 1923 as president of the Russian Supreme Court.

6. Mikhail Petrovich Tomsky (1880–1936 or 1937): Old Bolshevik. In Soviet Russia, active as trade union official. Committed suicide after being charged in a 1936 show trial with "right deviation."

7. Aleksandr Georgievich Beloborodov (1891–1938): factory worker and Bolshevik from 1907 on. In 1918, active in Yekaterinburg as head of the local soviet. Played an active part in arranging the murder of the imperial family. In 1923, commissar of internal affairs. Accused of "Trotskyism." Perished in Stalin's terror.

8. I. T. Smilga (1892–1938): Old Bolshevik. Participated in Bolshevik coups in October 1917 in Finland and Petrograd. During the civil war, served in Revolutionary-Military Council of the Republic. In 1917–20, member of the Central Committee. Later worked in VSNKh. Perished in Stalin's terror.

9. Mikhail Ivanovich Kalinin (1875–1946): Old Bolshevik. In March 1919, appointed to the Central Committee of the Communist Party and to chairmanship of the All-Russian Central Executive Committee. In 1925, promoted to the Politburo.

10. Georgy Yereemevich Yevdokimov (1884–1936): Old Bolshevik. In the 1920s, headed the Petrograd Soviet and served as member of the Central Committee. Subsequently expelled from the party. Arrested in 1934 and sentenced to death at the 1936 "Trotskyite-Zinoviev" show trial.

11. Karl Berngardovich Radek (1885–1939): journalist who acted as Lenin's agent in Germany in 1919 and later. Perished in Stalin's terror.

12. Grigory Leonidovich Piatakov (1890–1937): joined the Bolsheviks in 1910. After 1917, active in Communist and Soviet affairs in the Ukraine. Member of the Central Committee. Expelled from the party as a "Trotskyite" and in 1937 condemned to death in a show trial.

13. Vikenty Semyonovich Mitskevich (Kapsukas) (1880–1935): Lithuanian Social Democrat. In 1915, joined the Bolsheviks, and in 1917–18 was active in attempts to sovietize his homeland. Later worked in the Comintern.

14. Karl Kristianovich Danishevsky (1884–1939): In 1907, elected to the Bolshevik Central Committee. In 1917–18, active among Latvian Communists and military units. Later worked in economic enterprises. Arrested as a "Trotskyite" and shot.

15. Andrei Sergeevich Bubnov (1883–1940): Old Bolshevik, member of the Petrograd Military-Revolutionary Committee in October 1917. Held various posts in the Soviet government; was elected member of the Central Committee in 1924. Later headed the

Political Administration of the Red Army. In 1929, was appointed commissar of enlightenment. Purged iñ 1937.

16. Most likely Vasily Vladimirovich Shmidt (1886–1940): Old Bolshevik, metalworker. Elected to the Central Committee in 1919. Purged in 1937; died in prison or in a camp.

17. Yemelian Yaroslavsky (1878–1943): Old Bolshevik. Active in the atheist movement in the 1920s and 1930s. Wrote a Stalinist *History of the Communist Party.*

18. Fyodor Andreevich Artyom (1883–1921): Old Bolshevik. After 1917, active in the Ukraine. Died in a railway accident.

19. Ivan Nikolaevich Smirnov (1880 or 1881–1937): Old Bolshevik. Held various posts after 1917. In 1927, expelled from the party for "Trotskyism" and ten years later sentenced to death for the same crime.

20. Mikhail Fyodorovich Vladimirsky (1874–1951): Old Bolshevik. Active in Bolshevik power seizure in Moscow in 1917. Elected in 1917 to the Central Committee. Subsequently occupied posts in Russian and Ukrainian party and state institutions.

21. Ilia Benediktovich Tsivtsivadze (1881–1938): Old Bolshevik active in Russian and Georgian Soviet institutions.

22. V. M. Smirnov (1887–1936): accused of "Trotskyism" and expelled from the party in 1927. Perished in Stalin's terror.

L enin and Kamenev react to the strike by printers in Moscow.

Document 35
Draft by Kamenev and Lenin of a Resolution Concerning the Printers' Strike

[Before 28 April 1919]

1. Require the Moscow Cheka to carry out merciless arrests among the strikers and delegates, ignoring previous considerations.

2. Call Khalatov[1] to the Council of People's Commissars by nine o'clock.

L. Kamenev

3. Require Kamenev **immediately** to send for Red printers from Petersburg.

1. A. B. Khalatov (1896–1938): food supply official in Moscow.

I n the summer of 1919, Trotsky suffered one humiliation after another. His strategic plan calling for adoption of a defensive stance on the eastern front to reinforce the front against Denikin[1] was spurned. His candidate for commander in chief of the Red Army, I. I. Vatsetis,

was rejected in favor of S. S. Kamenev,[2] Stalin's protégé. He was criticized for his management of the Commissariat of War. The following
letter was his response to these reverses. Lenin and his associates insisted
that Trotsky stay at his post; and to smooth his ruffled feathers, Lenin
gave him a carte blanche endorsement to use whenever his orders were
questioned.[3]

1. Anton Ivanovich Denikin (1872–1947): tsarist general. After the death of Kornilov,
assumed command in April 1918 of the White Volunteer Army in southern Russia. In 1919,
came closest of all the White leaders to defeating the Red Army. In April 1920, after being
crushed by the Red Army, resigned his command. Died in the United States.

2. S. S. Kamenev (1881–1936): tsarist officer. Switched to the Bolsheviks; from July 1919
until 1924, served as commander in chief of the Red Army.

3. The response of the Central Committee to Trotsky's resignation, but not Trotsky's
letter, was published in Leon Trotsky, *Stalin* (London, 1947), pp. 314–15.

Document 36
Trotsky's Statement and the Central Committee Resolution

[5 July 1919]

To the Central Committee, RKP

The conditions of my work at the fronts
deprive me of the opportunity to participate regularly in the work of the
military center and the Politburo [Political Bureau] of the Central Committee. This, in turn, frequently deprives me of the opportunity to assume
personal responsibility before the party and the [party] workers of the War
Office for a number of the center's steps that I consider risky and outright
dangerous violations of the military system established in our country and
approved by the party congress.

Considering at the same time, like the majority of the Central Committee, that my further work at the front is indispensable, I request:

a. That I be relieved of the title of member of the Central Committee's
Politburo and chairman of the Revolutionary-Military Council (people's
commissar of war).

b. [That I be] confirmed in my position as a member of the Revolutionary-
Military Council.

Trotsky, Central Committee Member

Draft Resolution of the Organizational and Political Bureaus of the
Central Committee, RKP(b), proposed by Lenin

The Orgburo [Organizational Bureau] and Politburo of the Central Committee, having reviewed and thoroughly considered the statement by Com-

rade Trotsky, have reached the unanimous conclusion that they are entirely unable to accept the resignation of Comrade Trotsky and to satisfy his petition.

The Org- and Politburos of the Central Committee will do everything in their power to make [his] work on the southern front optimally convenient for Comrade Trotsky and optimally productive for the republic—[work] which is the most difficult, most dangerous, and most important at the present time [and] which Comrade Trotsky has himself chosen. In his capacities as people's commissar of war and chairman of the Military-Revolutionary Committee, he can work closely with that commander of the southern front (Yegorov[1]) whom he himself has appointed with the approval of the Central Committee.

The Org- and Politburos of the Central Committee grant Comrade Trotsky the full opportunity to use every means to accomplish what he deems a correction in the [party] line in military matters and, if he so desires, to try to speed up the convocation of the party congress.

Firmly convinced that the resignation of Comrade Trotsky at the present moment is absolutely impossible and would inflict the greatest harm on the republic, the Org- and Politburos of the Central Committee resolutely urge Comrade Trotsky not to raise this issue again and to continue to perform his functions and, if he so wishes, reduce these functions to the minimum because of his need to concentrate his work on the southern front.[2]

In view of this, the Orgburo and Politburo decline both the resignation of Comrade Trotsky from the Politburo and his resignation from the post of chairman of the Revolutionary-Military Council of the Republic (people's commissar of war).

> Lenin, Kamenev, Krestinsky, M.
> Kalinin, L. Serebriakov, Stalin,
> Stasova[3]

1. A. I. Yegorov (1883–1939): lieutenant colonel in the tsarist army, in his youth affiliated with the SRs. In June 1918, joined the Bolshevik Party. In late 1919, as commander of the southern front, directed the campaign that led to the defeat of Denikin. Subsequently marshal of the Soviet Union. Perished in Stalin's terror.

2. Up to this point, the document was written by Lenin. The following paragraph and the first three signatures are in the hand of Krestinsky.

3. Last two signatures written by Stasova.

T he note below dispels the widespread notion that French Communists did not take money from Moscow.

Document 37
Note to G. K. Klinger[1]

9 August 1919

9 August 1919
Comrade Klinger,

I am sending a letter to Balabanova.

You should pass it on—**but** under supervision.

You should send (letters, documents, money) to France **not** to Longuet[2] but to **Péricat**,[3] care of the newspaper *L'Internationale,* **without fail.**

Yours, Lenin

1. G. K. Klinger (1876–1943): Old Bolshevik. Worked in the munitions industry in 1917–18, then in the Comintern. After the Second Comintern Congress in 1920, was assigned to the Executive Committee of the Comintern (IKKI).

2. Jean Longuet: nephew of Karl Marx; one of the founders of the French Socialist Party. In 1918, served as editor of *L'Humanité.* Opposed Allied intervention in Russia but refused to join the Comintern.

3. Raymond Péricat: French trade union leader.

Document 38
Telegram to Frunze[1]

[30 August 1919]

To Frunze   **Coded**

Discuss separately with extreme care how to seize the oil in Guriev.[2] This is imperative. Use both bribery and threats to exterminate every Cossack to a man if they set fire to the oil in Guriev. Reply immediately and in detail.

Lenin

1. Mikhail Vasilievich Frunze (1885–1925): Old Bolshevik. Served in the civil war, commanding Red Army forces on the eastern front and in Turkestan. In 1924, candidate member of the Politburo. In 1925, replaced Trotsky as commissar of war. Died shortly afterward under suspicious circumstances.

2. Guriev is a town on the Ural River in the Ural Cossack region, near the Caspian Sea. Its population at the beginning of the twentieth century was 13,700, nearly all Cossacks. Frunze's troops captured the region, including the nearby Emba oil fields, in the winter of 1919–20.

Trotsky's note to the Central Committee holds interest for two reasons. First, it shows how little familiarity Trotsky had with the operational plans of the Red Army, which he nominally headed. Written less than two months before the Red Army would decisively defeat General Denikin (and save Tula), it reveals that Trotsky either was unaware of the actual preparations for the Soviet counteroffensive or misunderstood them. Second, Lenin's cavalier dismissal of his advice indicates that he did not hold Trotsky's military abilities in high esteem.

Document 39
Memorandum to the Central Committee from Trotsky

[1 October 1919]

Top Secret

[For] the RKP Central Committee[1]
The Southern Front
THE SITUATION ON THE SOUTHERN FRONT

The *a priori* formulated plan of operations on the southern front has turned out to be indisputably faulty. The failures on the southern front are explainable, first and foremost, by the defectiveness of the basic plan.

1. The plan rested on equating the Denikin White Guard danger with the Don and Kuban Cossacks. This made more or less sense as long as Denikin's center was located at Yekaterinodar and the limit of his successes was the eastern border of the Donets Basin. The further things developed, the more incorrect this equating [of the two] became. Denikin's objectives are offensive; the objectives of the Don and Kuban Cossacks are defensive within the boundaries of their regions. With the advance of Denikin into the Donetsk region and the Ukraine, elementary considerations dictated the necessity of cutting off his forces advancing westward from their original base—the Cossacks. A strike against Kharkov-Taganrog or Kharkov-Berdiansk represented the shortest line along territory populated not by the Cossacks but by workers and peasants, and promised the greatest success with the least expenditure of forces.

2. The Cossacks in their majority would have remained hostile to us, and the liquidation of the particular Cossack counterrevolution in the Don and Kuban regions would have remained an independent task. With all its difficulty, this was a localized task and we could have resolved it in due course.

The Don, as a base, is exhausted. A large number of Cossacks have perished in the incessant battles. As concerns the Kuban, it is opposed to Denikin. With our direct assault on the Kuban, we push the Kuban Cossacks closer to the Denikinites. A strike against Kharkov-Taganrog would have cut off Denikin's Ukrainian troops from the Kuban, provided temporary support to the Kuban separatists, and created a temporary lull in the

Kuban in anticipation of the outcome of our struggle with the Denikinites in the Donetsk and the Ukraine.

3. A direct attack along the line of the greatest resistance turned out, as predicted, to play entirely into the hands of Denikin. The Cossack communities of the Veshensk, Migulin, and Kazan villages mobilized themselves to a man, vowing not to surrender. Thus by the very direction of our advance, we supplied Denikin with a significant number of soldiers.

4. To verify an operational plan, it is not superfluous to review its results. The southern front received forces the likes of which not a single one of the fronts has seen: at the moment of the offensive, there were there no fewer than 180,000 bayonets and sabers, and a corresponding number of field guns and machine guns. As a result of a month and a half of fighting we have a pathetic marching-in-place in the eastern half of the southern front and heavy retreat, loss of units, and organizational disruption in the western half. **In other words, our situation on the southern front is worse now than it was when the command proceeded to implement its *a priori* plan.** It would be childish to close one's eyes to this.

5. Attempts to dump responsibility for this on the condition of the armies of the southern front, on the organization of the *apparat* [staff], and so on, are fundamentally groundless. The armies of the southern front are in no way inferior to the armies of the eastern front. The Eighth Army fully matches the Fifth Army. The weaker Thirteenth Army is at any rate not inferior to the Fourth. The Ninth Army is at approximately the same level as the Third. To a large extent these armies were formed by the same kind of [party] workers, and talk of any organizational and combat differences between the southern and eastern fronts sounds exceedingly false to anyone who has observed these armies during the periods of their successes as well as their failures.

6. The only truth is that Denikin is an incomparably more serious enemy than Kolchak.[2] The divisions transferred from the eastern to the southern front turned out in no way better than the divisions on the southern front. This applies fully to the commanding staff. On the contrary, in the first period the divisions of the eastern front, as a general rule, turn out to be weaker, until they acquire the knack in the new conditions against a new enemy.

7. But if the enemy in the south is stronger, then we, too, are incomparably stronger than [we] ever [were] on any other front. Hence, the reasons for failure must be sought entirely in the operational plan. We proceeded along the line of greatest resistance—that is, we sent units of average steadiness to localities populated entirely by Cossacks who are not attacking, but defending their villages and homes. The atmosphere of a "people's Don" war has a debilitating effect on our units. Under these conditions, Deni-

kin's tanks, skillful maneuvering, and so on, turn out to be an enormous advantage in his hands.

8. In that realm where less force on our part could have produced incomparably greater results in the Donetsk and the Ukraine, we gave Denikin complete freedom of movement and thus handed him the opportunity to acquire an enormous reservoir of new formations.

9. All talk that Denikin will muster nothing in the Ukraine is nonsense. If in the Ukraine there are few politically educated proletarians, which hampered our formations, there are in the Ukraine very many officers, sons of landowners and the bourgeois, and brutalized kulaks. Thus at the time when we are thrusting out our chest in the Don, increasing the Cossack barrier facing us, Denikin, almost unopposed, is busy on the whole territory of the Ukraine creating new formations, particularly cavalry.

10. The fallacy of the plan is now so obvious that the question arises, How could this plan have emerged at all?

The origin of the plan has a historical explanation. When Kolchak threatened the Volga, the chief danger lay in Denikin's joining Kolchak. In his letter to Kolchak, Denikin appointed a meeting [between them] in Saratov.[3] Hence the task posed by the old command to create a strong striking force in the Tsaritsyn-Saratov [Volga] water basin.

The eastern front considered it impossible at that time to have its units transferred. The high command at the time accused the eastern front of delay. The latter maintained that the delay would not be too long or dangerous, since the units would be supplied immediately to the left Volga flank of the southern front.

Echoes of the old plans of the enemy, plus secondary considerations of saving time in transferring the units from the eastern front, led to the creation of the special Shorin[4] group. All the other considerations (of the decisive blow to the chief Don, Kuban bases, etc.) were dragged in by the hair *post factum*, when the inexpediency of the *a priori* plan began to be felt ever more acutely.

11. Now, in order to whitewash the real results, a new hypothesis has been advanced: "If the main forces had not been concentrated on the Tsaritsyn-Novocherkassk line, Denikin would be in Saratov and the Syzran Bridge would have been blown up." All these imaginary fears are supposed to compensate us for the real danger threatening Briansk, Orel, and Tula after our loss of Kursk. Moreover, the fact is ignored that it would have been just as hard for the Don Cossacks to advance on Saratov as it is for us now to advance on Novocherkassk.

12. The danger to Tula is at present almost a direct one: the enemy has advanced his base to the point where he can soon disorganize Tula with the raid of an air squadron.

13. The division of the southern front into a southeastern and a southern one consolidates organizationally the fundamental strategic mistake. At present, between the commander in chief and the two southern groups there no longer stands one person responsible for the southern front as a whole and able to exert lawful pressure on the high command for the purpose of securing the Tula sector.

14. Despite the formal release of the commander in chief from the obligations of the original plan, the *de facto* situation remains such that even essential changes (the transfer of Budenny's corps, the movement of the Ninth Army to the west, etc.) are evaluated in the Central Committee and the Revolutionary-Military Council as "assaults" on the basic plan and implemented with extreme delay. Under these circumstances, even the deliberately treacherous policy of open gates to Tula/Moscow could be carried out without great risk.

Conclusions. It is necessary to realize the actual extent of the danger. It is essential to order the commander in chief to take steps **that will really save Tula from perdition.**

Trotsky

In accord with the statement made to me by Trotsky, the above written statement was entered not for the purpose of discussion at the new session of the Central Committee, but as an attachment to the **protocol of the plenum of 26 September 1919.**

N. Krestinsky

Received 1 October. Lenin: (nothing but bad nerves; [the issue] was not raised at the plenum; it is strange to raise it now).[5]

1. Written by Lenin.
2. Aleksandr Vasilievich Kolchak (1873–1920): polar explorer; admiral in tsarist army. In 1918, served as minister of war in the Siberian Directory; in November of that year, after the directory had been overthrown, was appointed supreme ruler. Commanded the White armies on the eastern front. Defeated; arrested by the Bolsheviks and executed, very likely on Lenin's personal orders.
3. Reference to a letter from Denikin to Kolchak found on the person of General Grishin-Almazov when he was captured by the Bolsheviks as he tried to make his way to Siberia. In it, Denikin wrote that he hoped his and Kolchak's armies would join in Saratov.
4. Vasily Ivanovich Shorin (1870–1938): ex-tsarist officer. Played an active role as Red Army commander in the civil war. Retired from active duty in 1925; perished in Stalin's terror.
5. Written by Lenin.

Although the exact circumstances of the following communication are unclear, it almost certainly refers to secret preparations for military action in the Middle East against British possessions.

Document 40
Letter to Sh. Z. Eliava[1]

16 October 1919

16 October
Comrade Eliava!

An **independent** base, even if a small one, must be quickly set up in Turkestan: ammunition must be produced (we are sending the machine tools), military equipment must be repaired, coal, oil, and **iron** mined.

Rudzutak[2] and I have agreed that he will come on 17 October and bring along certain things. Apply pressure with all your might and inform me and anyone else necessary over the radio in code.

We will not spare money, and will send sufficient gold and foreign gold coins if you will arrange to buy military equipment (from English soldiers and officers, from merchants via Persia, and so on) and also establish ties through Persia, India, and so on, with Europe and America. To this end you must immediately begin looking for dedicated people capable of getting through to the right coastal locations and from there finding connections with steamships from neutral countries, with merchants, sailors, smugglers, and so on. Of course, the matter must be conducted in an extremely conspiratorial manner (as we knew how to work under the tsar). Weapons, connections with America and Europe, and aid to the peoples of the East in the struggle against imperialism. When you have the opportunity (an extremely reliable one), send me your reply and thoughts and inform me about the most important events and needs by radio (in code).

Greetings!

N. Lenin

1. Sh. Z. Eliava (1888–1937): Georgian Old Bolshevik, member of the Turkestan front Revolutionary-Military Council, starting on 15 August 1919. Served as chairman of the Commission for Turkestan Affairs of the VTsIK (All-Russian Central Executive Committee) and the Sovnarkom from its inception. (See *Dekrety*, vol. 6, p. 457.) Perished in Stalin's terror.

2. Ian Ernestovich Rudzutak (1887–1938): Old Bolshevik, specialist in labor questions. In 1920, became candidate member of the Central Committee; later appointed to the Politburo. Perished in Stalin's terror.

In mid-October 1919, at the time of Yudenich's[1] second offensive, the Bolsheviks seriously contemplated evacuating Petrograd and even took some measures in that direction. The prospect of abandoning Petrograd to the Whites was kept in greatest secrecy then and afterward.

1. Nikolai Nikolaevich Yudenich (1862–1933): tsarist general. Headed the White army in northwestern Russia in 1919; tried twice unsuccessfully to capture Petrograd.

Document 41
Telegram to Zinoviev, Trotsky, A. D. Naglovsky,[1] and Krasin

17 October 1919

For Military Purposes
Travel Warrant B
Petersburg. [To] the Defense Committee, Zinoviev
[To] the chairman of the Revolutionary-Military
Council, Trotsky
[To] the Evacuation Commission, Naglovsky
To Krasin, member of the Defense Council

Supplementing the resolution of the Defense Council of 17 October, you are informed that Groman[2] has departed for Petrograd, together with Comrade Krasin, to direct personally the removal of property designated as such by the evacuation committee of the Defense Council. Comrade Groman is to follow instructions issued by Comrade Krasin's commission concerning the shipment of parts of inactive plants.

17 October 1919

Chairman of the Defense Council,
Lenin
Chairman of the Evacuation Committee
of the Defense Council, V.
Avanesov[3]

1. Aleksandr Dmitrievich Naglovsky (1885–?): worked in the Commissariat of Transport and in 1919 served as chairman of the Committee for the Evacuation of Petrograd.
2. Vladimir Gustavovich Groman (V. Gorn) (1874–1932?): ex-Menshevik. Headed supply matters in Petrograd in 1917 and later worked in Gosplan. A leading defendant in the 1931 "Counterrevolutionary Menshevik Organization" show trial; sentenced to a prison term.
3. Varlaam Aleksandrovich Avanesov (1884–1930): worked in 1919 on the reorganization of soviets in the Volga region. Member of the Defense Council.

The resolutions in Document 42 were meant to guide Soviet authorities during the reoccupation of the Ukraine following the defeat of Denikin. According to the protocols of the Politburo meeting held on 21 November 1919, Lenin's theses were adopted with minor modifications. Particularly interesting is Article 7 in Lenin's draft, which calls for excluding Jews from the Ukrainian Soviet government.[1] This exclusion follows the practice of the White armies during their 1919 occupation of the Ukraine.

1. Article 7 was accepted in "revised form," presumably to incorporate Lenin's second wording. See f. 17, op. 3, d. 42, l. 1. The question of including the Borotbists (Ukrainian Left SRs close to the Bolsheviks) was left in abeyance because of the opposition of Trotsky and Krestinsky.

Document 42
Draft Theses of the Central Committee RKP(b) Concerning Policy in the Ukraine

[Prior to 21 November 1919]

Theses accepted (in principle, for editing)

1. Greatest caution regarding nationalist traditions, strictest observance of equality of the Ukrainian language and culture, all officials to be required to study the Ukrainian language, and so on and so forth.

2. Temporary bloc with the Borotbists[1] to form a center[2] before the convocation of the Congress of Soviets, with the concurrent launching of a propaganda campaign for the complete merger [of the Ukraine] with the RSFSR.[3]

For the time being, an independent Ukrainian Soviet Socialist Republic, in close federation with the RSFSR, on the basis of 1 June 1919.[4]

3. In connection with the advance of Red Army troops into the Ukraine, intensified work on the [class] differentiation of the village; singling out three groups; recruiting poor peasants (+ middle peasants)[5] into the administration. Rendering the kulaks completely harmless.

4. Immediately and without fail admit to all revolutionary committees and local soviets no fewer than half of the local peasants, first from among the poorest[6] and second from the middle ones.[7]

The strictest requirement of accounting for the implementation of this demand by all nonlocal [party] workers, by all those sent from the center,[8] by all members of the intelligentsia, etc.

Detailed working out of procedures for this accounting, and oversight of their actual implementation.

5. The countryside must be disarmed without fail and at all costs.

6. Food work in the Ukraine:

first, give priority to feeding Kharkov and the Donets Basin;

second, delay extraction of the surpluses from the Ukraine to Russia,

Lenin in Paris, 1910

Lenin in Stockholm, 30–31 March 1917 (OS), En Route to Russia (*Lenin in the middle, carrying an umbrella*)

Lenin Speaking on His Return to Russia, April 1917

Trotsky at Brest-Litovsk, December 1917 or January 1918

Lenin Confers with Bukharin and Zinoviev During a Break Between Sessions of the
Second Comintern Congress at the Kremlin, July or August 1920

Kamenev and Lenin in Gorki, September 1922

The Paralyzed Lenin in Gorki, Summer 1923

Lenin's Funeral Cortege, January 1924 (*Dzerzhinsky in front*)

stretching it out as much as possible (that is, getting by in Russia with our [own] surpluses);

third, use **any** extraction of surpluses to feed the local poor peasants no matter what, giving them without fail a share [of what is] taken from the kulaks;

fourth, in general, conduct the food policy more cautiously than in Russia, sparing the middle peasant more, taking fewer surpluses, etc.[9]

7. Treat the Jews[10] and urban inhabitants in the Ukraine with an iron rod, transferring them to the front, not letting them into government agencies (except in an insignificant percentage, in particularly exceptional circumstances, under class control[11]).

8. [Place] the teachers' union [spil'ka], the cooperatives, and other such petty bourgeois organizations in the Ukraine under special surveillance, with special measures for their disintegration, for the singling out of Communists, etc.

9. Initiate immediately especially energetic training of a special cadre of [party] workers for the Ukraine with specially reinforced surveillance and screening.

Quickly carry out such preparations both through all the individual people's commissariats and through the Orgburo.

1. In the margin "N.B.: include them in the Third International?" was crossed out by Lenin.

2. The word was substituted for *government* by Lenin. The following line was crossed out by Lenin: "In a minority; one can also include other parties, [but] all in a minority."

3. In the margin appears the phrase "in a veiled manner."

4. This paragraph was struck out by Lenin. In the margin: "The Ukrainian workers and peasants will decide their own fate."

5. Substituted by Lenin for "and only [the poor peasants]."

6. Lenin added "in a majority."

7. Lenin added "in a minority."

8. Lenin struck out *Russia*.

9. This was added in the margin: "The principles of food supply policy are the same as here."

10. In the margin Lenin added: "Express it politely: Jewish petty bourgeoisie."

11. This phrase was substituted by Lenin for "special supervision."

The intriguing part in Document 43 is the query about the creation of a "Galician striking force." It confirms information from other sources that the Red command was preparing to invade Poland in early 1920, before the Polish assault, in order to advance into western and southern Europe to aid revolutionary movements there.

Document 43
Telegram to Stalin

14 February 1920

14 February 1920

Kharkov, the Revolutionary-Military Council
of the Southwestern Front. To Stalin

Please speed up completion of the repair of the telephone lines; I have already given an instruction to this effect.

Advise more precisely **what measures you propose for the creation of a Galician striking force so that we will not have to shuffle divisions. Our diplomacy ought not to make noise but to keep silent about Galicia. Have you gotten in touch with Tukhachevsky[?].[1] Insist on the restoration of transport.**

Lenin

1. Mikhail Nikolaevich Tukhachevsky (1893–1937): army officer. Joined the Bolsheviks in 1918; defeated Kolchak the following year; led the Red Army in the assault on Warsaw in 1920. In 1921, commanded the Red troops that crushed the Kronshtadt rebellion. In 1931, was made marshal of the Soviet Union; was later arrested, accused of high treason, and shot.

The hints in Document 43 become clearer when read in conjunction with Lenin's statement in Document 44 that "a civil war in Germany may force" the Red Army "to move west to aid the Communists" there.

Document 44
Telegram to Stalin

[17 March 1920]

Coded by direct wire

To Stalin

I have just read the telegram from the commander in chief sent to you last night immediately upon receipt of your thoughts and in response to them. I find that the commander in chief is entirely correct that the operation in the Crimea cannot be delayed and that the Polish Fifty-second[1] is indispensable on the western front.[2] We have just received news from Germany that fighting is under way in Berlin and that the Spartacists have seized a part of the city.[3] It is not known who will win, but for us it is essential to speed up maximally the capture of the Crimea in order to have entirely free hands, as a civil war in Germany may force us to move west to aid the Communists.

Lenin

1. Reference to the Fifty-second Rifle Division of the Red Army, assigned to the Polish front.

2. On 15 March 1920, S. S. Kamenev, commander in chief of the Red Army, conveyed to the commanders of the western and Caucasian fronts a government directive that the Crimea was to be taken without delay and without weakening the southwestern army facing Poland. See f. 2, op. 1, d. 13,315, l. 3.

3. Lenin here confuses the right-wing Kapp putsch, which erupted in Berlin on 13–17 March 1920, with a Spartacist putsch. (See note 14 to Document 59.) The Spartacists (pro-Soviet German socialists who before long turned openly communist) raised the banner of revolt in the Ruhr on 19 March. Their revolt was suppressed as well.

The following exchanges concern the delegation of British trade unionists due in Moscow on 18 May 1920.[1]

1. See also British Labour Delegation to Russia, 1920, *Report* (London [1920]); Stephen Graubard, *British Labour and the Russian Revolution, 1917–1924* (Cambridge, Mass., 1956), 211–22; and *RUBR*, 203–5.

Document 45
Exchange Between Chicherin, Lenin, and Radek

6 April 1920

Letter from Chicherin to Lenin

6 April 1920

Respected Vladimir Ilich,

Shortly, a delegation from the [British] trade unions will make a sudden appearance on our border: it will have to be received very cordially. It will have some first-rate, high-caliber minds. It is essential to make political preparations for their visit; this is a complicated matter requiring time and attention. Someone should be assigned to work especially on this.

With communist greetings,
Georgy Chicherin

Note from Lenin to Chicherin

Comrade Chicherin!

        I am submitting the [following] proposal tomorrow to the Central Committee. Your opinion?
                      Lenin

> Briefly: in essence, organize **badgering** and **badger,** but in **extremely polite** forms.

Draft Resolution of the Central Committee RKP(b)

I propose the following **secret** resolution to the Central Committee:

1. For the reception of the trade union leaders, create a commission consisting of Radek, Melnichansky,[1] Fainberg,[2] + two others who have been to England and America, + Chicherin.
2. Task of the commission
    a. Arrange for the printing (if only of twenty to fifty copies) of English-language pamphlets for the "guests."
    b. Arrange for **reliable** interpreters, who should take turns, in order to be **inseparable** from the "guests."
    c. Organize **a campaign** in the Soviet press (brief articles, five to ten lines, **completely** exposing the guests as social traitors, **Mensheviks,** accomplices of English colonial plunder, and so on).
    d. Wage the same campaign at workers' rallies by **inviting** the guests to lectures and **asking** them "questions." Invite them to hundreds of factories in St. Petersburg and Moscow.
    e. Make the focus of the whole campaign (in newspapers, in flyers, at rallies) **precisely** the exposure of the guests **as Mensheviks,** in order to undercut the impact of their **inevitable** Menshevik speeches in England.

Corrections and Additions Drafted After a Telephone Conversation Between Lenin, Chicherin, and Radek

The campaign of discreditation should not be directed at all the guests. On the contrary, their leftist and rightist elements should be distinguished, so that the former refute the latter.

The campaign of discreditation must clearly emanate from below and not be obviously inspired by us. Therefore, the press must be restricted to calm, objective, factual reporting about the guests that will serve as material for the campaign of discreditation. The latter should be waged from the grass roots by dispatching delegations of workers with printed mandates that will be given to the guests, and posing questions at meetings. On the whole, the leaflets and other publications for the guests should be designed in such a way that they carry them back and distribute them in England.

Besides the campaign of discreditation, political preparation must be made in the form of publication of commissariats' reports and preparation of everything that will be shown to the trade unionists.

1. Grigory Natanovich Melnichansky (1886–1937): Old Bolshevik, in emigration until October 1917. On his return to Russia, worked in the Moscow Trade Council; subsequently served on diplomatic missions to Japan and in Rabkrin (the Workers and Peasants' Inspectorate) and Gosplan. Perished in Stalin's terror.

2. I. I. Fainberg (1886–1951): joined the Bolshevik Party in 1918. One of the founders of the Communist Party of Great Britain. Active in the Comintern until 1935.

Q uite insignificant in itself (like Document 79), Document 46 is included here to give an idea of the trivial issues with which Lenin chose to occupy himself. The cited telegram was written by semiliterate persons.

Document 46
Telegram to the Atkarsk District Land Department

[20 April 1920]

Atkarsk, District Land Department
Copy: Saratov, Province Land Department

I have received the following telegram from Atkarsk: "A member of Atkarsk District Executive Committee insistently demands a reduction for the following communities of delivery of pigs and sheep[:] from 1 Malo Voronets 120 sheep, 27 pigs, [from] 2 Malo Voronets, 180 sheep, 45 pigs [and from] Tashov 54 sheep and 24 pigs. Owing to the untimely demand, full delivery of sheep to the depot could not be made because of a severe decline in agriculture, a continued wave of losses [first] of cattle [and] then of sheep from the 1919 plague. All of the offspring are bound to perish. For your information, at the present time they weigh no more than twenty pounds, so that their delivery will bring little substantive benefit. The same for the pigs, because except for breeding stock with meat up to three poods[1] also yield no result [sic]. We urgently ask you not to reject our petition, and to cancel the delivery through the local Talov region's executive committee of the Atkarsk District. Ignat Kornienko, chairman of the soviets of 1 Malo Voronets; Trofim Volkov, 2 Malo Voronets." I request the land department to investigate immediately, on site, the status of these communities regarding livestock production. Report the results immediately.

Chairman of the Sovnarkom, Lenin

1. One pood equals 16.32 kilograms.

T he document that follows concerns the secret negotiations between Captain Ignacy Boerner—the envoy of Joseph Pilsudski, the Polish head of state—and the Polish Communist Julian Marchlewski,[1] representing the Soviet government. The talks concerned the possibility of a truce between Poland and Soviet Russia.[2]

1. Julian Marchlewski (1866–1925): Polish Communist. Active in the German Spartacus League and later in the Comintern. In 1919, served as a representative of the Soviet government in negotiations with Poland. In 1920, chaired the Moscow-sponsored Polish Revolutionary Committee, which in the event of the Red Army's victory was to assume governmental authority in Poland temporarily and sovietize her.

2. On 5 May 1920, Lenin familiarized himself with Marchlewski's 4 May report on the progress of negotiations with Pilsudski's envoy Captain Boerner about a truce with Poland, which he marked "5/5 from Marchlewski, secret, into the archive." See BKh, vol. 8, p. 522.

On the same day, Lenin forwarded this report to Trotsky with the following note: "Comrade Trotsky. I am sending you a letter from J. Marchlewski. We must have a talk by phone (before today's speeches) when you have read the letter. Yours, Lenin" (TP, vol. 2, pp. 160–61).

On 7 May the Politburo did not meet; it convened only on 10 May, but the note (Document 47) counseling against publication of the Marchlewski report was not recorded. The practice of including in the protocols Politburo decisions taken by polling the members was introduced in 1921.

See Document 1A (in the Appendix), a report from Marchlewski on his secret talks with Boerner the preceding fall, when the Poles promised the Russians that they would (passively) help them defeat Denikin.

Document 47
Note to Trotsky

7 May 1920

7 May 1920
Comrade Trotsky:

Comrade Marchlewski is also **against** publication of his negotiations with Boerner.

This should be bolstered by a Politburo resolution.

Add your vote and send it to all the Politburo members. (Send Marchlewski's text as well.)[1]

Yours, Lenin

Vote of the members of the Central Committee RKP(b) Politburo against the publication of the negotiations with Boerner.

> Lenin
> Trotsky
> L. Kamenev
> **Against** publication. J. Stalin
> (awkward to publish)

1. Trotsky added at this point: "Return the same day to Comrade Lenin. Trotsky."

O n 12 June 1920 the Central Committee of the Finnish Communist Party, with headquarters in Petrograd, requested the Sovnarkom to allocate to it the sum of ten million Finnish marks in gold for propaganda and educational activities in Finland and among Finns in Scandinavia, the United States, and other countries. It further requested one million marks to purchase the printing press of the Finnish Socialist Party, since there were no other outlets for communist literature.[1] Krestinsky allocated five million Finnish marks for these purposes.

1. See also f. 2., op. 2, d. 1,299, l. 1.

Document 48
Lenin's Annotation on a Letter from the Central Committee of the Finnish Communist Party

18 June 1920

I fully support the request of the Finnish Communist comrades and strongly urge you to speed up its implementation. If necessary, we will speak to each other on the phone today.

18 June

Lenin

H ere is Lenin's reaction to Chicherin and Litvinov's[1] recommendation that Fridtjof Nansen[2] be admitted into Soviet Russia in connection with his responsibilities as the League of Nations' chief commissioner for prisoners of war.[3]

1. Maksim Maksimovich Litvinov (1876–1951): Old Bolshevik; in 1930–39, Soviet foreign minister.
2. Fridtjof Nansen (1861–1930): well-known polar explorer and humanitarian who took an active part in helping refugees after World War I.

3. Lenin's note (Document 49) was written on the following letter from Chicherin dated 23 June 1920:

Respected Vladimir Ilich,

Litvinov reports that Nansen is coming to see him and wishes to receive permission to come to Moscow. Litvinov insists on an immediate reply. He thinks it is possible to allow Nansen in, only not in the capacity of a representative of the League of Nations, of course, but as a private person, without secretaries and other attendants. Nansen wants to work on the question of the Central Powers' prisoners of war. This, of course, is a minor question at the present time, but for us a meeting with Nansen is important in other respects. You no doubt recall that Nansen was always one of the most outstanding representatives of the leftist intelligentsia which insisted on reconciliation with Soviet Russia. The role of such radical intellectuals is, of course, somewhat complicated, and the Entente governments at one time tried to entangle and exploit Nansen for their own purposes. Litvinov rightly notes that if we manage to take Nansen into our hands, he could prove highly useful to us. His renown in the leftist bourgeois world and his major role would make close contact with him highly valuable for us politically. Litvinov correctly notes that the main thing that has to be watched is that no pernicious escorts accompany Nansen. Nansen alone can be very useful, but the escorts attached to him could be extremely harmful. We agree with Litvinov and think it is possible to allow Nansen to come here as a private person without escorts.

Document 49
Note to the Politburo

24 June 1920

I think he [Nansen] should not be allowed in as **yet.** We have no one to keep track [of him]. We will **miss** [something].

If the other Politburo members are for letting him in, I make this amendment: **absolutely** no one with him.

24 June

Lenin

F ollowing the crushing of the White Volunteer Army of the South, Soviet authorities in the Cossack regions of the northern Caucasus carried out mass executions and deportations.[1]

1. See V. L. Genis, "Raskazachivanie v Sovetskoi Rossii [De-Cossackization in Soviet Russia]," *Voprosy istorii* [Questions of history], 1 (1994): 42–55.

Document 50
Telegram to the Terek Regional Revolutionary Committee

[25–30 June 1920]

Vladikavkaz, Regional Revolutionary Committee

Until receipt of instructions from the center, immediately stop the implementation of your resolutions on the forced resettlement of Cossacks from the Terek, Sunzha, Vorontsovo-Dashkov settlements, and also the forced confiscation of arable lands from the Cossacks for distribution to mountain tribes. Wire to the People's Commissariat of Agriculture the reasons behind these resolutions. Wire implementation.

Chairman of the Sovnarkom, Lenin
People's Commissar of Agriculture,
Sereda[1]

1. Semyon Pafnutevich Sereda (1871–1933): Old Bolshevik; before the Revolution, a zemstvo statistician (zemstvos were organs of local self-government between 1864 and 1917). Served as commissar of agriculture from 1918 until 1921, after which he worked in Gosplan.

T he following documents reveal the strategy and tactics employed by Moscow in sovietizing Lithuania during the Red Army's sweep into Poland in the summer of 1920. Lenin's remarks appear in the margin of a letter to him from Chicherin. His laconic instruction, "We must [. . .] first sovietize Lithuania and then give it back to the Lithuanians," spelled out the formula used by Stalin to create the so-called satellite regimes in the Baltic region and the rest of Eastern Europe in 1940 and after World War II. Soviet Russia signed a peace treaty with Lithuania on 12 July 1920.[1]

The first article of the treaty affirmed the sovereignty of independent Lithuania and formally renounced all rights that Russia had previously held over the Lithuanian nation and its territories. And yet even as he signed this document, Lenin insisted on communizing Lithuania. On the day after the document was signed, the Red Army occupied Vilna and the Central Committee of the Communist Party of Lithuania appealed to the people to overthrow the "bourgeois" government and create Soviet authority there.[2]

1. On the terms of the treaty, see Albertas Gerutis, ed., *Lithuania: 700 Years* (New York, 1969), 164–65.
2. Jerzy Ochmański, *Historia Litwy* [History of Lithuania] (Wrocław, 1967), 255.

Document 51
Letter from Chicherin to Lenin, with Lenin's Marginalia

[10 July 1920]

Most respected Vladimir Ilich,

        I am sending you the text of the treaty with Lithuania. Marchlewski objects strenuously to the paragraph concerning the eastern border of Lithuania. In addition to Vilna, we are leaving to Lithuania parts of Oshmiansky and Lida Districts to the east of Vilna. The point is that when we were discussing with the Lithuanians joint action against the Poles, it was necessary to make them [the Lithuanians] a small territorial concession. Later it was decided that if we got together with them on all other questions, then they would retain this territorial concession. This question was put to the members of the Central Committee, and not only was it settled positively, but it was emphasized, especially by you, that territorial concessions were of no great significance and could be easily resolved. It would be quite impermissible and universally harmful to our reputation if, as a result of our military successes, we suddenly reneged on our final decision and suddenly refused [to cede] to Lithuania the parts of Oshmiansky and Lida Districts recognized as hers. This would be extremely impolitic because it would transform Lithuania from a benevolent neighbor, which she now is, into an indubitable and possibly active enemy.

Marchlewski also objects to our paying Lithuania three million.[1] At one time, the Central Committee gave our delegation carte blanche in this respect for up to five million, but the delegation conceded to Lithuania not five but only three million. This was an apparent reward to Lithuania for maintaining a very friendly stance [toward us] at the difficult time of the new intervention and for shattering through her conduct, before the eyes of the whole world, the Polish legend that Poland allegedly represents all the borderland nations. Reading English newspapers, I become convinced that the favor done us at the time by Lithuania was politically very significant; it is precisely this role of Lithuania that moved us to give [offer] her a maximum of five million, but instead, we are giving her only three.

The third incriminating point concerns the forest concession.[2] It surfaced at the very last moment, and Ioffe turned in this matter to the Supreme Council of the National Economy. The latter approved the plans for concessions, and Lomov[3] sent Ioffe several specialists, who worked out this question jointly with him. The text of the corresponding article of the treaty has been composed by our Supreme Council of the National Economy and fully corresponds to its intentions.

The agreement is to be signed on Monday, insofar as on Monday evening Ioffe is to depart for Riga to continue negotiations with Latvia. These negotiations have already passed the point of danger, in light of the changes in the military situation. It must be said that our talks with Finland and Latvia have proved, from the military point of view, most useful to us.

As concerns Marchlewski, he has fought very long against conceding even Vilna to Lithuania, on the groundless consideration that it will allegedly be more difficult for us to make peace with Poland if we turn Vilna over to Lithuania, inasmuch as this will allegedly deprive us of the possibility of giving Vilna to Poland, as if we could not in this event declare our disinterest, since we have in no way undertaken to defend Lithuania's new borders by force of arms.

The Lithuanians are now saying that they would like to conclude with us that convention about joint action, about the completion of which they had previously procrastinated. Ioffe justly points out that the small assistance which they would give us is outweighed by political inconveniences, because they can interpret this military help in the same sense as Petliura[4] did in his day with Denikin—i.e., that they will enter Vilna ahead of us, whereas without their military help we will take Vilna very soon. The agreement says nothing about the time[5] when we must turn Vilna over to them, and from the military-strategic point of view there is no hurry to do so. The Lithuanian delegates themselves express their **full readiness to have us occupy Vilna**[6] but only state the desire to run the civil administration. The latter, of course, is impossible; i.e., our regime is **incompatible with theirs.**[7] Once our occupation is in place, it will be necessary to have local Soviet authority and to create a Vilna Revolutionary Committee. Our relations with Lithuania require only that this Revolutionary Committee be regarded as local [and] not claim authority over all Lithuania. **In the opinion of Ioffe, who has in his day familiarized himself with Lithuania, under such conditions the sovietization of all Lithuania will proceed very fast.**[8] A Soviet Revolutionary Committee in Vilna and, generally speaking, in our occupation zone will confiscate estates from Polish landlords, and this cannot fail to have an effect on the peasantry of all Lithuania. We ourselves,[9] of course, will not meddle in Lithuanian affairs.

Thus, if a military convention with Lithuania is at present no longer expedient, then in reality something else is occurring. As a result of the Polish withdrawal, Lithuanian armies have already established contact with ours and greet them in the friendliest manner. They even propose joint action. The commander in chief has ordered to proceed with such action **under the condition that the Lithuanian armies be subordinate to ours.**[10] If such local agreements are made, that will only help us.

With communist greetings,
Georgy Chicherin

1. That is, gold rubles as an indemnity for the Soviet invasion of Lithuania in 1919. Lenin wrote in the margin: "All these concessions are unimportant. Important is the sovietization of Lithuania."

2. The treaty allowed Lithuania to cut timber on a hundred thousand hectares of Russian land, to use in reconstructing her economy.

3. Georgy Ippolitovich Lomov (1888–1938): Old Bolshevik. In 1918–21, served as deputy chairman of the Supreme Council of the National Economy and expert on timber.

4. Semyon Vasilievich Petliura (1877–1926): Ukrainian right-wing nationalist Social Democrat. In 1919, headed a Ukrainian military force that distinguished itself mainly

by carrying out pogroms against Jewish civilians. In 1920, collaborated in Pilsudski's invasion of the Ukraine. Was assassinated in Paris by a Jewish patriot.

5. Lenin wrote in the margin: "The crux of the matter is: we **must** occupy and **sovietize.** Judge, and judge **only** from this point of view: must one delay the treaty or can one sign [it?]. Occupy and organize **a revolution in Lithuania.**"

6. Underlined by Lenin. The Red Army occupied Vilna on 14 July 1920 in its advance on Warsaw.

7. Lenin underlined these words and then wrote and crossed out above them the word *inadmissible.*

8. Lenin underlined this passage and wrote in the margin: "This is now a *conditio sine qua non.* Please contact Ioffe about this today. Can one not insert something like it (the sovietization of Lithuania) into the treaty? If one cannot do this explicitly, then one must **ensure** [it] in fact; otherwise, I am **against** the treaty. Lenin.

N.B.: We must ensure that we **first** sovietize Lithuania and **then** give it back to the Lithuanians."

9. That is, the Russian Soviet government.

10. Underlined by Lenin.

T his telegram (Document 52) was sent at the time of the Soviet invasion of Poland.

Document 52
Telegram to I. S. Unshlikht[1]

[15 July 1920]

Smolensk, Revolutionary Council of the Western Front.
Secret. For Unshlikht only.

Communicate your assessment, and that of the other Polish comrades, of the following tactic:

1. We announce very solemnly that we assure Polish workers of a border east of the one offered by Curzon[2] and the Entente.

2. We are exerting all efforts to finish off Pilsudski.

3. We are entering Poland proper for only the briefest time to arm the workers and will depart from there at once.

4. Do you consider a Soviet revolution in Poland likely, and how soon[?].

Lenin

1. Iosif Stanislavovich Unshlikht (1879–1938): a Pole by origin. Served in the civil war and the war with Poland on the western front and held posts in the short-lived Lithuanian-Belorussian Republic. In 1921, was appointed one of the two deputy chairmen of the Cheka. Perished in Stalin's terror.

2. Lord Curzon (Curzon of Keddleston) (1859–1925): viceroy of India (1898–1905) and British foreign secretary (1919–24). In July 1920, at the height of the Polish-Soviet

war, proposed a border between the two countries which came to be known as the Curzon Line. It rested on the ethnic principle. In advancing into ethnic Poland, the Soviet government rejected the British proposal.

L enin presented these theses to the plenum of the Central Committee on 16 July 1920 during discussions of Curzon's Note of 11 July.[1] On the basis of Lenin's theses, approved by the plenum, Chicherin sent a response to Curzon on 17 July.[2] In it he rejected British mediation in the Polish-Soviet conflict, on the grounds that Britain had done nothing to prevent the Polish invasion of the Soviet Ukraine and that she was pressing Moscow to sign a truce with the White general Wrangel.[3]

The plenum also voted to send a delegation to England, headed by Kamenev. Kamenev was expelled from England on 1 September 1920, for smuggling in and selling precious stones and platinum, the proceeds of which (£75,000) he handed over to George Lansbury, the pro-Soviet editor of the *Daily Herald*.[4]

1. See *Dokumenty vneshnei politiki SSSR* [Documents of the foreign politics of the USSR], vol. 3 (Moscow, 1959), 54–55; and Richard H. Ullman, *The Anglo-Soviet Accord* (Princeton, N.J., 1972), 153–55.

2. *Dokumenty vneshnei politiki*, vol. 3, pp. 47–54; Ullman, *Anglo-Soviet Accord*, 166–69.

3. Pyotr Nikolaevich Wrangel (1878–1928): tsarist general, one of the leaders of the southern White army. In 1920, took command and evacuated most of its remnant to western Europe.

4. Ullman, *Anglo-Soviet Accord*, 270–73, 303–7.

Document 53
Draft Resolution of the Central Committee RKP(b) Plenum

[Prior to 17 July 1920]

1. Help the proletariat and the laboring masses of Poland and Lithuania to emancipate themselves from their bourgeoisie and landlords.

2. To this end—[mobilize] all forces, and especially press efforts to strengthen and speed up the offensive.

3. Also to this end—mobilize all Polish Communists, to a man, for the western front.[1]

4. Solemnly and officially announce to the Polish people that we guarantee them **in any event** as the border of the independent Polish republic a line **farther** east than that offered by Curzon and the Entente.

5. Other terms of peace will depend on the guarantees that the Polish people give us not to serve as an instrument of French, English, and other capitalists in [their] attempts against Soviet Russia.

6. Reject, with a detailed explanation, any mediation in negotiations with Poland and the other powers by both the League of Nations and England.

the direct and indirect pressure from the imperialists
"   "   participation of the Entente, etc.

7. We declare openly that if Poland seeks them,[2] we will **accept** peace negotiations, without rejecting negotiations for a truce.

8. England has made the proposal for a truce with Wrangel a separate issue. Clarify the **connection** between Poland and Wrangel in the Entente's offensive plan.[3]

N.B.: 9. Inasmuch as England is clearly revealing here the desire to annex the Crimea (develop, prove, expose), we state that we will not go along with this, and protest.

10. Inasmuch as England clearly **maintains** Wrangel and serves as his employer (his summons to London) (England does not want to have Wrangel himself even as a member of the peace conference), therefore [. . .][4]

1. Lenin added in the upper corner: "**Note:** 1. Exemptions are to be permitted only in exceptional cases by the Politburo. **Note** 2. The Central Committee recommends helping to create Soviet authorities in Poland and aiding them."

2. The following phrase is crossed out: "(directly or through another **uninvolved** power)."

3. The following phrase is crossed out: "(develop, prove this connection)."

4. Lenin crossed out the words *we reject,* which were here, added a footnote mark, and at the bottom of the text of the manuscript noted: "Add from the transcript." Lenin meant that the following passage should be inserted: "then renew consent to the old English proposal for Wrangel's capitulation on the terms offered (saving his life)."

Document 54
Telegram to Stalin

23 July 1920

23 July 1920   **Coded**
Kharkov. To Stalin

The situation in the Comintern is splendid. Zinoviev, Bukharin, and I, too, think that revolution in Italy should be spurred on immediately. My personal opinion is that to this end, Hungary should be sovietized, and perhaps also Czechia and Romania. We have to think it over carefully. Communicate your detailed conclusion. German Communists think that Germany is capable of mustering three hundred thousand troops from the lumpen[1] against us.

Lenin

РОССИЙСКАЯ
ФЕДЕРАТИВНАЯ
СОВЕТСКАЯ РЕСПУБЛИКА.

Председатель Совета
РАБОЧЕЙ и КРЕСТЬЯНСКОЙ
ОБОРОНЫ.
— о —
Москва, Кремль.

23 VII 19
№

Шифром

Харьков

Сталину

Положение в Коминтерне превосходное Зиновьев Бухарин

а также и я думаем что следовало бы поощрить революцию тотчас в Италии моё личное мнение что для этого надо советизировать Венгрию а может быть также Чехию и Румынию надо обдумать внимательно сообщите ваше подробное заключение немедленно Коммунисты думают что Чехия способна выдавить тогда наши войска не липнутся против нас

Ленин.

DOCUMENT 54. Telegram to Stalin, 23 July 1920

1. *Lumpenproletariat,* or "scamp proletarians," are marginal laborers said to be willing to sell themselves to the "bourgeoisie."

I n two telegrams dated 4 August 1920, Smilga and other Communists operating in Lithuania on behalf of the Soviet government described the economic situation in Vilna as desperate and requested immediate help in the form of food and money. They also recommended coming to terms with Letuvos Tariba, the national government of independent Lithuania created in 1917, and turning Vilna over to it. Document 55 indicates that the Politburo agreed to the latter proposal. Vilna for a while came under Lithuanian sovereignty, but it was seized by a Polish armed force and annexed to Poland in October 1920.

Document 55
Telegram to Smilga

[4 August 1920]

In reply to No. 135 and No. 138, we advise that the Politburo agrees with you and asks you to set deadlines for turning over Vilna and other locations.[1] Definitely demand that Tariba immediately undertake to supply food to the population, since we cannot provide grain, gold, or Nicholas [rubles].[2] We consider all this not a refusal to sovietize Lithuania but a postponement and an alteration in the form of sovietization.

1. The following phrase is crossed out: "Try to bargain."
2. "Nicholas rubles" (*Nikolaevki*) were banknotes issued under Nicholas II, which continued to circulate during the early years of the Soviet regime at a great premium to Soviet notes.

W ritten at the height of the war with Poland, the following document records the decision of the Soviet leadership to delay military offensives in Transcaucasia.

Document 56
Exchange Between Lenin and Krestinsky

[Before 9 August 1920]

Lenin to Krestinsky

Your opinion?
Delay the sovietization of Armenia.

Krestinsky to Lenin

We have already delayed the sovietization of Armenia; we should also delay that of Georgia.

Frumkin[1] is right—he has turned into a "Bufferite."[2]

1. M. I. Frumkin (1878–1939): Old Bolshevik. Held various posts in Soviet government, including membership in the Caucasian Bureau (Kavburo). Joined the "right opposition," was expelled from the party in 1937, and perished in Stalin's terror.

2. Refers to a faction formed in 1920 and headed by Bukharin during the dispute over the Workers' Opposition and the group of Democratic Centralists.

L enin's memorandum (Document 57)[1] is in response to Chicherin's expressions of anxiety that Soviet diplomatic codes might be deciphered.

1. Handwritten on Chicherin's letter, which reads:
21 August 1920
Respected Vladimir Ilich,
I have always regarded our codes with skepticism, have not reported the most secret things at all, and several times have cautioned others against making such reports. Comrade Kamenev's opinion that it is difficult to decipher the codes is not correct. We know from our official Sabanin, the son of an old cipher clerk in the Ministry of Foreign Affairs, that Russian cipher clerks positively deciphered all foreign codes. In the last years of tsarism there was no foreign cable that was not decoded, and this in consequence not of betrayal but of the skill of Russian code clerks. And foreign governments have even more complicated codes than the ones we use. [Even] if we constantly change the key [of the cipher], the system itself is known to tsarist bureaucrats and the military who are at present in the camp of the White Guards abroad. I consider the deciphering of our coded communications quite feasible. The most secret reports should not be conveyed other than through special couriers.
We will check whether, according to the dates, the codes mentioned by Kamenev are not a forgery. Only after receiving the text can a final answer to that question be given. With communist greetings, Georgy Chicherin.

Document 57
Note to Chicherin

[21 August 1920]

I propose

1. Changing the system immediately.

2. Changing the key [to the cipher] **every day**—for example, according to the **date** of the dispatch or according to the day of the year (the 1st . . . the 365th day, and so on and so forth).

3. Changing the system or its details every day (for example, five numbers for a letter; one system with the **first** number fictitious; a second system with the **last** number fictitious, and so on).

If you change a) the key and b) such details at least weekly, then it will be impossible to decipher.

T he following is a response to Chicherin's letter of 21 August 1920 to the Politburo, in which he raised the possibility of advancing bolder slogans to incite English workers, so that they would not only deter Britain from helping Poland but form volunteer units to fight Pilsudski and Wrangel.[1] Kamenev was in London at the time, negotiating with the British government. (He was expelled on 1 September; see the headnote to Document 53.)

1. F. 2, op. 2, d. 391.

Document 58
Draft of a Politburo Resolution

[21 August 1920]

I agree. Assign Chicherin on behalf of the **Politburo** to give this directive to [L. B.] Kamenev (to put forth offensive slogans and **in general** to switch from pacifism to revolutionary-communist slogans).

Lenin

N. Krestinsky

Trotsky

T he longest document in the present collection, Document 59 is a stenographic record of a speech Lenin delivered on 20 September 1920 to a closed meeting of the Ninth Conference of the Communist Party. Both *Pravda*[1] and *Izvestiia* carried summaries at the time that stressed the positive results of the Polish campaign as outlined by Lenin, but the text was omitted from the conference protocols as well as from all editions of Lenin's works. It was published for the first time seventy-two years later in *Istoricheskii arkhiv*.[2]

The purpose of the address was to explain the defeat of the Red Army in Poland and the reasons that had motivated the Politburo to violate the ethnic border of that country. It is the only known document in which Lenin indicates that the invasion of Poland had as its objective not only the sovietization of that country but also an immediate advance on Germany and possibly England, both of which Lenin viewed as in the grip of a 1917-like revolution. The key sentences explaining why the Red Army was sent into Poland proper read: "The defensive period of the war with worldwide imperialism was over, and we could, and had the obligation to, exploit the military situation to launch an offensive war"—not just against Poland, a pawn in Allied hands, but against Europe. "We use every opportunity to go from the defense to the offense." The speech also explains the Soviet strategy of destroying the Versailles treaty by forming an alliance with right-wing German elements ("a bloc of consistent and extreme patriots and Communists"), which was consummated two decades later in the Hitler-Stalin pact.

The speech is unusually rambling even for Lenin, filled with elliptical sentences, and at times obscure. Some of the confusion is due to the poor quality of the stenographic recording.

1. *Pravda*, 29 September 1920, p. 1.
2. *Istoricheskii arkhiv* [Historical archive], vol. 1 (1992), 14–29.

Document 59
Political Report of the Central Committee RKP(b) to the Ninth All-Russian Conference of the Communist Party

[20 September 1920]

Comrades, naturally the focus of attention in a report that has to be made at this time must be the war with Poland and all the vicissitudes that we have experienced recently. Allow me to begin from somewhat afar, from the period before this Polish war had become a fact.

You know that before the Polish war we had treated the matter with extreme caution and proposed peace to the Poles, to the Polish bourgeoisie, most solemnly, especially in a manifesto on behalf of the [V]TsIK under peace terms of the utmost advantage to them, the Poles, a peace not advantageous to[1] a great number of workers and peasants, and nationalities, who lived under the yoke of the Polish landowners and bourgeoisie.[2] We offered peace on the basis of the Pilsudski line—that is, the line where the Poles stood prior to the offensive of 26 April of this year; that is, a line which gave them all of Belorussia and a good chunk of the Ukraine, because at that time they had Volyn Province, far to the east of Rovno, which they have now wrested from us. We agreed to conclude a peace along that line, considering the peaceful economic work to which we had reassigned the army and tens of thousands of workers and peasants to be far more important than the opportunity to liberate Belorussia and part of the Ukraine or eastern Galicia by military means. Here, in international political and economic respects, it has been repeatedly confirmed and will continue to be confirmed that precisely [because of] the fact that our new diplomacy is entirely unconventional, unanticipated, and unprecedented in the history of the monarchical and bourgeois states, it can in no way as yet be accepted by the other countries. When [we] the Bolsheviks make straightforward statements, literally no one in a single country is capable of understanding that we are really conducting diplomacy on the basis of open statements and methods of special diplomacy. That is, the Bolsheviks are saying: ["]We are willing to accept the Pilsudski line, which must mean that the Bolsheviks are incredibly weak and the concession is incredibly great.["]³ We supported the utterly insane chauvinism of the Polish bourgeoisie and landowners, the utterly insane chauvinism in France and other imperialistic countries, all of which reasoned that in ordinary diplomacy such a thing could not be. Is it really done that way? This signifies weakness. Thus the offensive was decided on not only by the Poles but by France as well, because we said outright in an entirely unconventional manner: ["]In order to avoid war, we are prepared for an offensive,["] whereas in the negotiations conducted previously by Marchlewski, as a formal representative of the Polish Red Cross, such a line as the preliminary condition meant an enormous concession. This concession was interpreted as [a sign of] our weakness and led to war. You recall the beginning of the war, which brought success to the Poles, until the conquest of Kiev; according to preliminary calculations, they ruled a territory with a population of nearly four million. You will recall that after this success, the deployment of [our] forces brought success, and our troops, switching to the offensive, quickly reached Poland's main border.

Here begins a major turning point in the history of the Polish war, which in fact became a turning point for the world. We must proceed from this in order to clarify subsequent history and proceed to the main point that now concerns every party man, the most urgent question, namely, the profound defeat, the catastrophic defeat that we have suffered in consequence of the whole unfolding of the operation.

On 12 July, when our troops, having crossed an enormous space in an unceasing offensive, approached the ethnic border of Poland, the English government, in the person of Curzon, addressed a note to us demanding that we halt our troops at a line fifty versts from the ethnographic border of Poland, on the condition that the peace be concluded on that line. This line ran from Bialystok and Brest-Litovsk, giving us eastern Galicia. It was very advantageous for us. It was called the Curzon Line. And that was when we found ourselves facing the basic question. The Central Committee had to make a most important decision. And that is the starting point to which I will have to return in my report in order to provide an assessment of the

most important and basic question. We faced the question of either accepting this proposal, which would have given us an advantageous border and
thus [allowed us to] assume a position that was, generally speaking, purely
defensive, or [else] to exploit the élan of our army and the advantage we
enjoyed to help in the sovietization of Poland. Here stood the basic question of a defensive or an offensive war, and we in the Central Committee
knew that this was a new, fundamental question, that we stood at a turning
point of the whole policy of Soviet power.

Until then, in waging war with the Entente—because we knew perfectly
well that the Entente stood behind every limited offensive by Kolchak and
Yudenich—we realized that we were waging a defensive war and could
win the battles with the Entente, but that we could not win the final victory
over the Entente, which was many times stronger than we were. We merely
tried to exploit as broadly as possible the splits emerging between the
various countries of the Entente, in order to defend ourselves in due course.
The story with Yudenich and Denikin proved something unprecedented,
something incredible from the point of view of the correlation of forces. We
split them apart, and the smartest politicians of the world—not only those
who gave themselves airs from the colonial perspective, like England,
[and] overweening France, worried about their billions from the former
tsarist house (and there are still such strange people there hoping for their
return); not only politicians who have gone too far, who think of grabbing
something from Russia, not only big politicians interested in Russia, but
also those without a direct interest—they [all] found themselves in a state
of collapse. Although a hundred times stronger than we, they did not take
advantage of this opportunity, because they had collapsed internally; because they could not take a single step, they could not solve the simple
problem of uniting three or four elements, uniting, coordinating three or
four mighty "Great Powers," with vast superiority by comparison with us
not only financially but in terms of the navy and so on. We had nothing, but
they could not unite even with respect to finance, and this gave us the
advantage. And this was at a time when the whole bourgeoisie was burning
with fury and hatred of Bolshevism, and yet it turned out that we were
stronger than they. They let the enemy in, bit by bit. Shouting that they did
not want the return of the tsar, they could not prevent the purely monarchical policy of Yudenich and Denikin and thus drove away the element that
should have backed them (the peasant and kulak elements).

And so, in sum, our conviction ripened that the Entente's military offensive against us was over, that the defensive war with imperialism had
ended, and that we had won it. The stake was Poland. And Poland thought
that as a great power with imperialist traditions, she was capable of changing the nature of the war. This meant that the assessment was as follows:

the period of defensive war was finished. (Please take fewer notes. This should not get into the press.) On the other hand, the offensive showed us that because the Entente was powerless to crush us militarily, powerless to utilize its troops, it could only push various small countries against us, countries that have no military worth and that maintain a landowner-bourgeois system only at the cost of such violence and terror as the Entente provides them with. There is no doubt that the Menshevik democratic capitalism that still maintains itself in all the countries bordering on Russia, formed out of the previous territories of the former Russian Empire, starting with Estonia, Georgia, etc., maintains itself with the help of what England delivers. She provides cannons, soldiers, uniforms, and money to keep the workers in subjection.

We faced a new task. The defensive period of the war with worldwide imperialism was over, and we could, and had the obligation to, exploit the military situation to launch an offensive war. We had defeated them when they advanced against us; we would now try to advance against them in order to assist the sovietization of Poland. We will help to sovietize Lithuania and Poland, as was said in our resolution, when the resolution was raised in the Central Committee, and we certainly did not fail to understand the rather awkward nature of this resolution, in the sense that it seemed impossible to vote against it. How could you vote against assisting sovietization? If we compare our attitude toward Poland with our attitude toward Georgia and Latvia, the difference becomes completely clear. We did not pass resolutions to assist the sovietization of Georgia or Estonia by military means. We passed the opposite resolution, that we would not help. This caused a number of conflicts with the revolutionaries and Communists of these countries. They made speeches against us full of bitterness, asking how we could conclude peace with the White Guard Latvian henchmen who subjected to torture and hanged on the gallows the best Latvian comrades, who had shed their blood for Soviet Russia. We heard similar speeches from the Georgians as well, but we did not assist the sovietization of Georgia and Latvia. But we cannot do this now, either—we have other things to attend to.[4] The overwhelming task is the salvation and strengthening of the [Soviet] republic. We charted this policy with regard to Poland. We decided to use our military forces to assist the sovietization of Poland. Our subsequent overall policy flowed from this [decision]. We formulated it not in an official resolution recorded in the minutes of the Central Committee and representing the law for the party and the new congress, but we said among ourselves that we must probe with bayonets whether the social revolution of the proletariat in Poland had ripened.

Here we raised a practical question, which as it turned out was theoretically not entirely clear for the best communist elements of the international community, that is, the Communist International. When the Comintern Congress convened in July [1920] in Moscow, we were settling this question in the Central Committee. We could not raise this question at the Comintern Congress because that congress had to proceed openly—that was its enormous revolutionary, global political significance, which will become much more evident than has been the case up until now.

At the congress there were elements, including the German Independents,[5] who have launched a most vile policy against the Soviet government. It was impossible at that time to throw them out. We had to show the worldwide communist party that we did not want to allow them into our ranks. Thus at the Communist International Congress we had to speak openly. Therefore, this question was deliberately not raised at the congress.

The shift to the offensive against the Entente's allies could not be raised there, because the stage of development needed to discuss this question had not yet been reached there. We had to be patient. [Die] Rote Fahne [The red banner] and many others cannot tolerate even the thought that we will assist the sovietization of Poland with our own hands. These people consider themselves communists, but some of them remain nationalists and pacifists. Of course, the communists who have suffered more, such as the Finnish comrades, have not retained a shadow of those prejudices. I say they did not retain them because they had suffered a longer period of war. When an English workers' delegation visited me and I told them that every decent English worker should desire the defeat of the English government, they understood nothing. They made faces that I think even the best photograph could not capture. They simply could not get into their heads the truth that in the interests of the world revolution, workers must wish the defeat of their government.

The fact that in Poland the proletarian population is well matured and the rural proletariat is better educated tells us: you must help them sovietize.

So this was the stage at which events found us and where our party stood. This was a most important turning point not only in the politics of Soviet Russia but also in world politics. Until now we have acted as a single force against the whole world, dreaming only of how to spot rifts among [our enemies], so that the foe could not crush us. But now we said: ["]We have now become stronger, and we will respond with a counterattack to each of your attempts at attack, so that you know that you risk not only squandering some millions, as you squandered them on Yudenich, Kolchak, and Denikin, but you risk that each of your attacks will expand the territory of the Soviet republic.["] Until now, Russia has been only an object that people pondered and judged how best to divide among Yudenich, Kolchak, and Denikin. But now Russia has said: ["]We will see who is stronger in war.["] This is how the question has been posed now. This is a shift in politics as a whole, world politics. Here a historian will have to note that it is the beginning of a new period.

What were the results of such policies[?] Of course, the main result was that now we have suffered an enormous defeat. In order to come to this, I must describe what came before. As far as we were able to probe with a bayonet the readiness of Poland for social revolution, we must say that this readiness was slight. To probe with a bayonet meant gaining direct access to the Polish farm laborers and to the Polish industrial proletariat, to the extent that it remained in Poland. The industrial proletariat remained in Warsaw, Łódź, and Dąbrowa,[6] which were very far from [our] borders. On the other hand, in order really to probe the degree of the Polish proletariat's readiness, first of the industrial proletariat and second of the farm laborers, who were subjugated,[7] we had to clear of Polish bourgeois forces and occupy not only the regions of Warsaw but also the regions with the industrial proletariat. These regions, however, start even [farther away][8] than Warsaw, which we did not manage to occupy. Thus we were able to probe Poland's readiness for a socialist revolution only to an extremely small extent. We encountered a great national surge of petty bourgeois elements who, as we got closer to Warsaw, were terrified for their national existence. We did not really manage to test the true mood of the proletarian masses among either farm laborers or the industrial proletariat.

On the other hand, a picture emerged in international politics that was extremely instructive and turned out to be the crux of the event. Comrade Kamenev, who has observed certain upheavals in London, will shed light on one side of the story in full detail. We did not succeed in probing the development and readiness for the socialist revolution of the proletariat in Warsaw. Our advance proved that Poland could not beat us, but we were very close to [beating them].[9] It turned out that all this changed international politics. In approaching Warsaw, we came so close to the center of world imperialist politics that we started to make them [politics] ourselves. This sounds incomprehensible, but the history of the Council of Action in England[10] has proved with absolute precision that somewhere in the proximity of Warsaw lies not the center of the Polish bourgeois government and the republic of capital, but that somewhere in the proximity of Warsaw lies the center of the entire current system of international imperialism, and that we are now at a point when we are beginning to sway this system and making politics not in Poland, but in Germany and England. Thus in Germany and England we have created a completely new zone of the proletarian revolution against worldwide imperialism, because Poland, as a buffer between Russia and Germany, Poland, as the last[11] state, will remain entirely in the hands of international imperialism against Russia. She is the linchpin of the whole Treaty of Versailles. The modern imperialist world rests on the Treaty of Versailles. Having defeated Germany and settled the question of which of the two powerful international groups—the English or the German—will determine the fate of the world in the coming years, imperialism ended up with the Versailles peace. They have no other means of solidifying international relations, political as well as economic, than the Versailles peace. Poland is such a powerful element in this Versailles peace that by extracting this element we break up the entire Versailles peace. We had tasked ourselves with occupying Warsaw; the task changed and it turned out that what was being decided was not the fate of Warsaw but the fate of the Treaty of Versailles. This was how the question was posed by the entire German bourgeois Black Hundred[12] and French press. The approach of our troops to the borders of eastern Prussia, separated [from Germany proper] by the Polish corridor that reaches Danzig, showed that all Germany was seething. News began to come out that tens and hundreds of thousands of German Communists were crossing our borders, and telegrams flew [from] German Communist regiments. We had to make decisions not to publicize the help [of the German Communists] and to continue asserting that we were waging war [against Poland]. Now when newspapers arrive that do not share the views of the Bolsheviks and that portray the situation in eastern Prussia, there is an extremely interesting picture that reminds me of certain periods of the Russian revolution of 1905, when in Russia[13] there appeared the average type of a Black Hundred revolutionary.

At the time, the revolution of 1905 in Russia was taking the first major steps to dig up and arouse the largest and at the same time the most backward elements, which, through their agitation against us, tried to incite the peasantry. At that time, this agitation was waged by the Black Hundred clergy and officers, and it turned out that this newly emergent Black Hundred political organization for the first time united the peasants, attracting them to [the idea of] organization. These aroused peasants came one day with Black Hundred demands and the next day demanded all the land-owners' land. And the same thing is happening at present in Germany. I did not bring with me a dispatch from one of the German anti-Bolshevik newspapers (which of course I could not read out in its entirety, for lack of time) [which reports] that all of eastern Germany is seething, and all the Kappists[14] (that is, the ones who were for Kapp—[like] our Kornilov[15]) all of these Kappists are for the Bolsheviks, and you get a situation where they talk with a backward German lad who understands nothing of politics, he hesitates and says that Wilhelm[16] has to be brought back because there is no order, and in the same breath, he says the opposite, that one has to follow the Bolsheviks. And we see that eastern Germany is seething, that it is forming into some kind of unnatural bloc headed by Kornilovite generals, who, as people of military mentality, have a slogan: ["]War with France, regardless of everything, it does not matter with whom and under what conditions.["] These officers—people who are politically illiterate, who do not know that war has certain consequences (how could they know that?)—such German officer[s] would have to study various revolutions for ten years in order to learn anything. So they have this idea of war with France no matter what. And thus it happened that we had power, and significant power, against the Entente.

So at the time we replied to Curzon, ["]You refer to the League of Nations. But what is the League of Nations? It is not worth a damn.["] Another question: Who will decide the fate of Poland? The question can be decided not by what the League of Nations says but by what the Red Army soldier says. This is what we replied to Curzon, if we translate our note into plain language. This is how it was understood in Germany, and an unnatural characteristic[17] bloc emerged, a bloc that was not formed by agreement, that was not recorded anywhere or voted on, but a bloc in which the Kappists and the Kornilovites, the entire mass of patriotically inclined elements joined up with the Bolsheviks. That was how the problem stood then, and the German Communists could not resolve this problem at the time; they could not resolve it because at the time they were sitting here in Moscow and resolving the most primitive question of how to create elements of a real communist party in Germany, resolving the basic question of the attitude [to take] toward the right-wing Independents, whose leaders resembled our Martov,[18] while the workers were Bolshevik-minded. They were busy solving this worldwide question that had arisen in all the countries. And at that time the events in Germany overtook all resolutions of these matters and there loomed a bloc of consistent and extreme patriots and Communists, who consciously acknowledged a bloc with Soviet Russia. So there came into being such a bloc that only two forces exist [now] in world politics: one is the League of Nations, which produced the Versailles treaty, and the other is the Soviet republic, which undermined this Versailles treaty, and the unnatural German bloc was on our side.

Here emerged a gigantic fact of international politics that I have observed by bits and pieces a number of times, and upon which I had to dwell when summarizing the results of the campaigns of Yudenich, Kolchak, and Denikin and speaking of the terms for concluding peace with Estonia, Georgia, and Latvia. What transpired internationally was not only that we had beaten Kolchak and Denikin and conquered the prosperous Russian peasantry—the anticommunist peasantry, which, by the way, had decided the fate of Kolchak and Denikin. But we conquered the petty bourgeoisie and the big bourgeoisie of the little countries, which were formally independent, but crushed by the Entente. That decided Estonia [to] sign a peace with us, the first country to conclude peace with us. She is thoroughly bourgeois, she is entirely in the pocket of English and American billionaires, she was wholly against peace with us, and [yet] she concluded peace with us because international imperialism seemed too much for her.

In Germany, the Communists stuck to their slogans. When the German leftists got to saying such an absurdity as that a civil war was not necessary but that on the contrary what was needed was a national war against France, it was an unheard-of stupidity. To put the question this way bordered on treason. Without civil war you will not get Soviet rule in Germany. If you form a bloc with the German Kornilovites, they will dupe you. In Germany there is a small, weak Communist Party and a strong party of Scheidemannites,[19] [that is,] right-wing Mensheviks. [It is] an enormous proletarian party headed by [people like] our Martovs. It is fence-sitting politics. And the first result was that along with the small states that all joined us despite their hatred of the Bolsheviks, along with the executions of their own Bolsheviks—Estonian, Finnish, Latvian—they were forced to conclude peace with us and said that in the international respect, we little countries are closer to Soviet, Bolshevik Russia. We proved in practice that for Germany—where the sentiment of the most backward and Black Hundred–like masses capable of saying "better Wilhelm"—in respect to international relations there is no other force but Soviet Russia. The national aspirations of Germany consist of two quantities, not to distinguish between which is to commit a huge mistake. One quantity is to throw off the Versailles treaty, which is suffocating them. On the other hand, the German imperialists who sided with this said: ["]We want only to throw off the Treaty of Versailles["][20]—but in fact they wished to restore imperialist Germany. We have been sounding out the international situation not only in regard to the little countries but also in regard to Germany. In my Petrograd speech at the opening of the Comintern Congress, I had occasion to speak about the international situation, and I said that the earth's population had now reached one and three-quarters billion,[21] of which a quarter of a billion was in the colonies and three quarters of a billion in the countries that had been defeated, which means that 70 percent was in the colonies.[22] I said that even with such a rough definition, if we were speaking of world politics, then seven-tenths of the population, given a correct policy, would back Soviet Russia.[23] Here someone may ask, How can they be for Soviet Russia if they are not Communists? But how were Estonia and Georgia for us, when they were shooting their own Communists?

We have now proved with our international policy that we have an alliance with all the countries living under the Versailles treaty, and that is 70 percent of the whole population of the earth. If in Germany people merely trembled and waited, in England the situation shaped up differently. In England Curzon has issued an ultimatum to us: ["]Either leave [Poland] or we fight.["] They have grown used to thinking that they who have signed the Treaty of Versailles can run the whole world. When we replied to this that we did not recognize the League of Nations, the French newspapers said: "An impudent response." It is an expression from the terminology of the schoolroom, where the teacher tells the children that they behave impudently; in international politics such terms should not be used. The fact is that the League of Nations has not shown itself to be such. It has turned out that in order to fight us, first of all you have to ask the English worker. As a result of our declaration, it has turned out that the English proletariat has raised itself to an entirely new revolutionary level. Standing outside Warsaw and unable to take this Warsaw and probe it to see how ready the Polish workers were for revolutionary action, we probed the English workers and raised them to a new level of revolutionary action. When the ultimatum was issued to us, the British workers, nine-tenths of whom are the vilest Mensheviks, replied to this with the formation of the Council of Action. The English press grew worried, crying that this was "dual power," and it was right. England was at the same stage with regard to political relations as Russia after February 1917, when alongside the government existed the soviets, which had the Conciliation [Control] Commission and actually verified the government's every step, and when the bourgeoisie of the whole world said that you could not exist like that. And now this Council of Action turns up in England and this Council of Action has prevented England's war with us. None of the threats that Lord Curzon made to us could be implemented, and the workers' movement of England has risen to incredible heights.

The Council of Action has created an organ for all the working masses, which took its place alongside the bourgeois [government] and does not collaborate with it. At the head of this Council of Action stand glaring Mensheviks and glaring right-wing SRs, the [very] people whom we have hounded in the past. They needed the Second Congress of the Comintern in Moscow, where representatives of all countries assembled. Only now has the complete text of the resolutions been published, where this policy is accepted on an international scale. And what relationship has emerged[?]. It is said that we have proposed unprecedented terms. Then a split occurred there: at any rate, a split between the Bolsheviks and the Mensheviks in all the countries of the world, without exception.

At a time when, with the help of the Comintern, we accomplished that which in decades could not be done even under the conditions of a complete split with international imperialism, in England the Mensheviks and the Bolsheviks united in the Council of Action. We were painfully forced to resolve problems of incredible difficulty. The progress of the workers' movement is worth a split with the Mensheviks and, at the same time, cooperation with them in the Council of Action.

At first glance, this seems to be a contradiction and opportunism, but we say: ["]You will have to continue the Russian Revolution in its basic outlines.["] The Council of Action in England entirely resembles our VTsIK of the time when the decisions were made by Gots,[24] Dan,[25] and the others—that is, an alliance of all workers, without distinction between Menshevik and Bolshevik Parties. An alliance that competes with the bourgeois government, where the Mensheviks are forced to act like Bolsheviks. We understand that the manifesto of 1917, released by the Mensheviks and SRs at the first VTsIK, said that the war was imperialist, that we should defend the minority. They were confused, and the masses were brought over to us, and thus Plekhanov was right.

They say: ["]We are for constitutional democracy, and you are for a private [sic] democracy.["] There is also the Council of Action, but that is an extreme case. This is something that we had to read [sic], because this concerns the relations of the most imperialist country, with unusually solid traditions of Menshevism. If in our country Menshevism has a fifteen-to twenty-year history, [in England] all the trade union organizations have a thoroughly democratic system, headed by the Mensheviks. It was all destroyed by the English Mensheviks, and they had to advance to the period of the dictatorship of the proletariat. We gained the opportunity to tell the English and French workers that you must teach them to be communists. The Comintern taught this. English politics is beginning to teach politics to the French.

At the same time, you must learn, on the basis of mass organizations, to form blocs with the English Bolsheviks when they are forced to behave constitutionally, so that the English masses learn this in practice. [. . .][26] It was hard for us to decide, and we in Russia ourselves suffered terribly over [the question of] how many times the Mensheviks and the SRs would dupe the Russian workers before they would cease to believe them. They duped the Russian workers before the February Revolution, they duped them from May until the July offensive, duped them once again, and finally, by October, the Russian worker had matured to such an extent that he did not allow himself to be duped any longer. How many times it will be necessary for the English workers to be duped by the English Mensheviks is not written in any book and cannot be written. This will be seen, but the English Bolsheviks must know how to stand together with the masses at all times, educating them, demonstrating to them and telling them: "You are being duped again; there, you have been duped once more." And we see in the course of current events in England, and Comrade Kamenev will summarize his impressions, that the English Mensheviks already sense themselves to be the government. They know that the bourgeois government in England will not last, that it will be overthrown. They see a government post before them. "Welcome, [we say to them,] but you will also fall from this government post as your bourgeois government has fallen, and you will fall so hard that you will never climb up again."[27]

Such are the results of our international policy and the relations taking shape in western Europe.

Now I must come to the main and dismal point that has emerged from this summary. We have been so pushed at the front, we have fallen back to such an extent, that battles are being fought near Grodno, and the Poles are approaching the line from which Pilsudski previously boasted that he would advance on Moscow. And which remained only boasting. It must be said that despite the fact that we have been pushed back, our troops have nevertheless worked miracles. They have been thrown back hundreds [of versts] to the east and west, but they have not been pushed back to the place where we previously offered to make peace with Pilsudski. And now Pilsudski will have to make peace on terms that are worse for him and better for us than under our first offer. But nevertheless we have suffered an enormous defeat; a colossal army of a hundred thousand is either prisoner of war or [interned] in Germany. In a word, a gigantic, unheard-of defeat.

What does this mean? It means that a mistake has undoubtedly been committed; after all, we had victory in hand and we let it slip. This means a mistake was made. This question faced each one of us, and we in the Central Committee searched for the answer: What was the mistake? Where is it and where to find it? The mistake clearly had to be either in policy or in the strategy of war. But you know that strategy and policy are inseparably linked. During the civil war, we in the Politburo had to decide purely strategic matters, matters that were purely strategic to such an extent that we looked at each other with a smile—how we had turned into strategists. In our midst were even people who had never seen war even from afar, and even so, we had to be involved in strategy, because strategy is subordinate to politics and [the two] are inextricably linked. Now, as in the era of the Yudenich and Denikin offensives, we have decided purely strategic matters many times; this no longer surprised us. Now, however, we have to remember that every strategy is nothing but politics.

Where should we now look for the mistake? Perhaps the mistake was political, perhaps it was strategic as well. I do not claim in the slightest to know military science; I apologize in advance to the comrades who know this science in theory and practice. I will analyze this matter from the perspective of where to look to see if it was possibly a political or a strategic mistake.

I will state now that the Central Committee analyzed this question and left it open. In order to make this question the object of investigation, to resolve it in the proper manner, we have to devote to it greater efforts than we have at our disposal, because we are entirely preoccupied with the future. So we decided to let the historians resolve the past; let them figure out this question later. This is the conclusion we reached. The mistake was either in policy or in strategy, or both. Perhaps the mistake was in the reply to Curzon's Note of 12 June, when we said, plainly: "To hell with the League of Nations, we are going forward."

Of course, we diagnosed incorrectly. A correct diagnosis is demanded of revolutionaries who are in a difficult political situation, who are used to settling matters victoriously, when there is unprecedented heroism and a surge of the masses. In deciding this matter, we predetermined a general offensive line. Fundamentally, it was correct—we are certain of that; it was fundamentally sound and really coincided with a new period in world history, when Russia, which up until then had been an object of decision making [by others]—would Yudenich or Kolchak devour it, and how[?]—[this] Russia was now determining England's domestic policy. And perhaps a different reply should have been given here. We [could have] said that we basically accepted Curzon's offer but we would haggle. And we [could have] haggled on the basis of our decision until such time as Kamenev was forced, owing to circumstances beyond his control, to haggle in such a way that he was kicked out [of England]. We received help from the Council of Action, so in the end Kamenev won, and not Lloyd George.[28] Perhaps we should have answered thus: ["]We accept in principle that we will remain on the fiftieth verst, or on the border that you indicate.["] This is determined by the condition of the military fronts. In gaining eastern Galicia, we had a base against all the contemporary states. Under those conditions we came to border on Carpathian Rus, which is seething more than Germany and provides a direct corridor to Hungary, where a small flash point is enough to spark a revolution. At the international level we preserved the aura of a country that is invincible and a great power. This is great praise. But here another policy took shape. We would not have gotten that seething which occurred, for certain we would not have gotten the Council of Action, and we would not have gotten the shift of England's whole proletarian and bourgeois politics to a new stage. But from the projected borders we would have won a solid, comfortable, firm base for operations against central Europe. I repeat, perhaps this was a political mistake, for which the Central Committee on the whole is responsible, and for which each one of us takes personal responsibility. This is a fundamental mistake. Strategy is subordinate to politics.

Another explanation is possible—namely, given that the Central Committee set the political line, determined the status of all Soviet organs, since it determined the bounds beyond which our command could not go [. . .].[29] You gave the assignment to help sovietization, to cross the ethnographic border and maintain the border with Germany from the place where we stood, from Bialystok. A strategy could have been developed to alter our strategic conditions and tasks. It is possible to argue that strategists should accurately implement the solution of the task. But talk, motives, and moods are one thing, and decisions another. You can talk, but if you do not carry out decisions, if you are not a decent people's commissar, then you will be chased out or put in jail. Without this awareness we would all have long ago fallen apart. Here strategy will perhaps enable one to understand and say: ["]But we do not have the forces to attack, and after crossing fifty or a hundred versts, having stopped, we would have stood in ethnic Poland, and we would have [had] a true, assured victory.["] If we had stopped, we would already for sure have had peace now, an absolutely victorious peace, while retaining all the aura and all that influence on international politics. It is possible that a strategic mistake was committed.

Such is the general framework within which all these errors naturally revolved in the minds of the Central Committee [members]. You will see why the prevalent opinion in the Central Committee was that no, we would not create a commission to study the conditions of the offensive and retreat. We do not have the resources to study this question. We now have a number of other matters that require immediate attention. We cannot commit a single, even second-class resource to this. We have to resolve other questions, the most complex questions of politics and strategy, because we recall how we beat Denikin, driving him to the Donetsk region and, unable to finish him off at all, were rolled back to Orel. We saw how we fought Kolchak. When we drove him to Ufa and then he drove us back to Samara, the entire European press set a new date for the fall of Moscow and Petrograd.

Interestingly, I saw in an American publication yesterday that some people had collected in a small publication full information on what the best American papers were writing about Russia.[30] You cannot conceive better agitation for the Bolsheviks. They study how often the date has been set for the fall of Moscow and Petrograd. This little pamphlet consists of what the American papers said from October 1917 to 1920 and, in a word, what came out of this. There is no better or more successful short history of this offensive than this publication; we will try to publish it in Russian.

You recall what [they wrote] about our Red Army after one hundred and fifty versts of defeats—how it [then] finished off Kolchak. It did the impossible, as a comrade from the Red Army told me, before this halt fifty versts outside Cheliabinsk, when it became incapacitated. Comrade Smirnov[31] said: ["]Look at the Russian soldier. If we had not gone forward, we could have mobilized new ones.["] In a desperate plight, with regard to [a lack of] boots—the advance was impossible; this was done, but it was accomplished by heroes who by nature can work miracles. The Red Army soldier began to work miracles. He marched eighty versts; will he march another oo, or should he be stopped at oo versts because he will not go any farther[?].[32] This was a strategic task of unprecedented difficulty, a new strategy. You see there elements of the task from which the Central Committee drew its conclusion. The Central Committee itself, while incredibly worried that we had made a mistake and suffered a defeat, is not undertaking to correct this mistake and appoint a commission. We must resolve the question of current policy—the negotiations in Riga.[33] We are facing an offensive in Grodno, while Wrangel has taken Aleksandrovsk and advances on Yekaterinoslav. We must muster all forces, live through this matter, and it would be good to double every effort.

This is the issue which attracted our attention and I must claim your attention for it. It is clear that the Polish offensive and that of Wrangel are the same offensive by the Entente. It is staking everything on this card. A letter came today from a comrade active in England who says the mood is changing there; yesterday the German formations[34] were for the Bolsheviks, but now they're for the Entente. But we have seen even greater turnarounds. We must deal with conditions as they are now. In all likelihood a winter campaign is predetermined. A whole number of clues indicate what Poland and the imperialists of the Entente are counting on. The French are betting on Wrangel and saying to the Poles: ["]You can be sure that if you get a border from the Bolsheviks that runs near Warsaw, your cause is dead. Wrangel is behind us, and we are your only friends.["] This policy is not very bright. The French and the Poles and Wrangel—it is not so easy to bring these three elements into friendly cooperation—it is even almost impossible to unite three governments, three forces against the Bolsheviks. It would seem easy and sufficient to do this, because they all hate the Bolsheviks. You have to imagine how Pilsudski, Wrangel, and the French imperialists are ready to devote every effort to crushing the Bolsheviks. All three are proclaiming [a campaign] against the Bolsheviks and can do nothing [and could not] even if they were ten times smarter and found themselves advisers who were ten times as smart. Now from the other side the French are exerting all efforts to support Wrangel, and he is having successes. He is receiving reinforcements. At the same time, the French have to hold the Polish front, and say: "Wait, don't conclude a peace." Poland is petty bourgeois, patriotic, and chauvinist; representatives of the PPS—the party of the landowners—and the PSL—the party of well-to-do peasants, the kulaks—say: ["]We prefer peace, because war brings ruin.["][35]

Even before the war, Poland's situation was one of deep crisis, and her representatives were saying that financially, they would come out of the war utterly ruined. This is correct, because they know perfectly well that they must pay for this war, that France recognizes the "sacred[ness of] private property."

There is a new report that sixty steamships have come again to Poland. I don't think that these sixty steamships will help them strengthen their position. Here the comrade who gave us a report said that the social composition of the Polish army has changed. This remark of his has passed unnoticed, but I am noting it now, because it is the whole point. If we beat Kolchak and Denikin, it was only because the social composition of their army had changed. Wrangel now feels that he is strong only because his army is made up of officers. And he himself knows that if he begins to rely on the masses, he will fall as quickly as the Kolchaks and Denikins fell in their day.

The Poles advanced on us with an army that initially was made up exclusively of young people, who can be thoroughly molded. But now they have already taken older people who have gone through a far harsher war. Now they have an army of adults—not of boys, but of people who cannot be taught just anything. The Poles have now crossed that line which Kolchak and Denikin crossed in their day, the line that guarantees first the maximum victory and [then] maximum defeat. Such are the conditions in Poland, and given those conditions, we are still saying that we have to avoid a winter campaign, because for us the lives of ten thousand Russian workers and peasants are of far greater value than anything else. We understand perfectly well that the stakes are high, that we are strong, that in taking Galicia, where Soviet rule is assured, in taking Galicia, which has a connection to Czechoslovakia and Hungary, where things are seething—by doing this—we are opening a direct road for revolution. This is worth fighting for; such a fact cannot be scorned. But at the same time we realize that a winter campaign will cost many lives, and we are saying that we must avoid a winter campaign. The chances of this are not great, because Wrangel and Poland, no matter how much they quarrel, still form part of the same international front. But here we will cut them off, as we have always done. We will counter all previous international customs. We know full well that the international predators will not believe us, but there are those who will always trust us. So we will start to cut straight through it, and we propose saying in the name of the session of the VTsIK that we do not want a winter campaign—that is, it is convenient to sign a peace within ten days. If so, then we renounce Galicia and propose a border significantly to the east of the Curzon Line. No matter how difficult these concessions are for us, it is more important for us to avoid a winter campaign, so that we will be strengthened in peaceful construction, but we propose doing this in ten days. But we are saying that in order to do this, your petty bourgeoisie, your patriotic-minded workers must defeat your bourgeoisie and landowners. And this is possible, because they are strong, because the peasantry were always patriotic lackeys. This is inevitable for economic reasons, by virtue of the inevitable private property, inevitable also politically, but in any event there are opportunities, and in any event a private meeting between us and these parties has already taken place. The representatives of these parties said: ["]We know that it was not the Entente that saved Warsaw and Poland; they could not save us—it was the surge of patriotism that saved them, and these lessons are not forgotten.["]

This chance we want to make use of. We are prescribing immense concessions and a short time period in order to resolve the question of a winter campaign. We want to avoid a winter campaign; therefore, we are proposing to the Poles to conclude a peace right now, and are placing the line to the east of Brest-Litovsk. We gain in the military respect in that we assure a rapid victory over Wrangel. That gain is sufficient. With regard to western European policy, we must move on from [consideration of] the first attempt at an active policy to its consequences. The consequences are not so terrible. The military consequences do not mean consequences for the Communist International. Amid the clamor of war the Comintern forged its weapon and honed it so that the imperialist gentlemen will not break it. The development of all the parties is going our way for the time being, just as prescribed by the Comintern. Without any exaggeration it can be said that on this score we can feel confident. The matter boils down to the pace of development, to the conditions of development.

We were not in a position to secure a decisive military victory that would have shattered the Versailles treaty. We should have been faced with a dismembering of the Versailles treaty of triumphant worldwide imperialism—but we were not strong enough to do this. Our fundamental policy has remained the same. We use every opportunity to go from the defense to the offense. We have already undermined the Versailles treaty, and we will smash it at the first convenient opportunity. Now, however, in order to avoid a winter campaign, we have to make concessions. I do not have available now the text of the declaration that is being proposed by the party conference for approval and submission to the session. I have presented its political content. To avoid a winter campaign, we are giving the Poles a brief ten-day period. Our chances are not great, but we win in either case. We have shown our troops that we have done everything to avoid the hardships of a winter campaign. For us the question of territorial borders is a twentieth-rate question by comparison with the question of the quickest end to the war. We have set the condition, and no matter how hard the winter campaign that will be imposed upon us despite our peace offer, we will still end it victoriously.

I have gone over the time limit allotted to me and will now very briefly turn to the domestic situation. We will end a winter campaign victoriously despite terrible exhaustion.

We have achieved great successes, and we have secured a position where from an economic perspective it is clear that we will have a base, a foundation, if we take grain. From 1917 to 1918, 30 million poods were stockpiled. The following year it was 110 [million]. We are secure now because we have more than 300 million poods of grain, and perhaps even as much as 360. That means from 25 to 30 million poods per month. These figures exceed the starvation figures in which we were mired in the years of starvation. Disposing of such a base, we will not look with such horror at the colored papers, at those millions, hundreds of millions, and billions [of banknotes] which must be signed every day and which show that this base, this trinket, is broken, that these are the remains, the scraps of very old bourgeois clothing. But when 260 million poods of grain a year are in the hands of the state, which requisitioned it from the peasantry by quotas [razvërstka] and as a fixed condition of industrial requirements, we have a base for construction, and then we will resolve freely the task of correct distribution [of food].

Our economic situation has improved significantly. We know that we have more than 100 million poods of petroleum. We know also that we have from 20 to 30 million poods of coal in the Donets Basin. We also know that the situation has improved with respect to firewood, which we were supposed to use last year to get by without coal and oil. That shows that the economic base, despite unprecedented losses, despite incredible fatigue, nervous exhaustion, bureaucratization, the deterioration of the entire party apparatus, despite all this, despite the difficulties of the forthcoming winter campaign, we are continuing to secure for ourselves a fundamental economic base. We have more basic food for the people and food for industry—that is, fuel—than last year. And this is why, taking into account the difficult situation we have endured, we are saying that if once again we unite our forces and concentrate them on the winter campaign, we are certain to achieve victory.

Now I must say something about concessions.[36] We have spoken a great deal about concessions. We have argued about whether they are permissible in principle or not. We have concluded that they are permissible if correctly set up. Of course, we will give the imperialists only what we cannot process ourselves. In England our comrades have concluded a concession for ten thousand *desiatinas*[37] of timber. In the north, in the Arkhangelsk region, we are organizing this work ourselves, and it is totally advantageous for us. We have been offered a redemption in fifteen years. This period is entirely acceptable. There is no reason to fear concessions—they are a gigantic plus.

I recently read a pamphlet by the American social-chauvinist Speerd,[38] truly like our Aleksinsky,[39] who writes that we will bring about obvious ruin if we sign a concession with the bourgeoisie. Such attacks by an American Aleksinsky are entirely unsubstantiated, and we must treat them completely calmly, because every intelligent worker will realize that we are right. We are striving to help Russia bring about a communist order, but we cannot get by with purely Russian efforts. We are saying that the revolution can be realized only through the efforts of the advanced workers of the advanced countries.

On this subject, no single [politically] conscious communist ever had any doubts. This transitional period, during which one side, which is weak, holds out against all the other sides, will be one of complex, entangled relationships. We can rest assured that we will not become entangled, but others will, because we have demonstrated our international policy in relation to the small powers. Then, of course, we will exist as a socialist republic ruined by imperialist war, with incredible riches, which we cannot develop within ten to fifteen years. To attract foreign capital to this, to pay with our riches only for the fact that we cannot overtake them, means to secure now [for ourselves] a basis for peaceful relations. England kicked out our trade union organization, quarreled with Kamenev, and expelled him. This is not so terrible. The communists knew how not to fear displays. And at the same time an agreement was signed to have us deliver [wood for] one million railroad ties. We are not capable of fighting under these conditions.[40] ["]We have the [wood for] railroad ties that we are not in a condition to process; we have the timber that we are not in a condition to use; but you can. Take our timber in the Ukraine [*sic*] that we are unable to utilize, and in gaining concessions from us you will create a foundation for a capitalist peace, both political and economic. You cannot attack, because any attempt at an offensive will mean a Council of Action in any country. The Comintern has dozens of ties and agents in every country. Representatives from various countries come to Moscow. We are independent of all other conditions of development.["] [. . .][41]

This weapon is permissible in principle, although it is double-edged. Not only have we become convinced of its fundamental permissibility, but in practice we have learned to manage it. American politicians write extended notes accusing us of being poor democrats. A famous American billionaire comes to visit and says: ["]Let's shake hands . . . ["][42]

We are likely to gain from this. Given the international situation, we must limit ourselves to a defensive posture with regard to the Entente, but despite the complete failure in the first instance, our first defeat, we will keep shifting from a defensive to an offensive policy over and over again until we finish all of them off for good.

1. Lenin crossed out the word us when he edited the first page of the stenographic record.

2. Refers to the appeal to the Polish people broadcast on 2 February 1920. *Dokumenty vneshnei politiki SSSR*, vol. 2 (Moscow, 1958), 355–57.

3. Lenin corrected the stenographic record up to this point; then he gave up, and the record was handed over to the journalist V. S. Popov-Dubovsky to use in compiling an account, which was subsequently published.

4. In fact, five months after these words were spoken, the Red Army invaded and conquered independent Georgia.

5. The German Independent Social Democratic Party (USPD), the left wing of the Social Democratic Party of Germany, a good part of whose members joined the Comintern and the German Communist Party in October 1920.

6. Lenin mistakenly referred to this Silesian mining town as Dąbrowice.

7. So in the stenographic record.

8. "Earlier," in the stenographic record.

9. This obscure phrase could also be read "but we were very close [to being beaten]."

10. Created in August 1920 by the Labour Party and the Trade Union Congress, to deter England from helping Poland in the war with Soviet Russia. In the document, Lenin refers several times to the Council of Action as the Committee for Action; the first term has, however, been used in this translation.

11. Presumably, farthest east.

12. Black Hundreds were pro-monarchist groups in Russia that carried out pogroms before 1917.

13. The stenographic record incorrectly says "Germany."

14. Kappists were followers of Wolfgang Kapp, a conservative politician who led a putsch in Berlin in mid-March 1920 in an effort to restore the monarchy. The attempted coup was suppressed.

15. Lavr Kornilov (1870–1918): Russian general. Aleksandr Kerensky appointed him commander of the Russian army in July 1917 but then fell out with him and in August accused him (falsely) of heading a counterrevolutionary plot. After the Bolshevik coup, Kornilov fled to the Don region, where he headed the Volunteer Army. Killed in combat.

16. Reference to the deposed Kaiser Wilhelm II.

17. So in the stenographic record.

18. L. Martov (Yuly Osipovich Tsederbaum) (1873–1923): a Menshevik leader. Emigrated in 1920.

19. Moderate German Social Democrats, named after their leader, Philipp Scheidemann (1865–1939).

20. In the stenographic record, "We not only want to throw off the Treaty of Versailles."

21. So in the stenographic record.

22. So in the stenographic record.

23. In his speech opening the Second Congress of the Communist International on 19 July 1920, Lenin said that the population of the United States, Japan, England, and several small countries that had prospered from the war amounted to a quarter of a billion. This figure he contrasted with the populations of colonial and semicolonial nations such as China, Persia, and Turkey, which constituted one and a quarter to one and a half billion people (PSS, vol. 41, pp. 216–18). These various billions and fractions of billions, unfortunately, do not add up.

24. A. R. Gots (1882–1940): a prominent SR, tried in Moscow in 1922 and sentenced to death. His sentence was commuted. Perished in Stalin's terror.

25. Fyodor I. Dan (1871–1947): prominent Menshevik; émigré.

26. According to the editors of Istoricheskii arkhiv, at this point in the stenographic record an omission occurs.

27. Compare this statement with Lenin's recollection at the beginning of Document 59 that when he talked to representatives of English labor and urged them to overthrow their government they were stunned: "They simply could not get into their heads the truth that in the interests of the world revolution, workers must wish the defeat of their government."

28. David Lloyd George (1863–1945): British liberal statesman; prime minister from 1916 to 1922.

29. Omission in the stenographic record.

30. Reference to a pamphlet by Walter Lippman and Charles Marz on the coverage of Soviet Russia in the New York Times, published as a supplement to the New Republic on 4 August 1920.

31. I. N. Smirnov (1881–1936): Old Bolshevik, active in Siberia; during the civil war, chairman of the Military-Revolutionary Committee of the Eastern Front.

32. The zeros appear in the stenographic record.

33. Peace negotiations with Poland.

34. Formirovtsy—which is meaningless—in the original text.

35. PPS: Polish Socialist Party; PSL: Polskie Stronnictwo Ludowe 'Wyzwolenie,' the Polish Peasants' Party.

36. To foreign investors.

37. Measurement of land equal to one hectare.

38. Meant is John Spargo, an American socialist critic of the Bolsheviks. See PSS, vol. 42, pp. 24, 43, and vol. 43, p. 189.

39. G. A. Aleksinsky (1879–1967): prominent Bolshevik. In the Second State Duma, headed the Bolshevik faction. Later broke with Lenin. Emigrated.

40. So in the stenographic record.

41. Omission in the stenographic record.

42. Omission in the stenographic record.

The day after Document 60 was written, Chicherin sent Ioffe a cable that reproduced Lenin's suggestions as formal instructions concerning peace negotiations with Poland.[1]

1. See also f. 2, op. 2, d. 429, l. 2–3.

Document 60
Draft of Politburo Directives to Ioffe and Berzin

2 October 1920

To Politburo Members

I propose approving the following directives:

For Ioffe:

a.[1] to agree to a line that gives Poland the **Lida-Baranovichi** railroad, on condition that peace (and a truce) will be signed for certain in the briefest possible time (approximately three days) (that is, with the precise stipulation "I am taking it back if you do not sign within this brief time").

The whole art and the whole task is to find out whether they agree in practice or are only fooling. If you fail to find out, do not give your consent.

b. After 5 October, either return to Moscow (if the signing of a peace treaty is **completely** hopeless), but do not break off [negotiations]; leave for two to three days, as a demonstration.

Or (if there is at least a shadow of hope of signing a peace treaty) do not leave, but state solemnly and **publicize:** 5 October has passed, **Poland is responsible for the winter campaign.**

For Berzin: make the concession proposed by Berzin, but only **under the precise stipulation** of paragraph a. Otherwise, take it back. You **cannot** allow yourself to be toyed with. In that case it is better to break off.

2 October

Lenin

1. In the margin: "N.B. also for Berzin."

O n its retreat from Poland, the Red Army carried out numerous pogroms against the Jewish population. Local Jewish Communists urged Lenin to intercede, but as his notation indicates, he refused to do so. Compare with Document 71 below. The report was made in October and the document forwarded to Lenin in November.

Document 61
Report on Red Army Pogroms, with Lenin's Reaction

[17–18 October 1920]

Proletarians of the world, unite!

RUSSIAN COMMUNIST PARTY (BOLSHEVIK), CENTRAL COMMITTEE

CENTRAL BUREAU OF THE JEWISH SECTION OF THE

RUSSIAN COMMUNIST PARTY CENTRAL COMMITTEE

No. 1515   Secret   Moscow, 18 November 1920
                        To Comrade Lenin

This letter certifies that we are dispatching for your information an excerpt from the report of an agent of KOPE on the new pogroms perpetrated by the First Cavalry Army.

> Central Bureau Secretary,
> [signature illegible]
> Administrator,
> [signature illegible]

Into the Archive[1]   **Copy of a copy**

EXCERPT

From the Report of the Agent of KOPE, Comrade ZILIST, concerning
Zhitomir, dated 1 October 1920

In recent days Zhitomir[2] has faced a new task. A new wave of pogroms has swept over the district. The exact number of those killed cannot be established, and the details cannot be established (because of the lack of communication), but certain facts can be established definitively. Retreating units of the First Cavalry Army (Fourth and Sixth Divisions) have been destroying the Jewish population in their path, looting and murdering.

ROGACHEV (more than thirty killed), BARANOVKA about fourteen dead, ROMANOV (not established), CHUDNOV (about fourteen) are new pages in the history of Jewish pogroms in the Ukraine. All the enumerated localities have been completely plundered. The district of Berdichev has also been sacked. The Forty-fourth Division did not lag behind. GOROSHKI and CHER-NIAKHOV have been completely plundered. After the departure of the Forty-fourth Division from Goroshki, a band raided it and finished up what the Tarashchantsy[3] had started. There are two dead and many wounded. Of the wounded, one died in Zhitomir.

Bands have also begun operating. IVNITSA, KOTELNO, KHODORKOV have been sacked. Emergency aid is vital.

A large sum of money and food must be sent.

True copy of original: [signature illegible]
True copy of copy: [signature illegible]
Copy of copy

> Administrator [signature illegible]

1. Written by Lenin.
2. Zhitomir, capital of Volyn Province. At the beginning of the twentieth century, it had 281,000 inhabitants, of whom 8 percent were Jews.
3. Members of the Tarashchan Division of the Red First Cavalry.

Российская Коммунистическая партия (Большевиков). Центральный Комитет.

Центральное Бюро Евсекции при Ц. К. Р. К. П.

№ 15/15

Москва _ноября_ 18 дня 19 20 г.

Секретно

Товарищу Ленину

при сем препровождаю для Вашего сведения выписку из докла-
да уполномоченного "Дон" о новых погромах, учиненных первой Конной арми-
ей.

Секретарь Ц.Б.Е. _Диманитейн_

DOCUMENT 61. Cover Memo to Report on Red Army Pogroms, 18 November 1920

A fter a meeting of the Politburo on 18 November 1920, Lenin sent the following telegram to Stalin, then in Vladikavkaz. The question concerned Georgia, whose conquest was strongly urged by Stalin and G. K. Ordzhonikidze,[1] over Lenin's hesitations. Stalin requested that the issue be postponed until his return to Moscow. At a meeting of the Politburo on 27 November, Stalin reported on the situation in the Caucasus, and it was decided to strengthen the Red Army in Azerbaijan, which had been conquered in April of that year and which was to serve as the springboard for the projected assault on Georgia.[2]

1. Grigory Konstantinovich Ordzhonikidze (Sergo) (1886–1937): Old Bolshevik, Georgian by nationality. During the civil war, served as political commissar. In 1920, chaired the Caucasian Bureau of the Central Committee, organized the conquest of the three Transcaucasian republics, and then served as Communist boss there. Committed suicide in protest over certain of Stalin's repressive actions.

2. For Stalin's request that the issue be delayed, see f. 558, op. 1, d. 2,001. On the decision of 27 November, see f. 17, op. 3, d. 125, l. 1.

Document 62
Telegram to Stalin

[18 November 1920]

To Stalin, copy to Trotsky

Have received your reports. **Chicherin has telegraphed** you in detail **that the commander in chief**[1] has responded to my inquiry that he **would propose sending to the Caucasus from the Crimea one rifle and three cavalry divisions, including the cavalry corps of Kashirin.**[2] One must **carefully consider whether it is worth it to fight Georgia,** then **to feed her and risk a break with England,** even a new **war.** Respond, and I shall submit [it] to the **Politburo.**

Lenin

1. S. S. Kamenev.
2. Nikolai Dmitrievich Kashirin (1888–1938): organized partisan bands in the Urals during the civil war.

Document 63
Dzerzhinsky's Report on the Treatment of White Prisoners of War, with Lenin's Annotations[1]

[November 1920]

Into the Archive[2]
To the Chairman of the Council of People's Commissars
Comrade **Lenin**

The situation of prisoners in Yekaterinburg along with the

other provinces is not particularly outstanding. General laxity in the management of forced labor camps can be observed everywhere: it results above all from the lack of organization of the center. The lack of organization of the center—i.e., the NKVD's [People's Commissariat of Internal Affairs'] Department of Forced Labor—is, in turn, caused by the total lack of employees. The responsible workers available in the department cannot cope with their tasks. The work proceeds with [the help of] an unsatisfactory contingent of rank-and-file employees selected from prisoners in Moscow camps.

Given the current state of affairs, massive work in filtering out the enormous number of White Guard prisoners of war is becoming virtually impossible. Meanwhile, the republic faces [the task of] having to organize the more or less long-term isolation in camps of some one hundred thousand POWs from the southern front and an immense number of persons deported from the rebellious Cossack settlements of the Terek, Kuban, and Don. At present, a wave of thirty-seven thousand Wrangel prisoners of war has reached Kharkov, a party of four hundred, including children and elderly persons aged from fourteen to seventy, is in Orel, after arriving there completely by accident and in an unorganized fashion from the Terek. The extent to which this transfer was really accidental and unorganized is shown by a telegram from the chairman of the Executive Committee: "dispatched without any documents or files . . . on the mere signature of the head of the Special Caucasian Labor Army with reference to an instruction from Orzhanikidze [sic]. . . ." (attachments 1 & 2).

The magnitude of the scope of this work in general is shown by the figure of twenty thousand White officers who have passed through the Moscow Cheka in the course of several summer months.

The current situation of the organization of the labor camps and their internal condition will also persist in the future, if the Department of Forced Labor works amateurishly, coping with ongoing problems on a case-by-case basis, without a centralized system of inventory for vacant places.

With the latest dispatch of prisoners to Yekaterinburg, the Cheka received a certification from the Department of Forced Labor that such a dispatch was feasible. Upon the receipt of the first reports of the conditions of the prisoners' confinement, the Cheka gave the appropriate instructions to Yekaterinburg. At present a commission is being formed, chaired by Comrade Skliansky, with representatives of the Cheka, the Commissariat of Justice, and the Department of Forced Labor, in order to resolve the matter of the organization of the labor camps on the widest possible scale, appropriate to the massive tasks in this area.

In order to take emergency measures regarding Yekaterinburg in accordance with your instruction, I, together with Comrade Kursky, will imme-

diately send a special authorized representative. Besides this, additional
directives will be given over the telegraph, in accordance with the telegrams already sent (attachments 3, 4, 5, 6, 7, 8, and 9).

Chairman of the Cheka, F. Dzerzhinsky

"   " November 1920
Moscow

1. See Document 3A (in the Appendix).
2. Written by Lenin.

On 4 December 1920, the Politburo discussed the draft of Chicherin's directives to P. G. Mdivani[1] concerning Turkey. It was
decided to work them out in consultation with Stalin.[2] At this time
Soviet Russia was establishing friendly relations with the government of
Kemal Atatürk,[3] helping him diplomatically to oust Allied contingents
from Turkish soil. At the same time, as the following document indicates, Moscow was also trying to subvert the Turkish Republic from
within.

1. P. G. ("Budu") Mdivani (1877–1937): Georgian Bolshevik, one of the leaders of the
Georgian opposition to Stalin and Ordzhonikidze in 1921–22. Was expelled from the party in
1928; later perished in Stalin's purges.
2. Stalin's draft is in f. 558, op. 2, d. 1. Document 64 is apparently Lenin's contribution to
the directives.
3. Kemal Atatürk (1881–1938): founder and first president of the Turkish Republic.

Document 64
Central Committee Resolution on Turkey

[Prior to 4 December 1920]

The line of the Central Committee approved today is as follows:

Do not trust the Kemalists;[1] do not give them arms; concentrate all
efforts on Soviet agitation among the Turks and on the building in Turkey
of a solid Soviet party capable of triumphing[2] through its own efforts.

1. Followers of Kemal Atatürk.
2. Lenin crossed out "inside the country."

As part of the commercial agreement with Great Britain, Soviet
Russia undertook not to carry out anti-British propaganda or engage in subversive activities in the British possessions. The following

document indicates that Lenin intended to pay no attention to this pledge. His draft served as the basis for a resolution by the plenum of the Central Committee, adopted the same day.[1]

1. See f. 17, op. 2, d. 56, l. 2.

Document 65
Draft of a Politburo Resolution

[26 January 1921]

1. Conclude an agreement on the principles advocated by Krasin.

2. Send a note immediately with a rather blunt and very detailed rebuttal of all Curzon's charges.

3. Task Sokolnikov[1] with creating a Khorassan Soviet Republic **unexpectedly** by spring.[2]

4. Dispatch special envoys to Baku and Tashkent, to explain to them that the attack on British imperialism must be pursued even more vigorously, although not in our name, but in that of Azerbaijan and Bukhara. This must never be mentioned in notes or letters.

5. Require the Orgburo within a week to augment the apparatus of the People's Commissariat of Foreign Affairs with two or three additional highly trained and conspiratorial party workers.

6. Confirm in every note, covertly and overtly, that the envoys are required to see to it that nothing is done against England.

7. Henceforth, communicate everything that is hostile to England only in a special code, whose deciphering the envoys are not to entrust to any secretary but do without fail in person.

8. Inform all the eastern peoples, only verbally, through envoys, without a single piece of paper, that we shall dupe England.

9. Mention, among the countries of interest to us, the Caucasus, Armenia, and if possible the western states.[3]

1. Grigory Yakovlevich Sokolnikov (1888–1939): Old Bolshevik. Sent in 1920 to Bukhara to organize seizure of that state. In the 1920s, played an active role in Soviet Russia's financial apparatus; helped design monetary reform. In 1923, commissar of finance; in 1929–32, Soviet envoy to Great Britain. Perished in Stalin's terror.

2. *Khorassan* is a mistaken rendering of *Khorezm* (Khiva), which was conquered by the Red Army on 2 February 1920, one week after Lenin's order. This once semisovereign principality, under a Russian protectorate, was proclaimed a Soviet republic in April of that year; later incorporated into the Uzbek Soviet Socialist Republic (SSR).

3. By "western states," Lenin apparently means those newly independent republics of eastern Europe which had once been part of the Russian Empire.

T he next document reveals Lenin's tactics for the defeat of the so-called Workers' Opposition and Democratic Centralists, who felt that the Communist Party was being overbureaucratized and over-centralized. The former group, led by Aleksandr Shliapnikov, the head of the Metallurgical Union, consisted of Old Bolsheviks. They wanted power to pass from party bureaucrats to actual workers. Lenin vehemently opposed this platform because he considered workers to be fundamentally unsocialist and unrevolutionary. At the Ninth Party Congress (March 1920) he had the delegates pass a secret resolution outlawing the formation of "factions" in the party, a faction being defined as an organized caucus or pressure group. This ban was instituted to prevent the Workers' Opposition and the Democratic Centralists from gaining followers.

Lenin, however, had no scruples about holding secret factional meetings of his own at the next party congress to organize a strategy for defeating the opposition. As a result of this tactic, the so-called Platform of Ten drafted by Lenin defeated the opposition platform by a wide margin, following which the Workers' Opposition was ordered to dissolve.[1]

1. See *RUBR*, 450–57.

Document 66
Summary of Lenin's Remarks at the Conference of the Delegates to the Tenth Congress of the RKP(b)—Supporters of the Platform of Ten

13 March 1921

13 March 1921

Is the majority entitled to be a majority[?]. If it wants to be, then how should it be done[?]. For example, [of] three hundred, two hundred are the majority, and one hundred the minority. There arises the question of a split. A union is possible.

If the majority does not come to an arrangement, then the minority can win. This does happen. We are not a faction. We came as a faction, but we do not constitute a faction here. We should use our right in elections. In elections of delegates we have fought to win at the congress. And this we should do.

When the discussion got under way, then all saw the political mistake, and rightly so. It was a most dangerous discussion. The masses have taken it up, so they, too, have disagreements.

We must be firm, hard. Those who hesitate will join us.

Now as to Kronshtadt. The danger there lies in the fact that their slogans are not Socialist-Revolutionary, but anarchistic.

An All-Russian Congress of Producers[1]—this is not a Marxist but a petty bourgeois idea.

If you wish to introduce the opposition into the Central Committee to further its disintegration, then permit us not to permit it.

The "Workers' Opposition" expresses the vacillations of the nonparty masses.

The "Democratic Center" exists only in Moscow and unites only the intelligentsia. But it hinders work.

Moscow is the best city in the sense that it has a mass of intelligentsia, creators of theses, ex-officials, etc.

I have been accused: ["]You are a son of a bitch for letting the discussion get out of hand.["] Well, try to stop Trotsky. How many divisions does one have to send against him?

The organization [apparat] is bad. Everyone hates the glavki.[2] But no one agrees to disperse them. It is politics for the organization, not the organization . . .

Our policy. From the point of view of the interests of the vanguard to the rear guard, of the whole class toward the peasantry [sic].

Yesterday about trade unions, and today to revamp the whole [military] command staff. Where are we to get the commissars[?].

We will come to terms with Trotsky.

The apparatus is for politics, not politics for the apparatus.

Trotsky wants to resign. Over the past three years I have had lots of resignations in my pockets. And I have let some of them just lie there in store. But Trotsky is a temperamental man with military experience. He is in love with the organization, but as for politics, he hasn't got a clue.

1. A slogan popular in 1918–20 among anti-Bolshevik workers and socialist intellectuals eager to circumvent the soviet apparatus, which was completely under Communist control.

2. Glavki were the organs of the Supreme Council of the National Economy in charge of particular branches of industry.

L enin's telegram (Document 67) is a good example of the kind of "mobilizations" of civilian labor that were carried out routinely under War Communism.[1]

1. See RR, 706. Similar orders were issued to the Soviet authorities in Saratov and the Kalmyk regions. See f. 2, op. 1, d. 17,812 and 17,814.

Document 67
Telegram to the Tsaritsyn Province Labor Committee

[25 March 1921]

Via Direct Wire

To Tsaritsyn Province Labor Committee

You are directed as a battle order to take decisive measures to mobilize three thousand men and eight thousand women for the Astrakhan Fishing [Concern] without fail, completely [and] without any changes, by deadline, as per resolution of the Main Labor Committee dated 11 December 1920. Implementation is your personal responsibility. Telegraph daily to Main Labor Committee on the progress of mobilization.

Lenin, Chairman of the Defense
Council

A fter the military debacle in Poland, the Soviet regime sought to purchase weapons surreptitiously in Germany. Its main agent in these dealings was Krasin, who had considerable pre–World War I experience in dealing with German businessmen.

Document 68
Exchange Concerning Weapons Purchases in Germany

18 May 1921

Secretary of the Deputy
People's Commissar for
Foreign Affairs

5/18/577 252 18/5 23/10
No. 86 To Chicherin, Moscow
Decode personally

For Lenin: it is possible to obtain one million German rifles of the latest model. Each has two hundred[1] rounds of ammunition. Delivery can probably be arranged by ship to one of our northern ports. The price of each kit is about two hundred marks—i.e., ten gold rubles. I estimate delivery charges at approximately half a million in gold. The business can be carried out only on the basis of the strictest conspiracy after you have opened a credit line for my disposal here. Wire immediately whether you are interested. In subsequent correspondence I will refer to this merchandise as flue pipes. No. 365. 18 May

Krasin, Litvinov
Gukovsky:[2] $1.5 \times 200 = 300$ mln.[3]

To Comrade Trotsky

I think we should take **100,000** rifles × 2,000 rounds of ammunition per rifle. Perhaps they will come in handy and we will resell [them] for more.

Lenin

1. In the original, the word is garbled.
2. I. E. Gukovsky (1871–1921): Old Bolshevik; at the time commissar of finance.
3. This and the succeeding lines are written by Lenin.

Document 69
Exchange Between Lenin and Litvinov

29 June 1921

Note to Litvinov

Secret
29 June
Comrade Litvinov,

Please give me your response **on this same** sheet of paper and send it to me in extreme secrecy.

Lenin

Reply from Litvinov

Assuming that the question addressed to me concerns the prospect of sales, I reply:

1. The sale of **valuables** has run into immense difficulties. The capacity of the market, given the current economic crisis, is extremely limited. Only an insignificant portion of the valuables turned over to the People's Commissariat of Foreign Trade has been sold. This commodity must be removed from the calculations of our hard-currency plans.

2. **Platinum.** With the disappearance of this metal from the world market, the demand has also disappeared. The current price is extremely low. In Copenhagen last year I was offered £42 an ounce; now they are offering £15. We must await an increase in the demand and a rise in the price.

3. **Bonds.** It is easy to sell Chinese debentures, but Alsky[1] unfortunately does not indicate how many are on hand. They are quoted on the London exchange at 60 to 62 percent [of face value], but for our Russian issues one can get [only] up to 50 percent. We are getting the full value for the coupons. Since they are bringing us an income (5 percent,[2] and 50 percent and even 60 percent at the market price [sic]), it is more important to leave them for last, meanwhile selling off our dead capital, like gold.

We have only a trifling number of other bonds.

Conclusion. We must rely mainly on the sale of gold, especially foreign gold.[3] Everything else does not amount to anything.

M. Litvinov

29 June 1921

1. A. O. Alsky (1892–1939): joined the Bolsheviks in 1917. Deputy commissar of finance, 1921–27.

2. That is, 5 percent interest at the bonds' nominal value.

3. Possibly a reference to the gold deposited by Romania with the Russian Imperial Treasury during World War I.

W hen, in March 1921, the Soviet authorities abolished forced requisitioning of food in favor of a food tax, thereby launching what became the New Economic Policy, they did not intend to introduce free trade in foodstuffs but rather to have the peasants barter their surplus grain for the government's stock of manufactured goods. This plan had to be abandoned because of the unavailability of manufactured goods. The following dispatch indicates that as late as July 1921, Moscow was still attempting to thwart a free market in foodstuffs.[1]

1. See Maurice Dobb, *Soviet Economic Development Since 1917* (London, 1948), 131; *RUBR*, 391–93.

Document 70
Telegram from Lenin and Molotov to Siberia and Kirghizia

2 July 1921

By Direct Wire

Omsk, Siberian Bureau of the Russian Communist Party Central Committee, Siberian Revolutionary Committee, Siberian Food Committee

Orenburg, Kirghiz Regional Committee, Kirghiz Sovnarkom, Kirghiz People's Supply Commissariat

I convey the following Central Committee resolution:

We order the most resolute measures to halt the free exchange of grain products, not stopping at the complete shutting down of bazaars, etc., and enforcing wide-scale compulsory barter, for which the Siberian food authorities must be bolstered by military force.

2 July

Council of Labor and Defense Chairman, Lenin
Central Committee Secretary,
V. Molotov[1]

1. Vyacheslav Mikhailovich Molotov (1890–1986): longest-lived Old Bolshevik, heavily relied on by both Lenin and Stalin. Secretary of the Russian Central Committee and (after 1926) member of the Politburo. Beginning in 1939, commissar (then minister) of foreign affairs. Actively involved in carrying out Stalin's crimes. In 1957, expelled from the Soviet government for "anti-party activity."

Document 71
Report on Pogroms, and Lenin's Reaction

6 July 1921

No. 172   Central Committee Archive. Miscellaneous[1]
Proletarians of the world, unite!
RUSSIAN COMMUNIST PARTY (BOLSHEVIK), CENTRAL COMMITTEE
CENTRAL BUREAU OF THE JEWISH SECTIONS OF
THE RUSSIAN COMMUNIST PARTY CENTRAL COMMITTEE

No. 1,404   Moscow, 6 July 1921
Urgent

To the Politburo of the Central Committee
Copy to Comrade Lenin
Into the Central Committee Archive[2]

In sending **materials on the pogroms in Gomel and Minsk Provinces,**[3] the Central Bureau of the Jewish Sections of the Russian Communist Party Central Committee calls special attention to the conclusion of the collegium member of the Jewish Department from Belorussia: " . . . the Jewish population is gaining the impression that **the Soviet government is not capable of defending the civilian population from bandits** (see Report No. 9).

"Jewish farmers in Kovshits advise that neighboring peasants believe that the attacks and **pogroms against the Jews are made with the knowledge of the Soviet government and this contributes to an increase in the number of bandits.**"

The question of arming trade union members with the active participation of the people's commissariats and the Jewish Sections should be resolved without delay, because the Jewish population is being systematically exterminated and compelled to attend to its self-defense under the leadership of elements that are politically and socially alien to us (Zionists, Tseirei-Tsion).[4]

We consider it necessary:

1. To conduct an investigation of the recent pogroms in Gomel and Minsk Provinces.

2. To appoint commissions for the urgent resolution of the matter of arming trade union members.

Secretary of the Central Bureau
[of the Jewish Section]
[Signature illegible]

1. An unidentified person penned this line across the top of the original document.

2. This line was written by Lenin.

3. Underlined by Lenin with annotation "N.B." Subsequent underlinings are also in Lenin's hand.

4. Tseirei-Tsion was the organization of Young Zionists.

C hicherin wrote Lenin on 24 July that France was assuming a threatening posture toward Soviet Russia, possibly to divert attention from Russia's famine and force her to make military preparations.[1]

1. For Chicherin's note, see f. 2, op. 2, d. 733. In responding to Lenin's instructions, Chicherin disagreed with the proposal that Lenin should give a "threatening" interview or dispatch Tukhachevsky to Minsk. Such steps would only serve to strengthen the impression abroad that to overcome domestic problems Soviet Russia planned to attack her neighbors. Instead, Chicherin suggested sending friendly notes to neighboring states. See f. 5, op. 1, d. 2,057, l. 36.

Document 72
Note to Chicherin

25 July 1921

Comrade Chicherin!

A number of practical proposals must be considered and presented to the Central Committee.

Etwa[1] 1) Charge the All-Russian Extraordinary Commission [VCheka] with strengthening intelligence; a report should be made **in writing** within **a week.** 2) Also—the Revolutionary-Military Council of the Republic (or its registry?). 3) The draft (text) of a **threatening** interview with Lenin or Trotsky (threats: ["]If you meddle, we'll thrash you!["]). 4) A trip by Tukhachevsky to Minsk, also with a threat and with pomp. 5) Directives to the press (draft the directives).

With communist greetings,
Lenin

25 July

1. German for "something like."

W ritten when the famine that had struck Russia was reaching its climax and millions were starving, this telegram indicates that Lenin was unaware of the causes of the famine, one of which was arbitrary confiscations of seed grain, and continued to rely on coercion to secure food for the urban population and the Red Army.

Document 73
Telegram from Lenin and Molotov to All Provincial and Regional Party Committees of the RKP(b)

[30 July 1921]

To All Provincial and Regional Committees:

In confirming the circular telegram to the provincial executive committees and the provincial food committees signed by Sovnarkom Chairman Lenin and Deputy People's Supply Commissar Briukhanov[1] under No. 251, the Central Committee directs the attention of the provincial committees to the following: 1) the food situation of the republic is extremely difficult, owing to crop failures in a number of provinces. For a number of reasons, free trade and free barter do not solve the supply problems. A rise in prices for agricultural produce can be observed everywhere [along with] a relative drop in the prices of manufactured goods. 2) For this reason, at the present time one should not exaggerate the significance of commodities exchange and relegate [food] taxation to a second place, which would be criminal shortsightedness. The chief condition for resolving the food crisis lies in the successful collection of taxes in [the form of] food. In light of the above, the Central Committee categorically orders the provincial committees: 1) to take immediate steps to restore and strengthen the food [collecting] apparatus, safeguarding it throughout [each] province from dislocation [and] the turnover in food workers without the consent of the supply commissars and the Supply Commissariat; 2) to reinforce the food apparatus by means of additional mobilizations of party and professional forces in order to establish a tax inspection staff within two weeks without fail, with at least one person per district; 3) given the novelty of the matter and for the guidance of the village soviets, to provide at least one comrade per district as an interim inspector; 4) to organize [and] unfold extensive agitation [among] the rural population, explaining the economic benefit of timely and full payment of taxes; 5) to enlist rural Communist cells to assist the rural soviets in the collection of taxes; 6) to raise the authority of the food agencies in party and Soviet circles and among the population; [the agencies' reputation] has suffered

greatly in the period of transition to the new [economic] policy, and measures should be taken to stop the indiscriminate, unfounded accusations
against food workers; 7) to take steps to reinstate comrades engaged in food
work whose guilt has not been proven; 8) not to lose sight of the fact that the
successful collection of taxes, which are an obligation, is ensured by the
right granted under the law to district and provincial supply commissars to
levy judicial [or] administrative punishments on tax evaders, as well as the
right to limit and even temporarily prohibit free barter; 9) to appoint to
chairmanships of the supply sessions of Revolutionary Tribunals reliable
comrades who have had a connection with food work in the past and who
are familiar with it; 10) to establish full contact between food agencies and
party organizations and also food agencies of executive committees, especially of the rural soviets and district executive committees; 11) to provide
the food agencies with the necessary party authority and the total power of
the state apparatus of coercion. The Central Committee [hereby] orders the
provincial committees, along with the executive committees and provincial food committees, to inform the Central Committee at least once a week,
with copies to the Supply Commissariat, on the progress of preparatory
work and the implementation of these directives. Especially responsible
comrades of the Central Committee and Supply Commissariat are to be
appointed to monitor the information. Responsibility for the correct and
timely preparation of the supply apparatus is placed personally on the
secretaries and members of the provincial [party] committees, chairmen of
the provincial executive committees, and the provincial supply commissars.

> Signed: Chairman of the Council of Labor
> and Defense, Comrade Lenin
> Central Committee Secretary,
> Molotov

1. Nikolai Pavlovich Briukhanov (1878–1942): Old Bolshevik. Appointed deputy
commissar of supply in July 1918. In 1926–30, commissar of finance. Perished in Stalin's
terror.

The communication that follows relates to secret negotiations
between Moscow and Germany concerning weapons purchases,
as well as plans to turn over to the Germans the reconstruction
of Petrograd's industrial and port facilities. These plans never mate-
rialized.

The letter makes explicit Soviet Russia's policy of secretly collab-
orating with those elements in Germany which wanted to "overturn the
Versailles treaty," that is, the Nazis and other nationalists.

Document 74
Letter to Chicherin

6 August 1921

6 August, Saturday
Comrade Chicherin:

I have received your letter of 5 August about the **second** conversation with Neumann,[1] and I conclude: (Kopp[2] +) Neumann are blackmailing us. Brazenly and intolerably.

This must be stopped.

I propose a plan approximately as follows:

1. Yet another conversation between you and Neumann: you **cut him off** sharply. Only a fool could interfere in our relations with Kopp and in the role of Stomoniakov.[3] We do **not** talk to such fools. Not another word dare be said about **this!**

2. Only a fool does not understand that **it is advantageous** also to us (and to **those** Germans who want to **overturn the Versailles peace** and not to kowtow to the Entente) that Stomoniakov **cover his tracks.**

3. If the agreement is not concluded as yet, the **Germans** are wholly to blame, because they are dragging it out. Their job is to supply the draft of an agreement and to deliver coal and grain to Petrograd.

4. We will tolerate their red tape a little longer, but not much.

5. We will turn the Petrograd **port** over to the **English if** the Germans do not sign our agreement with them within the briefest time and if they do not find a Dutch **front man.**

If they sign the agreement, we will give **that** Dutchman the port for a -1 (a = British price).

6. After the conversation, write a letter to Neumann **in this vein** (so that **he dare not misquote you; send** a copy to all **leaders** in this matter in Germany **via courier**). [State] directly in the letter: ["]Whoever wants an alliance **against** England, we are for him. Whoever is for red tape can go to hell.["] The letter can be signed with the pseudonym Katerina.

They must be taught a lesson!!

Yours, Lenin

P.S. Of course, we are for **military**-industrial plans, but conspiratorially. And an agreement **right away.**

1. Reference to Oskar, Ritter von Niedermayer (1885–1948), a German officer who used the alias Neumann and was very active in Soviet-German military collaboration in the 1920s. See TP, vol. 2, 442–43, and Manfred Zeidler, *Reichswehr und Rote Armee, 1920–1933* [The German Army and the Red Army, 1922–1933] (Munich, 1993), 48, 51–52.

2. Viktor Leontievich Kopp (1880–1930): the Soviet representative in Berlin, starting in late 1919. Later served as Soviet envoy to Japan and Sweden.

3. Boris Spiridonovich Stomoniakov (1882–1941): a Bulgarian-born Bolshevik who enrolled in Soviet service in 1917 and worked from 1920 to 1925 as Soviet trade representative in Berlin. Subsequently served in the Commissariat of Foreign Affairs.

I n August 1921, the Soviet government reached an agreement with Herbert Hoover, U.S. secretary of commerce and head of the American Relief Administration (ARA), to provide large-scale aid to the starving Russian and Ukrainian populations. Hoover made it one of his conditions that the Russians not interfere with his personnel. Lenin was infuriated by Hoover's demands and called him "impudent" and a "liar" who deserved to be "publicly slapped," but Lenin had no choice and ultimately accepted Hoover's terms.[1] As the following document reveals, he also ordered that the ARA be infiltrated and its employees spied on.

1. See *PSS*, vol. 53, pp. 110–11; *RUBR*, 416.

Document 75
Note to Molotov

23 August 1921

Secret
To Comrade Molotov

23 August
Comrade Molotov!

In view of the agreement with the American Hoover, we can expect the arrival of a lot of Americans.

We must take care of surveillance and intelligence.

I propose that the Politburo resolve:

To create a commission with the task of preparing, working out, and conducting through the VCheka and other agencies the strengthening of surveillance and reporting on foreigners.

The members of the commission are: Molotov, Unshlikht, Chicherin.

They can be replaced only with highly reliable party members, with Molotov's consent.

The commission can create subcommissions on special issues.

The main thing is to identify and mobilize the maximum number of Communists who know English, to introduce them into the Hoover commission and for other forms of surveillance and intelligence.

The decisions of the commission are to be approved through the Org-buro.

23 August

Lenin

Document 76
Letter to Berzin

8 September 1921

Comrade Berzin!

Your note about the slackening of revolutionary spirit among the working class of England is "not it," and "off the mark."

Regarding the "Committee to Aid the Hungry" you are also wrong.[1] They should have been arrested. Noulens should have been punched in the snout.[2]

Are you getting serious and systematic medical treatment? This is necessary. It must be strictly observed. Respond.

It is necessary to help the English Communists; of course, strictly conspiratorially. They must be taught how the Bolsheviks have worked (always). They should be given the most practical directives—print them (or better, find an intermediary and publish through him, in his name, while correcting the texts of his articles).

Have you seen **Cedar & Eden Paul?**[3] Couldn't it be done through them? Is **Price's** useful book **going well**—*My Reminiscences of the Russian Revolution?*[4] Why are they not reprinting **Reed** in England (*Ten Days That Shook the World*);[5] **Fraina** (*The Proletarian Revolution in Russia*)?[6]

The English Communists must be taught over and over again to work as the Bolsheviks worked: taught through articles, taught publicly without fail, in the press. They can be taught about the work of the party from the resolutions of the Third Congress of the Communist International.

With communist greetings,

Lenin

8 September 1921

P.S. Pick out **worthwhile** articles and pamphlets now and then and send them to me.

Lenin

1. The Committee to Aid the Hungry (Pomgol) was a volunteer group of prominent non-Communist Russians, formed in July 1921 with Communist permission and under Communist control to raise funds abroad to alleviate the famine. A few days after Herbert Hoover came to terms with Moscow concerning famine relief, Lenin ordered the non-Communist members of Pomgol arrested (*RUBR*, 416–17).

2. Joseph Noulens (1864–1939): in 1914–15, French minister of war, and in 1917–18, ambassador to Russia.

3. Cedar Paul and Eden Paul (1856–1944): well-known translators with pro-Soviet sympathies.

4. "Price's useful book" refers to the book by M. Phillipps Price, published in London in 1921. The author, the Russian correspondent of the *Manchester Guardian*, was highly sympathetic to the communists. Later on he admitted that he had been a "fellow-traveller" and in his dispatches had merely adopted communist jargon, "as if [he] had been listening to the speeches of Lenin and Trotsky" (*Survey*, 41 [April 1962]: 16).

5. John Reed (1887–1920): Harvard-educated journalist. Was in Russia in 1917 during the Bolshevik coup and turned communist.

6. Louis C. Fraina: American Communist who in 1918 had a collection of Lenin's writings published in New York under this title. He later admitted to having received $50,000 in Moscow for publication purposes. See Theodore Draper, *Roots of American Communism* (New York, 1957), 294.

Document 77
Note to Unshlikht

21 September 1921

21 September '21
To Unshlikht

I saw Radek today, who has just returned from Petrograd.

He says the city is unusually active. The port. Foreigners are engaged in massive bribery, [bribing also] **hungry and tattered Chekists.** The danger here is extremely great.

Immediately form a party commission (VCheka + Petrograd Cheka + Petrograd party organization and the Central Committee)—procure some money (gold will have to be supplied) and **feed and clothe** the Chekists in Petrograd, Odessa, Moscow, and so on.

Without fail and urgently.

Reply in detail.

With communist greetings, Lenin

The following exchange refers to the decision to allocate ten million rubles in gold for the clandestine purchase of weapons in Germany. Instructions to this effect were issued soon afterward to the Soviet agent in Germany, Viktor Kopp.[1]

1. On allocations for weapons purchases, see *RUBR*, 418. See Document 4A (in the Appendix) for Trotsky's cable to Berlin.

Document 78
Note from Trotsky to the Politburo, with Annotation by Lenin

4 October 1921

To the Politburo
To Comrade Lenin
To Comrade Molotov

The Central Committee Commission (Trotsky, Stalin, Ordzhonikidze, Gusev[1]) has concluded that it is necessary to allocate ten million rubles in gold and has drafted the text of the proposed enclosed telegram.

I urge an immediate decision on this matter by the Politburo, so that the telegram can be sent to its destination today.

4 October '21

L. Trotsky

Secret (Into the Archive)[2]

> Military proposals
> [of] October 1921
> and **ten** million.

1. Sergei Ivanovich Gusev (1874–1933): Old Bolshevik. During the civil war, active as commissar on the southwestern and southern fronts. Appointed head of Political Administration of the Red Army in 1921. Later worked in the Comintern.
2. This and the following lines are in Lenin's handwriting.

Document 79
Telegram to the Fuel Directorate of Tsaritsyn Province

4 October 1921

Tsaritsyn, Provincial Fuel Directorate

The following must be delivered urgently to Baku[1] to the address of the Council of Labor and Defense representative at the irrigation works in Mugan, Comrade Bogdatiev,[2] Directorate of Water Transportation of the Azerbaijan SSR: 1) 10,594 logs 4–5 vershok[3] × 13 arshin[4]—10,594 pieces, 2) 1,815 boards 1 1/2 vershok × 13 arshin, 3) 650 boards 1 1/4 vershok × 13 arshin, 4) 50 boards 1 1/8 vershok × 13 arshin, 5) 850 boards 1 3/4 vershok × 13 arshin, 6) 2,700 casks. Report implementation to the Council of Labor and Defense.

Chairman, Council of Labor and Defense, Lenin

Moscow, the Kremlin
4 October '21

1. See the headnote to Document 46.

2. S. Ya. Bogdatiev (Bogdatian) (1887–1946): Bolshevik active in 1917 in Petrograd. In 1921, in charge of land reclamation in Mugan.

3. Measure of length equivalent to 1 3/4 inches.

4. Measure of length equivalent to 28 inches.

Trotsky wrote Document 80, but Lenin signed it, in the name of the Politburo. It refers to secret negotiations with Germany concerning weapons sales and other cooperative measures.

Document 80
Exchange Concerning Weapons Purchases in Germany

21 October 1921

Politburo

I direct your attention to the purely subversive nature of the telegram from Comrade Krasin:

1. If he does not trust Kerzhentsev's[1] *apparat*, no one prevents him from taking this matter into his own hands—in order really to carry it out and not to sabotage it.

2. Discussions about the caliber of our rifles are simply ridiculous. After all, all our rifles and munitions are of this caliber. Is he really proposing to redo everything casually because of the purchase of 150,000 rifles? (N.B.: The caliber of the Japanese rifles is **smaller** than ours, and still they beat us). The Germans want to equalize our caliber to theirs (for purchase orders) [by enlarging it] a bit—that is why they are criticizing [us].

I propose sending Krasin the following telegram:

Re: your No. R834–835–836. 1. The Central Committee does not object to the ten-million [ruble] order being removed from the hands of Kerzhentsev, on the condition that you personally take this matter into your hands very energetically, in view of its exceptional importance and urgency.

2. Notions regarding caliber are without substance, and the order remains in full force.

3. Once again we affirm the necessity of filling the previous order for twelve million [rubles] as energetically as possible.

4. The required measures of caution must in no way lead to the de facto annulment of these exceptionally important orders.

21 October 1921

On assignment from the Politburo,
Lenin
Central Committee Secretary,
V. Mikhailov[2]

1. Platon Mikhailovich Kerzhentsev (Lebedev) (1881–1940): Old Bolshevik, journalist, and diplomat. In 1921–23, served as Soviet envoy to Sweden, where he seems to have worked as an intermediary in Soviet-German dealings. Later, envoy to Italy.

2. Vasily Mikhailovich Mikhailov (1894–1937): party member, beginning in 1915. Head of the Moscow Cheka, then political commissar in the Red Army. In 1921–23, secretary of the Central Committee. Perished in Stalin's terror.

I t cannot be established what this exchange refers to. The document is reproduced here because of Lenin's comments on Lev Kamenev.

Document 81
Remarks About Kamenev

1 December 1921

Note from Kamenev

VCheka   1 December '21

I am very glad. But this should be given as a **directive** from the Politburo, and Kamenev will write it.

Note by Lenin

Poor fellow, weak, frightened, intimidated.

L enin's instruction that Bukharin be kept "out of politics" can be interpreted in two ways: one, that Lenin was so concerned with Bukharin's heart condition that he wanted him to get a good rest; the other, that he thought him a poor politician and wanted him to stay out of politics for good. Supporting the second reading is Lenin's order that the message be transmitted "extremely conspiratorially, sown up, etc.," which would have been an unnecessary precaution if Lenin had been concerned with Bukharin's health. If this interpretation is the correct one, then the often heard argument that Bukharin was Lenin's natural heir and successor is severely undermined.

Document 82
Letter to Krestinsky

28 January 1922

Please dispatch this through P. P. Gorbunov[1] to Berlin, EXTREMELY CON-
SPIRATORIALLY, SOWN UP, etc.

Comrade Krestinsky! Thank you for your letter about Rykov. Take **all** steps for the **protection** of the Bukharins. Bukharin's wife will need a long stay in a sanatorium. It is said that she is seriously ill.

N. I. Bukharin must be kept **strictly** out of politics. Let him stay now until he improves his heart [condition] and then, **from time to time,** visits his wife. Verify: **out** of politics!

Greetings!
Lenin

28 January

1. Pavel Petrovich Gorbunov (1885–1937): joined the Bolsheviks in 1918. From February 1921 to February 1922, business manager of the Commissariat of Foreign Affairs; member of its governing board, starting in September 1918.

T he documents that follow (Document 83 and a number of others) are connected with the international conference held in Genoa in the spring of 1922 with Russian and German participation. The conference had its origin in a gathering in Brussels on 6–8 October 1921 attended by twenty-one states, including Germany but not Russia, to devise means to help Russia cope with her devastating famine. The organizers apparently felt that in her hour of dire need, with some thirty-five million citizens desperately short of food, Russia would be more amenable to settling her outstanding differences with the West, most important among them the matter of Russia's foreign debts, on which she had defaulted in 1918. The conference resolved that Soviet Russia should get aid on condition that she recognized her debts and guaranteed the security of future credits extended to her. Chicherin, the commissar of foreign affairs, responded later that month, agreeing to recognize Russia's prewar debts, provided that she received substantial Western aid and investments and that foreign powers ceased their intervention and recognized the Bolshevik regime de jure. He suggested an international conference to settle these questions and conclude a final peace treaty with the other powers.[1]

On 6 January 1922, the Supreme Allied Council met at Cannes. It resolved to convene an international conference in March, to which the onetime Central Powers as well as Russia would be invited. Its purpose was to find ways of promoting the economic reconstruction of Europe and settle some outstanding issues left as a legacy of the world war. The principles proclaimed in the Resolution of the Cannes Conference called for noninterference in the affairs of sovereign states; respect for foreign investments; acknowledgment of all public debts and obligations and a promise to compensate victims of confiscation or sequestration; renunciation by all nations of subversive propaganda in other states and acts of aggression against neighbors.[2]

Lenin hesitated over whether to have his diplomats attend; apparently he also considered having them go and immediately depart. Chicherin suggested that to avoid a "scandal" the Soviet government reject the terms set by the Allies at Cannes and on these grounds refuse to attend. For the Soviets to go and then leave immediately would lead to Western denial of the loans and a general worsening of relations with the West. He further urged that Moscow acknowledge its foreign debts as a precondition for both peace and loans.[3]

Lenin had originally thought of attending the Genoa Conference in person but gave up the idea for security reasons.

1. Carole Fink, *The Genoa Conference: European Diplomacy, 1921–22* (Chapel Hill, N.C., 1984), 5–6.
2. Ministère des Affaires Etrangères, Documents Diplomatiques [Ministry of Foreign Affairs, Diplomatic Documents], *Conférence Economique Internationale de Gênes: 9 Avril–19 Mai 1922* [The Genoa International Economic Conference, 9 April–19 May 1922] (Paris, 1922), 15–16.
3. Chicherin's communication is reproduced in Document 5A (in the Appendix).

Document 83
Letter to Molotov for All Politburo Members

30 January 1922

To Comrade Molotov for All Politburo Members

I have just received and read the ultrasecret letter from Chicherin to all Politburo members.[1] I think that Chicherin's idea should not be rejected out of hand; it must be discussed more carefully, the results of the work of the Piliavsky commission noted, and the magnitude of all the claims and all counterclaims weighed more carefully.[2]

I propose raising this question for discussion on Thursday without recording anything in the minutes, and making a final decision after a preliminary discussion at the Thursday session, additionally polling all the members of the Politburo later. It may be that Chicherin's proposal is the most rational.

Regarding the special security measures for ultrasecret communications, I propose appointing one of the party secretaries serving under Molotov (or Comrade Molotov himself) to ensure that ultrasecret papers are returned to him personally and burned by him personally.

30 January '22

Lenin

Dictation taken over the telephone.

L. Fotieva[3]

1. See Document 5A (in the Appendix).

2. Stanislav Stanislavovich Piliavsky (1882–1937), an employee of the Commissariat of Finance, drafted a report in September 1921 on Soviet Russia's financial counterclaims against the West. By charging the Western Allies for the costs of the civil war, the suffering experienced by the population, the failure to acquire Constantinople, and pogroms and other misdeeds, he came up with a global sum of 185.8 billion gold rubles, about $92.9 billion (RUBR, 218–19).

3. Lidia Aleksandrovna Fotieva (1881–1975): Old Bolshevik, secretary to Lenin personally from 1918 to 1924, and until 1939 to the Sovnarkom and the Council of Labor and Defense (STO).

Document 84
Letter to Molotov for All Politburo Members

31 January 1922

31 January

To Comrade Molotov for All Politburo Members[1]

Please consider as rescinded my telephonegram[2] of yesterday regarding Chicherin's letter. I was not feeling well. I wrote vaguely. I had hoped to correct it today.

But today I am feeling even worse.

I ask you to discuss whether it is necessary to

1. Postpone the reply to Chicherin until Thursday.

2. On Thursday decide only: let Chicherin and all the other members of the delegation thoroughly consider their proposals and various combinations for a decision by 22–23 February.

3. Appoint responsible persons for the preparation by 22–23 February of **financial** questions (the loan and so on and so forth) for the Genoa Conference.[3]

Lenin

The matter is placed on the agenda for the 2 February Politburo meeting. V. M. Molotov

Read. L. Kamenev

In favor of Comrade Lenin's motion, i.e., to postpone the matter until Thursday. Opposed to Trotsky's motion about Rakovsky.[4] Stalin

I join Stalin. M. Kalinin

1. This document refers to Document 83.

2. A telephonegram, *telefonogramma* in Russian, is an official communication relayed by phone and written down.

3. Kamenev underlined the third point and noted: "This is particularly important. L. K."

4. This allusion is unclear.

Document 85
Letter to Sokolnikov

4 February 1922

Secret

To Comrade Sokolnikov

Trotsky advises me that allegedly, according to your statement, the budget of our party for nine months is forty million [rubles] in gold.[1] I absolutely refuse to believe this; is there not some mistake? **I ask you** to send me secretly, **on this same piece of paper,** care of Fotieva, confirmation or clarification in a few lines.

If possible, add two to three figures about the budget of our party for the past three years.[2]

4 February '22

Lenin

Dictation taken over the telephone.

L. Fotieva

1. Trotsky's note to Lenin cannot be located.

2. In response to this request, Lenin received a projected budget for January through September 1922 which indicated that the party and its youth organization (Komsomol) had been allocated 17.4 million rubles; together with a reserve, the total funds came to nearly 20 million. Lenin noted: "Consider the incident closed" (f. 2, op. 1, d. 22,738).

Document 86
Letter to Stalin and Kamenev

4 February 1922

To Comrades Stalin and Kamenev[1]

1. I am attaching a letter from Trotsky regarding the party's budget. Trotsky is right.

A number of radical measures must be taken. Think about it. We will talk on Wednesday.

2. Do **not** confirm the experts.[2] They will put us to shame. First **examine** them: write an outline, within a week, of your program and tactics. Otherwise, the hell with them. For sure, they will put us to shame, the way Preobrazhensky[3] (chairman of the Financial Commission!!) shamed us with the budget.

We always manage to get shit for experts: first let us try to single out something sensible.[4]

3. Smolianinov[5] redid the "Mandate of the Council of Labor and Defense." Why? I do not know.

This is playing at redoing things instead of **businesslike work**: take in hand these good-for-nothings, these scum who do not want to submit reports. (I cannot do this both because I am sick and because I am extremely angry and capable only of kicking Smolianinov out).

I ask you to devote two to three hours to this matter.

4. The situation with the gold stock is a scandal. For God's sake, do not reconcile yourself to this outrage. Who is responsible? Novitsky?[6] Then let him stand trial for lying. Sokolnikov? Then a **written guarantee** should be gotten from him. If he gives himself away while lying, I will wage a furious fight at the congress. Teach these shit-heads to reply seriously and provide **completely** accurate numbers, or else we will put ourselves to shame and **inevitably** collapse.

Two figures: a) **all** the cash on hand
                              b) minus **all** obligations.
Then I see   c) thus, so much cash on hand.
4 February

                              Lenin

1. In the upper right corner of the first page Lenin wrote: "I am attaching also an addition to the directives."

2. The reference to "experts" is to members of the Soviet delegation to the Genoa Conference. On 4 February, Lenin sent a resolution about these experts to Molotov for the Politburo (PSS, vol. 44, p. 380). They agreed with Lenin's recommendation; see f. 17, op. 3, d. 230, l. 3.

3. Yevgeny Alekseevich Preobrazhensky (1886–1937): Old Bolshevik; Communist economist and theoretician. Perished in Stalin's terror.

4. A notation from Lenin follows: "See next page."

5. V. A. Smolianinov (1890–1962): Old Bolshevik. Worked on economic questions in the Council of Labor and Defense.

6. A. A. Novitsky (1894–1930): headed the Budget Administration of the Commissariat of Finance of the Russian Republic and bore responsibility for accounts concerning the Soviet gold reserve.

Document 87
Note to Sokolnikov[1]

[After 4 February 1922]

Comrade Sokolnikov!

In view of the fact that with the cordial assistance of Comrade Stalin the matter has been completely clarified, I acknowledge that you have not concealed anything, and propose to regard the incident as closed.

With wholehearted delight and communist greetings.

Lenin

1. See Document 86.

L enin refers in the following document to a report that the secretary of the British Labour Party, Arthur Henderson, had asked Lloyd George to raise at the forthcoming Genoa Conference the question of Georgia and her self-determination. (Georgia had been occupied by the Red Army the previous year.) The *Pravda* editorial to which Lenin refers suggested that in response, the Soviet delegation raise the question of self-determination for Ireland, India, and Egypt.

The important aspect of this document is Lenin's determination to wreck the Genoa Conference. Although not spelled out, the reason was the desire at all costs to prevent a rapprochement between Germany and the Allies, because Lenin counted on the animosity between them to facilitate the communist penetration of Europe. The goal was achieved by signing the Treaty of Rapallo with Germany on 16 April 1922, initially in secret, settling the relations between the two countries bilaterally, and in this manner undermining the Genoa Conference.

Document 88
Letter to Chicherin

10 February 1922

10 February 1922
Dear Comrade Chicherin!

I rejoiced today when I read *Pravda*—not the editorial, of course, which **ruined** a most magnificent topic—but the telegram about Henderson's "move."

Henderson is as stupid as Kerensky,[1] and for this reason he is helping us.

That was the first reason to rejoice.

The second: you must see how right I was to advance the "broad" Genoa program approved by the Central Committee.

I hope that now, after Henderson's move, you see this?

We will advance a very broad Genoa program, **courteously** emphasizing in so doing that we are not presenting an ultimatum, **because** in Genoa there cannot be any question of **subordination** to the majority, but only of the **agreement** of all. ["]You do not agree? It is up to you. We [then] shift to the narrow program!["] (In the broad program also insert: international labor legislation, measures to combat unemployment, and so on.)

Furthermore. This is ultrasecret. It suits us that Genoa be wrecked . . . but **not by us,** of course. Think this over with Litvinov and Ioffe and drop me a line. Of course, this must not be mentioned **even in secret documents. Return this to me, and I will burn it.** We will get a loan **better** without Genoa, if we are not the ones that wreck Genoa. We must work out cleverer maneuvers so that we are not the ones to wreck Genoa. For example, the fool Henderson and Co. will help us a lot if we **cleverly** prod them. Was Krasin summoned? Was it verified that he was summoned? When is he leaving? Speed it up, **verify it twice.**

Everything is flying apart for "them." It is total bankruptcy (India and so on). We have to push the falling one **unexpectedly, not** with our hands.

Yours, Lenin

P.S. Show this to Litvinov and Ioffe.

1. Aleksandr Fyodorovich Kerensky (1881–1970): radical Russian lawyer and states-man active in the prerevolutionary Duma. In March 1917, joined the Petrograd Soviet as well as the first Provisional Government. In May 1917, took over as minister of war, and in July as prime minister. Was overthrown by Lenin in October; went into emigration.

S tarting in 1920, the Kremlin had a private hospital and pharmacy that served only the Soviet leaders and stocked medicines imported from abroad.[1]

1. See I. V. Pavlova, *Stalinizm: Stanovlenie mekhanizma vlasti* [Stalinism: The emergence of the mechanism of power] (Novosibirsk, 1993), 52.

Document 89
Request to the Kremlin Pharmacy

13 February 1922

13 February 1922
To the Kremlin Pharmacy

Please issue me bromide in tablets, about twelve, in such a dosage that it will be possible to count on the effect of one tablet, and if it has no effect, then to take two.

V. Ulianov (Lenin)

T he note concerns the central bacteriological station of the German Red Cross in Moscow. Lenin requested N. P. Gorbunov[1] on 20 February 1922 to visit this installation and to invite the German doctors working there to enroll in Soviet service.[2]

1. Nikolai Petrovich Gorbunov (1892–1937): Secretary to Lenin and the Council of People's Commissars.
2. See *PSS*, vol. 54, p. 175.

Document 90
Note to Kamenev

[20 February 1922]

Comrade Kamenev!

In my opinion, one should not only preach "Learn from the Germans, you lousy Russian Communist loafers!" but also **take** Germans **as teachers.**

Otherwise, it's just words.

Why not start with those Germans who (as you saw) organized a model project in Moscow?

If you don't agree, drop me a line. If you do agree, send the attached to (Sovnarkom administrator) N. P. Gorbunov (because Semashko[1] will **not** follow through).

Lenin

1. N. A. Semashko (1874–1949): Old Bolshevik; Soviet commissar of health from 1918 to 1930.

Document 91
Exchange Between Lenin and Molotov

6–7 March 1922

Letter to Molotov

To Comrade Molotov

I request that you put the following proposal through the Politburo:

1. Require Comrades Kamenev and Stalin to perform the work of the Politburo in the course of four sessions per week, beginning Monday and ending Thursday, and on Thursday evening to leave until Monday morning.

2. Ask Comrade Gerson[1] (secretary of Comrade Dzerzhinsky) to set up for the rest period either the site where Comrade Lenin stayed before his current rest place (Comrade Stalin was there once also) or the place where Comrade Trotsky has spent his vacation, if he has already finished it.

I ask you, Comrade Molotov, to coordinate this proposal first with Comrade Zinoviev, as well as Comrade Kalinin, if he is now voting in the Politburo, and put it through immediately. Because I am completely certain that if such measures are not taken and moreover taken immediately, we will not preserve the working capabilities of Comrades Stalin and Kamenev for the party congress.

I await a reply by telephonegram care of Gliasser[2] or Lepeshinskaia[3] or Fotieva.

Lenin

6 March '22

Dictation taken over the telephone by Gliasser. 20:00 hours

Telephonegram from Molotov to Lenin

Telephonegram

The proposal by Comrade Lenin concerning weekly three-day leaves for Comrades Stalin and Kamenev until the party congress has been approved.

Molotov

7 March 1922

Voted: 2—in favor[4]

2—abstained (Trotsky and Kamenev)

1—opposed (Stalin)

1. V. L. Gerson (1891–1941): official of the Cheka and its successors from 1918 to 1937.

2. M. I. Gliasser (1890–1951): worked from 1918 to 1924 in the secretariat of the Council of People's Commissars.

3. E. S. Lepeshinskaia (1892–1959): in 1918–25, worked as secretary in the Council of People's Commissars and the Central Committee of the party.

4. Lenin and Molotov.

Trotsky's proposal to have the Communist Party remove itself from direct participation in economic management was used afterward by Stalin and his followers to undermine Trotsky's reputation in the party. Lenin dismissed it without discussion, relegating it to dead storage ("Into the Archive").

Document 92
Trotsky's Memorandum to the Politburo on the Party's Involvement in the Economy

10 March 1922

To All Politburo Members of the Central Committee of the Russian Communist Party: For the Information of Comrades Lenin, Kamenev, Stalin, Zinoviev, and Molotov

One of the most important questions, both for the party itself and for Soviet work, is the relation between the party and the state apparatus. In fact, this question is passed over in the theses [for the Eleventh Party Congress], and to the extent that it is touched on (in regard to economic training, and so on) nudges in the right direction.

Without freeing the party as a party from the functions of direct administration and management, it is impossible to cleanse the party of bureaucratism and the economy of indiscipline. This is the fundamental question. It is a ruinous "policy" when meetings of the provincial [party] committee decide, in passing, questions concerning the province's sowing campaign or whether or not to lease a factory. And it is in no wise better in the district committee or the central one. Such a method is propaganda in deed against serious specialization, against responsibility, against study of the matter in practice, against respect for specialized knowledge, against serious, unremitting, properly organized work.

When the Central Committee encountered, in different questions, the most egregious instances of direct interference by the provincial committees in judiciary matters, it fought such tendencies. But in all its practice, unconsciously, it has de facto instilled such a manner of acting, depriving all government organs of personal responsibility, removing responsibility for actual work, undermining self-confidence, and at the same time fostering the party's extreme bureaucratization.

We have now passed a resolution that will finally free the trade unions from the functions of economic management. With the change in economic policy, this is unquestionably correct. But for the sake of efficiency, i.e., for actual success, it makes no difference whether the interference comes from the trade unions or from the Central Committee, provincial committees, district committees, or party cells. If the New Economic Policy requires that trade unions be trade unions, then this same policy requires that the party be a party. Training for the correct implementation of commercial functions and economic functions in general is not the task of the party, but the task of the appropriate economic organs for which the party ensures solid leadership and provides the opportunity to select employees and train them without sporadic and incompetent outside interference. The party explains to the working masses the importance and significance of commercial operations as a method of socialist construction. The party combats prejudices that hinder the proper development of economic activity. The party fights attempts to use the New Economic Policy as a device for instilling bourgeois morals in the Communist Party itself. The party firmly establishes what is allowed and what is forbidden. But the party does not direct commercial operations, because it is incapable of doing that. The party does not train people for economic activity, and, in particular, commercial activity, because it is not capable of that.

The party has power in its hands, but it governs only through the properly functioning state apparatus. It sends back 99 percent of the matters submitted to it for decision, on the grounds that they contain nothing of concern to the party.

At the same time, the party concentrates its attention on the theoretical education of party youth to a far greater extent than in the past.

10 March 1922

L. Trotsky

True copy: Sh. Manuchariants[1]

Into the Archive[2]

1. Shushanika M. Manuchariants (1889–1969): Bolshevik from 1918 on; librarian for Lenin's private library.
2. Written by Lenin.

K rasin was responsible for disposing of Soviet valuables in Europe. These valuables were precious stones and bullion confiscated from churches in the spring and summer of 1922. Like Litvinov before him (see Document 69), Krasin advised Lenin that the market for jewelry in Europe was not favorable; Krasin suggested entering into a partnership with de Beers, Johnson-Mathey, or Warburg rather than selling independently at lower prices.[1]

1. Krasin's letter is deposited under the same shelf mark as Document 93.

Document 93
Exchange with Trotsky

11 and 12 March 1922

Note from Lenin

11 March
Comrade Trotsky!

Read this, please, and return to me. Shouldn't we put through a directive about this in the Politburo? (You have ordered the information about the number of "cleansed" churches, I hope?)
Greetings!

Lenin

Note from Trotsky

I have approximately the same answer from Comrade Krasin. It is completely clear that trading in hundreds of millions cannot be conducted "in passing." I suppose that we will have to send abroad the specialists from Fabergé and Moiseev[1] to determine the condition of the market, after whetting their interest in the profits.

12 March 1922

Trotsky

1. Peter Carl Fabergé (1846–1920): a prominent Petersburg jeweler. Moiseev cannot be identified.

This important document refers to the campaign launched in March 1922 to confiscate so-called consecrated vessels as well as other valuables from Orthodox churches and monasteries. The campaign had two purposes: to secure assets that the government badly needed because of the collapse of the economy under War Communism, and at the same time to break the power of the Orthodox Church and its hold on the peasant population. As the document makes explicit, Lenin hoped that the unprecedented famine which struck Soviet Russia and the Ukraine in 1921–22 would win the government peasant support against the church. The "events in Shuia" refer to one of many episodes in the campaign. Shuia, a textile center some three hundred kilometers northeast of Moscow, witnessed violence in mid-March when devout Christians sought to protect their church from soldiers sent to loot it. The soldiers fired at the crowd, reportedly killing several civilians. In Lenin's absence, on 16 March, the Politburo voted to delay further confiscations, and on 19 March Molotov sent instructions to this effect to all provincial party committees.[1] As soon as Lenin learned of this decision, he wrote the following letter, which overruled it.[2] D. A. Volkogonov states that he has seen an order from Lenin demanding to be informed on a daily basis about how many priests had been executed.[3] One Russian historian estimates that following Lenin's letter regarding Shuia, more than eight thousand persons were "liquidated."[4] There is no evidence whatever that the church planned a campaign of organized resistance to the government, as Lenin charged.

Document 94 was smuggled out of the Central Party Archive in the late 1960s and published in 1970 in Paris in *Vestnik Khristianskogo dvizheniia* [Herald of the Christian movement]. At the time, its authenticity was widely doubted because of the inhuman brutality of Lenin's instructions ("It is precisely now and only now, when in the starving regions people are eating human flesh, and hundreds if not thousands of corpses are littering the roads, that we can (and therefore must) carry out the confiscation of church valuables with the most savage and merciless energy, not stopping [short of] crushing any resistance"). But its republication twenty years later in the official *Izvestiia TsK* dispelled all skepticism.[5]

1. See f. 5, op. 2, d. 48, ll. 15 and 81.
2. For the background of this incident, see *RUBR*, 346–56.
3. *Literator,* 31 August 1990, p. 4.
4. Vladimir Yeremenko, in *Literaturnaia Rossiia* [Literary Russia], 14 December 1990, p. 17.
5. *Izvestiia TsK,* April 1990, pp. 190–93.

Document 94
Letter to Molotov for Politburo Members

19 March 1922

Top Secret
Do not make copies for any
reason, but have each
Politburo member (as well as
Comrade Kalinin) write his
comments on this document.
Lenin

To Comrade Molotov for the Politburo Members

Regarding the event in Shuia which is already on the agenda for discussion by the Politburo, I think a firm decision must be made immediately regarding a general plan of struggle in the given direction. Since I doubt that I will personally be able to attend the Politburo session of 20 March, I am presenting my thoughts in written form.

The event in Shuia should be related to the report that ROSTA[1] has recently sent to newspapers, not for publication—namely, a report on the steps taken by the Black Hundreds in Petrograd to defy the decree on the confiscation of church valuables. If one connects this fact with what the newspapers are reporting of the clergy's attitude toward the decree on the confiscation of church valuables, and further with what is known to us about the illegal appeal of Patriarch Tikhon,[2] it will become crystal clear that the Black Hundred clergy headed by its leader is quite deliberately implementing the plan to engage us in a decisive battle precisely at this moment.

It is obvious that the most influential group of Black Hundred clergy have conceived and adopted this plan rather resolutely at secret meetings. The events in Shuia are only one of the manifestations and implementations of this general plan.

I think that here our enemy is committing an enormous strategic mistake in trying to drag us into a decisive battle at a time when it is particularly hopeless and particularly disadvantageous for him. On the contrary, for us this moment is not only exceptionally favorable but generally the only moment when we can, with ninety-nine out of a hundred chances of total success, smash the enemy and secure for ourselves an indispensable position for many decades to come. It is precisely now and only now, when in the starving regions people are eating human flesh, and hundreds if not thousands of corpses are littering the roads, that we can (and therefore must) carry out the confiscation of church valuables with the most savage and merciless energy, not stopping [short of] crushing any resistance. It is precisely now and only now that the enormous majority of the peasant mass will be for us or at any rate will not be in a condition to support in any decisive way that handful of Black Hundred clergy and reactionary urban petty bourgeoisie who can and want to attempt a policy of violent resistance to the Soviet decree.

We must, come what may, carry out the confiscation of church valuables in the most decisive and rapid manner, so as to secure for ourselves a fund of several hundred million gold rubles (one must recall the gigantic wealth of some of the monasteries and abbeys). Without this fund, no government work in general, no economic construction in particular, and no defense of our position in Genoa especially is even conceivable. No matter what happens, we must lay our hands on a fund of several hundred million gold rubles (and perhaps even several billion). And this can be done successfully only now. All considerations indicate that later we will be unable to do this, because no other moment except that of desperate hunger will give us a mood among the broad peasant masses that will guarantee us the sympathy of these masses or at least their neutrality, in the sense that victory in the struggle for the confiscation of the valuables will be indisputable and entirely ours.

One wise writer on matters of statecraft[3] rightly said that if it is necessary to resort to certain brutalities for the sake of realizing a certain political goal, they must be carried out in the most energetic fashion and in the briefest possible time because the masses will not tolerate prolonged application of brutality. This notion is particularly reinforced by the fact that for us, after Genoa, Russia's international position in all likelihood will be such or may be such that harsh measures against the reactionary clergy will be politically irrational and perhaps even highly dangerous. At present, we are fully assured of victory over the reactionary clergy. Moreover, for the major part of our foreign opponents among the Russian émigrés abroad—that is, the SRs and the Miliukovites[4]—the struggle against us will be made more difficult if right at this moment, precisely in connection with the famine, we suppress the reactionary clergy with maximal speed and ruthlessness.

Therefore, I come to the categorical conclusion that precisely at this moment we must give battle to the Black Hundred clergy in the most decisive and merciless manner and crush its resistance with such brutality that it will not forget it for decades to come. I envision the actual campaign and the implementation of this plan as follows:

Only Comrade Kalinin should publicly undertake measures of any kind—Comrade Trotsky should at no time and under no circumstances speak out [on this matter] in the press or before the public in any other manner.[5]

The telegram sent on behalf of the Politburo about the temporary halt to the confiscations should not be withdrawn. It is advantageous to us, because it will plant the idea in the enemy that we are seemingly hesitating and that he has seemingly intimidated us (of course the enemy will soon learn about this secret telegram precisely because it is secret).

One of the most energetic, smartest, and most capable members of the All-Russian Central Executive Committee, or other representatives of central authority (better one than several), should be sent to Shuia and given verbal instruction through one of the Politburo members. The point of this instruction should be that he is to arrest in Shuia as many representatives of the local clergy, petty bourgeoisie, and bourgeoisie as possible, no fewer than several dozen, on suspicion of direct or indirect participation in violent resistance to the Central Executive Committee decree on the confiscation of church valuables. Immediately upon completion of this task he should come to Moscow and personally report either to the full session of the Politburo or to two members of the Politburo delegated for this purpose. On the basis of this report the Politburo will give a detailed directive to the judicial authorities, also verbal,[6] that the trial of the Shuia rebels resisting aid to the hungry be conducted with the maximum of speed and that it end in no other way than execution by firing squad of a very large number of the most influential and dangerous Black Hundreds in Shuia, and to the extent possible, not only in that city but also in Moscow and several other clerical centers.

I think it is expedient for us not to touch Patriarch Tikhon himself, although he is undoubtedly heading this entire rebellion of slaveholders. Regarding him, a secret directive should be issued to the GPU, so that all of this figure's connections are carefully and scrupulously observed and exposed, precisely at this moment. Dzerzhinsky and Unshlikht should be required personally to report on this to the Politburo weekly.

At the party congress arrange a secret meeting on this matter of all or nearly all the delegates, together with the chief functionaries of the GPU, the People's Commissariat of Justice, and the Revolutionary Tribunal. At this meeting, pass a secret resolution of the congress that the confiscation of valuables, in particular of the richest abbeys, monasteries, and churches, should be conducted with merciless determination, unconditionally stopping at nothing, and in the briefest possible time. The greater the number of representatives of the reactionary clergy and reactionary bourgeoisie we succeed in executing for this reason, the better. We must teach these people a lesson right now, so that they will not dare even to think of any resistance for several decades.

In order to oversee the most rapid and successful implementation of these measures, appoint a special commission right at the [Eleventh Party] congress, i.e., at its secret meeting, with the mandatory participation of Comrade Trotsky and Comrade Kalinin, without any publicity about this commission, so that the subordination of all operations to it is secured and conducted not in the name of the commission but through the customary Soviet and party procedures. Appoint the best—especially responsible—[party] workers for this measure in the richest abbeys, monasteries, and churches.

Lenin

19 March '22

I request Comrade Molotov to try to circulate this letter to members of the Politburo today (without making copies) and ask them to return it to the secretary immediately upon reading, with a brief notation about whether each Politburo member is in accord with the principle or if the letter raises any disagreements.

Lenin

19 March '22

Dictation taken over the telephone.

M. Volodicheva[7]

1. The Russian Telegraphic Agency.

2. Patriarch Tikhon (Vasily Ivanovich Belavin) (1865–1925): monk elected to his post by the All-Russian Church Council in October 1917. Attempted to keep the church out of politics but felt compelled to condemn the Bolshevik terror and antireligious policies. Was repeatedly placed under house arrest for this and in May 1922 was removed from his post by renegade clergymen whom the police had organized into a rump "Living Church." To prevent a split in the church, Tikhon eventually decided to collaborate with the Soviet authorities.

3. Reference to Machiavelli, The Prince, chapter 8.

4. Followers of Pavel Nikolaevich Miliukov (1859–1943), onetime head of the Constitutional Democratic Party, who in emigration broke with it and formed a bloc with the SRs.

5. Although Trotsky played a critical role in the 1922 antichurch campaign and may have even been its instigator, he was kept in the background throughout, in order not to feed rumors that the campaign was a Jewish plot against Christianity.

6. This instruction makes it abundantly clear that in Lenin's Russia the fate of political defendants was decided not by judiciary authorities but by the party.

7. Maria Akimovna Volodicheva (1881–1973): typist and assistant secretary in the Sovnarkom Council of Labor and Defense, 1918–24.

T he background of this strange note (Document 95) is as follows. On 20 and 22 January 1922, in connection with the forthcoming Genoa Conference, Chicherin proposed to Lenin that to satisfy possible American demands for "representative institutions" in Soviet Russia, a minor amendment be inserted in the Soviet constitution: in return for "appropriate compensation" (in other words, a large loan) non-proletarian elements (owners of private property) would be allowed some representation in the soviets. Lenin wrote in the margin of Chicherin's note "???" and "Madness!!"[1] He meant it literally, because he promptly dashed off a note to the Politburo stating that Chicherin's proposal indicated that he was "ill and seriously so": "We will be fools, if we do not immediately and forcibly send him to a sanatorium."[2] The subject was brought up several times in the Politburo, but in the end Chicherin was forgiven.

This seems to be the earliest mention of compulsory commitment to a medical facility as punishment for political deviation—a notorious practice of the Soviet government in the last two decades of its existence. Although there were instances of such confinement of political dissidents before the publication of this Lenin document, the policy became adopted on a wide scale only in the late 1960s.[3]

In the course of 1922, a special medical commission examined a number of prominent Bolsheviks and concluded that some of them suffered from nervous ailments of various kinds: Sokolnikov from neurasthenia (nervous breakdown), Kursky from neuralgia, and Zinoviev from nervous seizures. Stalin, however, was declared sane and sound.[4] It cannot be established whether this commission consisted of the German team to which Lenin refers, but that is likely to have been the case.

1. *BKh*, vol. 12, pp. 139–40.
2. *PSS*, vol. 54, pp. 136–37, 596.
3. Ludmilla Alexeyeva, *Soviet Dissent* (Middletown, Conn., 1985), 310–17.
4. Chuev, *Sto sorok besed s Molotovym*, 596.

Document 95
Note to N. P. Gorbunov

21 March 1922

To Comrade Gorbunov

Please raise the following proposal via Molotov at the Secretariat of the Central Committee and inform me whether it passes. In view of Krestinsky's departure for Moscow on 18 March with German specialists on nervous diseases to examine a group of senior [party] workers, I propose that the Secretariat of the Central Committee ask the doctor responsible for supervising the medical treatment of responsible [party] workers (and if there is no such doctor despite numerous Central Committee resolutions, then a special doctor must be appointed for this purpose without fail) to draw up a list of comrades requiring examination and take all measures to see that they are examined in good time by the visiting doctor, in consultation, if necessary, with those Russian doctors who have been treating them until now. This list should obviously include Comrades Chicherin, Osinsky,[1] Trotsky, Kamenev, Stalin, Briukhanov, and undoubtedly a whole number of others.

21 March '22

Lenin

Dictation taken over the telephone.

L. Fotieva

1. N. Osinsky (Prince V. V. Obolensky) (1883–1938): Old Bolshevik; economist; in 1917–18 chairman of the Supreme Council of the National Economy. A "Left Communist" and later a supporter of Trotsky, he was eased out of the party. Tried for allegedly trying to assassinate Lenin and executed.

I n April 1922, because of his recurrent bouts with illness, Lenin proposed to appoint two deputies (*zamestiteli,* or *zamy,* for short) to replace him when he was indisposed: one to chair the Sovnarkom; the other, the Council of Labor and Defense.[1] Rykov was nominated for the latter post, but to judge by this exchange, not without hesitation.

1. See T. H. Rigby, *Lenin's Government: Sovnarkom, 1917–1922* (Cambridge, 1979), 292–93; *RUBR,* 463–64.

Document 96
Exchange with Kamenev

[After 4 April 1922]

Note from Kamenev

Precisely because of his vile[1] speech today Rykov should not be included! But if we don't include him, I suppose he'll be an eternal sore.

L. Kamenev

Note from Lenin

If we don't include Rykov—he will be an **eternal** sore. **Then you will have to find another** deputy chairman of the Council of People's **Commissars.**

Kalinin is a candidate.

Lenin

Note from Kamenev

We'll have to take Rykov.

1. Lenin added a footnote to this word: "I don't understand why 'vile': a little bit of cunning!"

T he medicines Lenin requested were popular sedatives imported from Germany.

Document 97
Request to the Kremlin Pharmacy

6 April 1922

6 April 1922
Please send me two to three pipettes (or boxes?) with the following pills:
Somnacetin = *tabletten* [tablets]
Veronal = *tabletten*
in **Originaltabletten.**

Lenin

T he following document concerns the Soviet position at the Genoa Conference. It is a reaction to two telegrams[1] sent by Chicherin to the Politburo from Genoa on 15 April 1922, in which he reported the demand by the Allies that Moscow abandon counterclaims stemming from their intervention, in return for which they were prepared to annul both Russia's war debts and, until the expiration of an eight- to ten-year debt moratorium, interest due on prewar debts.[2] The nationalized assets were to be returned to their owners through a long-term lease or, exceptionally, restitution. According to Chicherin, Lloyd George had informed the Soviet delegation that this would be the extent of Allied concessions.

1. See Documents 6A and 7A (in the Appendix).
2. Russia's external debt at the time was estimated at 18.5 billion gold rubles ($9.25 billion); her "counterclaims" came to 39 billion gold rubles ($19.5 billion).

Document 98
Telegram from the Politburo to Chicherin

[17 April 1922]

To Comrade Chicherin

We have received both coded telegrams of 15 April over Chicherin's signature.

We define the limit to our concessions as follows. The war debts and the interest on prewar debts are covered by our counterclaims. We absolutely reject restitutions. In this area we propose as a maximum concession granting former foreign owners the preferential right to receive their former enterprises for rent or, [as a] concession, on terms equal (or meaningfully close to equal) [to those granted other foreigners]. Payment on acknowledged prewar debts is to begin in fifteen years (the maximum concession is ten years). A mandatory condition for all the enumerated concessions and in particular the concession on our counterclaims is an immediate large loan (approximately one billion dollars). The amount of the loan should be set through your special communication with Moscow.

We remind you that the final agreement must bring advantages to both sides; in particular, it must guarantee us a large loan. We propose moving the matter to the plenary session and there formulating all our counterclaims.[1]

Do not forget the concession which we have discussed hypothetically earlier and which we now are proposing firmly, namely, our commitment to take care of the interests of smallholders.

Lenin
Trotsky
Stalin
Zinoviev
Kamenev
Rykov

1. The beginning of the telegram and the signatures were written by Kamenev; from this point until the end it was written by Zinoviev.

The telegram that follows refers to transcripts of a meeting of representatives of the Second, Second and a Half, and Third Internationals held in Berlin between 2 and 5 April 1922. The gathering was the product of a short-lived attempt by Moscow to collaborate with the Socialist Internationals. Radek, apparently on his own initiative, pledged at this meeting that the leaders of the Socialist-Revolutionary

Party, about to stand in a show trial, would not be subject to the death penalty. Lenin repudiated this pledge.[1] The Berlin meeting passed a declaration acknowledging the possibility of conducting joint meetings and issuing common statements under slogans in favor of the eight-hour workday, against the offensive of "capital," and in defense of the Russian Revolution, aid to the hungry of Russia, Soviet Russia's renewal of political and economic relations with all other countries, and the creation of a "united proletarian front."

The declaration by representatives of the three Internationals was ratified at the 20 April session of the Comintern Executive Committee.

1. *PSS*, vol. 45, pp. 140–44.

Document 99
Telegram from the Politburo to Radek and Bukharin

[17 April 1922]

Coded!

To Radek. To Bukharin. Berlin

We received the transcripts. Both of Radek's speeches are very good. Tomorrow the Executive Committee will officially ratify the agreement. We propose immediately raising the issue of the progress of the negotiations in Genoa in the Commission of Nine. It has been shown that a rupture may take place any minute over the question of disarmament and the Entente's demand for acknowledgment of the private debts of big foreign capitalists. Point out that the demand for disarmament is among the demands of the Second and Second and a Half [Internationals]. If during the next twenty-four hours they will be dragging things out, come out yourselves with the [Comintern] Executive Committee manifesto and call on all workers to protest. In particular, advise the French Communists to step up their campaign against Barthou[1] and Poincaré.[2] We consider the proposal to offer an inch to Vandervelde to be incorrect; you have given him an inch already.

Zinoviev
Lenin
Trotsky
Stalin
Kamenev

1. Jean-Louis Barthou (1862–1934) served as French representative at the Genoa Conference.
2. Raymond Poincaré (1860–1934), who pursued a hard-line policy toward Weimar Germany, was at the time French prime minister and minister of foreign affairs.

The following telegram was drafted by Lenin in consultation with Stalin and Kamenev. Lenin refers to a note that Chicherin sent to Lloyd George on 20 April 1922, four days after the Soviet delegation had signed a separate treaty with Germany at Rapallo. In the note, Chicherin proposed that in return for the annulment of all Russia's wartime debts and of the interest on them, as well as "adequate" financial aid and de jure recognition of the Soviet government, Moscow would be prepared to allow the former owners to "use" their nationalized properties or, where this was impossible, arrive at some kind of compromise solution with them.[1] Other members of the Soviet delegation protested that these terms violated Politburo directives. Lenin agreed with these delegates.[2]

1. See *Dokumenty vneshnei politiki, SSSR*, vol. 5 (Moscow, 1961), 259–60.
2. *PSS*, vol. 45, pp. 164–65.

Document 100
Telegram from Lenin, Kamenev, Stalin, Trotsky, and Molotov to Chicherin and the Soviet Delegation in Genoa

25 April 1922

Coded

Genoa. To Chicherin for all members of the delegation

We consider Chicherin's maneuver in the form of his letter to Lloyd George to be correct, but we understand it precisely as a maneuver. The most important thing is to stress as clearly as possible that the break [in the Genoa negotiations] is provoked exclusively by the question of restoring private property. Regarding the losses of former foreign property owners, the limit to our compromise is as follows: first, according to the directive of 17 April, [they are to be offered] a right of priority to concessions where we recognize them as acceptable. If an enterprise is leased at all and the former foreign owner does not take it, then he loses the right to any compensation whatsoever. Second, the owners of enterprises that remain under the management of the [Soviet] government are to be compensated for the claims that we recognize, and in the amount set by us. These concessions must be made strictly dependent on the size and terms[1] of the loan. It is the task of our financial people to figure out the details. Break off at that point, emphasizing as trump cards for the resumption of future trading: first, the fundamental significance of the agreement with the Germans;[2] second, the rejection on principle of the restoration of private property.

Lenin, Kamenev, Stalin, Trotsky,
Molotov

P.S. In the most extreme case, we allow the following concession as well: instead of having only our side determine the recognition of claims and the amount of the owners' compensation, it is possible to propose that both are to be determined by agreement of the Soviet government with each individual owner. But we will make this concession only under two conditions: first, no arbiter for such agreements; second, very favorable terms for the loan.

Lenin, Kamenev, Stalin, Trotsky,
Molotov

25 April '22

1. "And terms" was inserted by Lenin into Kamenev's draft.
2. That is, the Rapallo treaty.

O n the same day (25 April), the Politburo resolved to ask Chicherin and Litvinov to draft a declaration for release in the event that the Genoa Conference broke up.[1]

1. *PSS*, vol. 45, p. 540.

Document 101
Letter from Trotsky, Politburo Vote, and Draft Resolution by Lenin

28 April 1922

Letter from Trotsky

Extremely Urgent
Top Secret

28 April '22
To the Politburo

      1. Since a breakdown is imminent in the matter of the confiscation of private capital, we should announce that in the event that the governments of the Entente were to confiscate all the capital of Russian capitalists abroad, we would treat this as an act of international reciprocity and would commit ourselves not to protest. I made this proposal to Comrade Karakhan;[1] he promised to forward it to Genoa. The purpose, of course, is purely agitational.

      2. The rupture [of negotiations at Genoa] will make a huge impression in our country. I believe that we should appeal to the people with a manifesto

on behalf of the Sovnarkom or the Central Executive Committee regarding the rupture that would explain all aspects of the matter. I think that the manifesto could even be constructed in such a way as to serve us abroad also (for workers as well as governments). Hence, **we should propose to our delegation that they jot down for us their principal ideas** for such a manifesto (otherwise we could miss important points).

L. Trotsky

Put to the vote of Politburo members.

J. Stalin

Voting of Politburo Members

Oppose the first point. Vote **in favor of** the second point.

J. Stalin

Agree with Comrade Stalin.

V. Molotov

Agree only with the last sentence.

Lenin

Draft by Lenin of Politburo Resolution

Just one thing must be done immediately: send a coded telegram to Chicherin with a request to send an outline or theses for a manifesto.

Lenin

1. Lev Mikhailovich Karakhan (1889–1937): a Bolshevik from 1917 on, deputy commissar of foreign affairs and later Soviet diplomatic representative in Poland. Perished in Stalin's terror.

The occasion for Document 102 was a letter Osinsky sent Lenin on 18 May 1922, requesting a lengthy leave to work on a book on agriculture.

Document 102
Letter to Stalin

19 May 1922

Comrade Stalin!

I enclose Osinsky's[1] letter. I think you should consult secretly with Yakovenko[2] and Teodorovich[3] to see if there is anything on the inside that looks like a fresh conflict or an exacerbation of an old [one] in the People's Commissariat of Agriculture.

If not, I **entirely** support Osinsky's proposal, and in fact **to the maximum.** Please put this to a vote in the Politburo if the secretariat does not object.

By the way, isn't it time to set up one or two model sanatoria not less than six hundred versts from Moscow? Gold should be spent on this; we are already spending [it] and will **keep on spending for a long time** on **unavoidable** trips to Germany.[4] But recognize as **model only** the sanatoria with a **demonstrated** capability of having **strictly scrupulous** doctors and administration—not the **usual** Soviet bunglers and slobs.

19 May

Lenin

P.S. **Secret:** In Zubalovo,[5] where you, Kamenev, and Dzerzhinsky are settled, and where I will be settled next door by the fall—**you must get** the rail line repaired and [arrange to] have the motorized trolleys running **absolutely regularly;** this will make possible rapid, **clandestine,** and cheap year-round shuttling. Apply pressure and check up on it. Also get the nearby state farm up and running.

1. Lenin added a footnote to this word: "Return this letter to me because of the second part: I shall issue an order."
2. V. G. Yakovenko (1889–1938): joined the Bolsheviks in 1917; served in 1922–23 as commissar of agriculture.
3. I. A. Teodorovich (1875–1940): Old Bolshevik. Served in the Commissariat of Agriculture.
4. Top Soviet officials were routinely sent to German sanatoria for cures.
5. Zubalovo was where Stalin, Dzerzhinsky, and Kamenev had their country dachas.

T he following note refers to Trotsky's refusal to supervise the work of Gokhran, the State Depository for Valuables.

Document 103
Note to the Politburo

22 May 1922

Trotsky's letter is not clear. If he is **refusing,** then we need a resolution of the Politburo. I favor not accepting Trotsky's resignation (from this matter).

22 May

Lenin

V V. Kramer, A. M. Kozhevnikov, Otfrid Foerster, and Georg Klemperer were members of a large medical team attending Lenin. Following Lenin's debilitating stroke during the night of 25–26 May 1922, Stalin, on Politburo instructions, requested the German government to arrange for the visits of Drs. Foerster and Klemperer. Klemperer examined Lenin on 11 June. Lenin took an intense dislike to him, and he was soon returned to Germany. Foerster, however, remained to the end and participated in the autopsy on Lenin.

Document 104
Letter to Stalin for the Politburo

15 June 1922

To Stalin for the Politburo

I beg you most humbly to liberate me from Klemperer. [His] extreme concern and caution can drive a person out of his mind and cause trouble.

If there is no other way, I agree to send him on a scientific assignment.

I strongly urge you to rid me of Foerster. I am more than extremely satisfied with my doctors Kramer and Kozhevnikov. Russians cannot stand German meticulousness, and Foerster and Klemperer have already participated enough in the consultation.

15 June

Lenin

I certify the authenticity. M. Ulianova[1]

1. Maria Ilinichna Ulianova (1878–1937): Lenin's sister, who lived with him at Gorki during his illness.

Document 105
Note to Stalin

7 July 1922

7 July
Comrade Stalin!

It seems that the doctors are creating a legend that must not be left without rebuttal. They have become upset over the severe attack on Friday and have done something totally ridiculous: they have tried to forbid "political" visits (understanding ill what that means!!). I was **extremely** angry and reprimanded them. Kamenev visited me on Thursday. We had an animated political discussion. I slept wonderfully and felt marvelous. On Friday, I suffered paralysis. I call for you urgently in order to **manage** to tell [what I have to say], in case the illness worsens. I manage to say everything in fifteen minutes and on Sunday again sleep wonderfully. Only fools can put the blame on political discussions. If I become excited at times, it is because of the **lack** of timely and political discussions. I trust you will understand this and will send that fool, the German professor and Co., packing. Come without fail to tell me about the Central Committee plenum, or [else] send one of the attendees.

With communist greetings,
Lenin

K amenev visited Lenin on 14 July 1922. The circumstances that led to this exchange concerning Trotsky are not known: from the context it appears that Kamenev reported to Lenin that the Central Committee, dominated by Stalin and Zinoviev, wanted to drop Trotsky because of his refusal to take on various responsibilities assigned to him.[1]

1. On 18 July 1922 Lenin wrote Stalin a brief note requesting him to remind Kamenev that he had promised to discuss Trotsky and let Lenin know their joint opinion (f. 2, op. 1, d. 25,996).

Document 106
Note to Kamenev

[Probably mid-July 1922]

I think exaggerations can be avoided. You write "(the Central Committee) is throwing or is ready to throw a good cannon overboard." Isn't that an immense exaggeration? Throwing Trotsky overboard—surely you are hinting at that, it is impossible to interpret it otherwise—is the height of stupidity. If you do not consider me already hopelessly foolish, how can you think of that???? Bloodied children before the eyes . . . [1]

A private meeting? I agree, but would advise **not now.** Shouldn't we wait two or three days? 1) To sound things out first and 2) to **guarantee** that the meeting will not arouse passions. I will not get into a fight, to be sure. But the others? Lenin

1. The phrase "bloodied children before the eyes" is a quotation from Pushkin's *Boris Godunov* and refers to the visions Godunov had after (allegedly) murdering the young tsarevich Dmitry in order to seize the throne.

DOCUMENT 106. Note to Kamenev Opposing Trotsky's Expulsion, mid-July 1922

The idea of deporting intellectuals hostile to the Bolshevik regime first occurred to Lenin in the spring of 1922. In a letter to Dzerzhinsky, he instructed the GPU to prepare lists of writers and scholars who were "helping the counterrevolution."[1] He wanted members of the Politburo to spend two to three hours a week inspecting publications and passing judgments on them, alone or with the help of experts. "Spies" and "perverters of youth" were to be apprehended and "systematically deported abroad." Apparently nothing was done to implement this order until Lenin raised the issue once again the next month in the following document. His wishes were carried out in the late summer of 1922, when the GPU arrested 120 intellectuals, including many prominent academics, a large number of whom were forcibly deported to Germany.[2]

The noteworthy aspect of Document 107 is the degree to which Lenin assumed the role of a thought policeman and followed the writings of various intellectuals in detail to determine whether they were fit to live in Soviet Russia.

1. The letter, dated 19 May 1922, is in *PSS*, vol. 54, pp. 265–66.
2. See Michel Heller, "Premier avertissement: Un coup de fouet. L'histoire de l'expulsion des personnalités culturelles hors de l'Union Soviétique en 1922," *Cahiers du monde russe et soviétique*, 20 (1979): 131–72.

Document 107
Letter to Stalin

[17 July 1922]

Comrade Stalin!

On the matter of deporting the Mensheviks, Popular Socialists, Kadets, and the like from Russia, I would like to ask several questions in view of the fact that this operation, initiated before my leave, has not been completed to this day.

Resolutely to "uproot" all Popular Socialists? Peshekhonov,[1] Miakotin,[2] Gornfeld?,[3] Petrishchev,[4] and the others. I think all of them should be deported. They are more harmful than any SR, because more cunning.

Also A. N. Potresov, Izgoev,[5] and **the entire** staff of *Ekonomist*[6] (**Ozerov**[7] and **many, many others**). Mensheviks: Rozanov (a physician, cunning),[8] Vigdorchik[9] (Migulo or some name like that), Lyubov Nikolaevna Radchenko[10] and her young daughter (said to be malicious enemies of Bolshevism); N. A. Rozhkov (he must be deported; he is incorrigible); S. A. [L.] Frank[11] (author of *Metodologiia*[12]). A commission under the supervision of Mantsev,[13] Messing,[14] and others should submit a list of several **hundred** such gentlemen, who must be deported abroad without mercy. We will purge Russia for a long time to come.

Regarding Lezhnev[15] (formerly of *Den'*[16]), we should reflect a great deal about whether he should not be deported. He will always be extremely crafty, as far as I can judge from the articles of his that I have read.

Ozerov, like **the entire** staff of *Ekonomist*, are the most ruthless enemies. The lot—out of Russia.

This must be done at once. Before the end of the trial of the SRs—no later.[17] Arrest several hundred and **without stating** the reasons—out with you, gentlemen!

All the authors from *Dom literatorov* [House of writers] and the Petrograd *Mysl'*;[18] Kharkov should be ransacked—**we don't know it,** it is a "foreign country" for us. We must purge **quickly, no later** than by the end of the SRs' trial.

Note the literary figures in Petrograd (addresses in *Novaia russkaia kniga*, no. 4, 1922, p. 37) and the list of private publishers (p. 29).[19]

With communist greetings,

Lenin

1. A. V. Peshekhonov (1867–1933): writer and economist originally close to the SRs, later one of the founders of the Popular Socialist Party. Served as minister of agriculture in the first coalition government in 1917. Emigrated.

2. V. A. Miakotin (1867–1937): historian and writer; cofounder, with Peshekhonov, of the Popular Socialist Party. Emigrated.

3. Arkady Georgievich Gornfeld (1867–?): literary specialist who wrote for *Russkoe bogatstvo* [Russia's wealth].

4. This individual could not be identified.

5. A. S. Izgoev (1872–1935): liberal publicist. Participated in the symposium *Vekhi* [Landmarks] in 1909. Expelled from Soviet Russia in 1922.

6. *Ekonomist* [Economist], a journal of the Russian Technical Society published in Petrograd starting in December 1921. Lenin called it "an organ of contemporary serf-owners." It was closed in the summer of 1922.

7. I. Kh. Ozerov (1869–1942): economist and academic.

8. N. S. Rozanov: physician; Trudovik deputy from Saratov Province in the Third Duma.

9. N. A. Vigdorchik (1874–1954): specialist on social insurance and hygiene; Social Democrat.

10. L. N. Radchenko (1871–1962): one of the oldest members of the Menshevik Party. At one time collaborated with Lenin; abandoned political activity in 1918.

11. S. L. Frank (1877–1950): prominent Russian philosopher; contributor to *Vekhi*. Expelled from Soviet Russia in 1922.

12. The book Lenin refers to is *Ocherk metodologii obshchestvennykh nauk* [Outline of the methodology of the social sciences] (Moscow, 1922).

13. V. N. Mantsev (1888–1939): Old Bolshevik. In 1922, chaired the Ukrainian Communist Central Committee and served in the Cheka.

14. S. A. Messing (1890–1946): Old Bolshevik. Worked in the Cheka and OGPU.

15. I. G. Lezhnev (1891–1955): Journalist.

16. *Den'* [The day] was a liberal daily published in St. Petersburg beginning in 1912 and closed by the Bolshevik Military-Revolutionary Committee on the day of the coup (October 26, 1917).

17. The "trial" of the Socialist-Revolutionary leaders opened in Moscow on 6 June 1922 and ended on 7 August.

18. *Mysl'* [Thought] was a publication of the St. Petersburg Philosophical Society under the editorship of E. L. Radlov and N. O. Lossky. After Lenin's letter, it was shut down.

19. *Novaia russkaia kniga* [New Russian book], published in Berlin, printed in its April 1922 issue, pp. 37–42, the names and addresses of numerous Petrograd writers and scholars whose fate had been in doubt. The same issue carried (on pp. 29–30) the names and addresses of forty-one private publishing firms in Petrograd.

Document 108
Letter to Stalin and Kamenev

[28 August 1922]

Comrade Stalin or Comrade Kamenev!
(letter for both)

Radek is in a hurry; he is grabbing papers out of Karakhan's hands. This is not the way to do it. Things are heating up. I advise appointing, let's say, two people (for example, Kamenev and Trotsky) and **forbidding** that anything be done diplomatically in the intervals between Politburo sessions without their **joint** consent.

With Germany we must now be "wiser than the serpent." Not one unnecessary word. Neither France nor England should be "teased" unnecessarily. Threats should not be made without cause (as in the 27 August *Pravda* editorial[1]). Think over every word beforehand ten and a hundred times.

The 27 August note should be answered with a **well-considered** note proposing **practical** help (concessions, state collective farms, and so on) and **not one word** calling for the nonfulfillment of the Versailles treaty.

With communist greetings,
Lenin

P.S. The closer the collapse, the greater the caution!!![2]

Nota Bene. Should not more submarines be quickly transferred to the Caspian Sea to defend Baku?[3]

N.B. N.B.

P.S. A provocation from England **is quite possible** in order to set **France** against us.

1. *Pravda,* 27 August 1922, p. 1.

2. Lenin added: "See verso of p. 1."

3. Lenin wrote these words on the back of page 1 with the notation: "page 1 verso." It is not clear what threat to Baku he had in mind.

L enin's proposal (Document 109) to appoint two deputies to the supreme state organ in view of his illness was approved by the Politburo on 14 September 1922. In its resolution, the Politburo expressed regrets at Trotsky's refusal and offered the position to Kamenev.[1]

1. See f. 17, op. 3, d. 312, l. 4. On the background and consequences of this episode, see Rigby, *Lenin's Government: Sovnarkom,* chapter 13, and *RUBR,* 463, 466–67. See also the headnote to Document 96.

Document 109
Letter to Stalin

11 September 1922

For the vote of Politburo members over the telephone.[1]
To Comrade Stalin, secretary of the Central Committee
In view of the fact that with the arrival of Tsiurupa[2] (his arrival is expected on 20 September) Comrade Rykov has been granted leave and [that] the doctors are promising me (of course, only in the event that nothing bad happens) a return to work (very gradually at first) by 1 October, I think it is impossible to dump all the current work on Comrade Tsiurupa, and propose appointing **two more deputies** (a deputy chairman of the Sovnarkom and a deputy chairman of the Council of Labor and Defense), namely, Comrades Trotsky and Kamenev. The work load should be distributed between them with my participation and, of course, that of the Politburo as the highest instance.

11 September 1922

V. Ulianov (Lenin)

Vote of the Politburo members taken over the telephone.[3]

1. "In favor" (Stalin).
2. "Categorically refuse" (Trotsky).[4]
3. "In favor" (Rykov).
4. "Abstain" (Tomsky).
5. "Do not object" (Kalinin).
6. "Abstain" (Kamenev).

1. Stalin underlined "over the telephone" twice, added "Top secret," and signed "J. Stalin."
2. Aleksandr Dmitrievich Tsiurupa (1870–1928): Old Bolshevik; commissar of supply from 1918 to 1921. In 1921, was appointed deputy chairman of the Sovnarkom and the Council of Labor and Defense.
3. The line was written by Stalin.

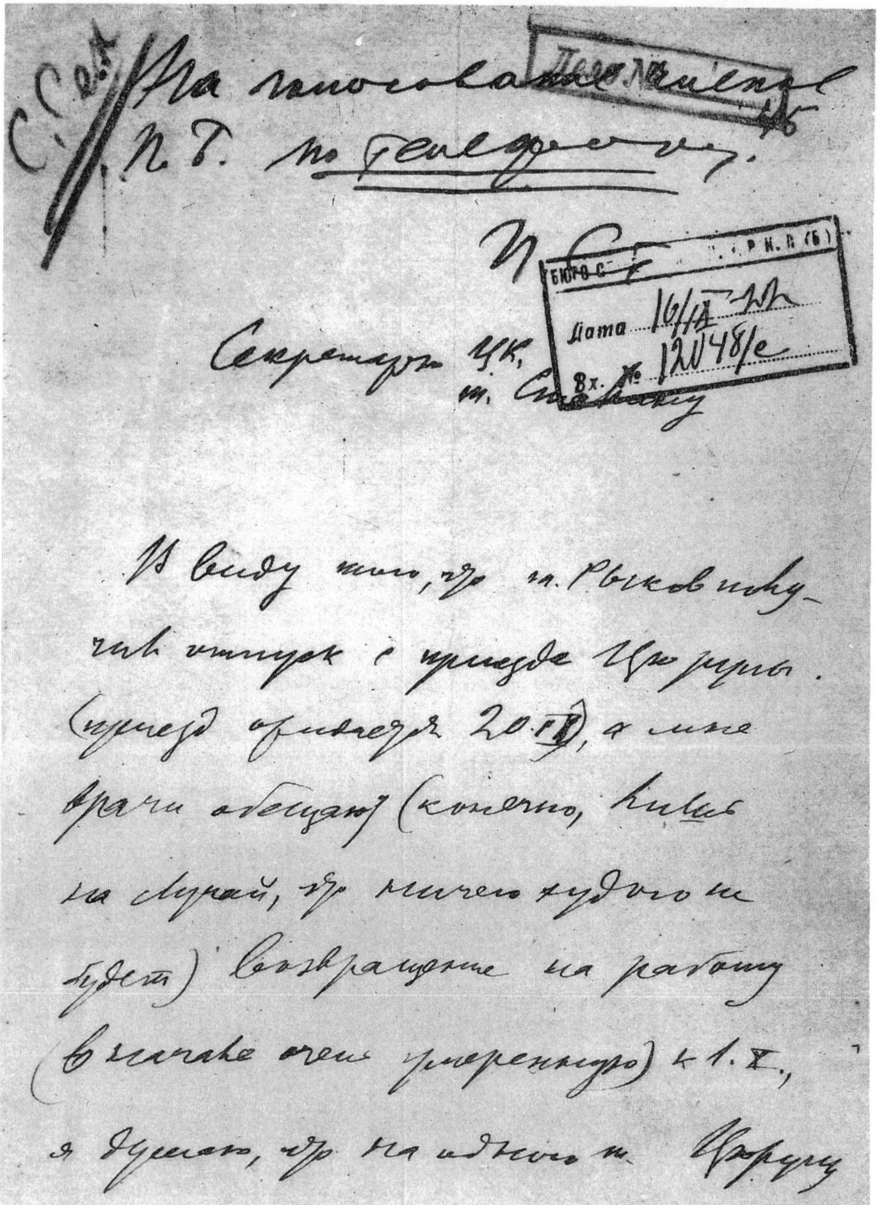

С Сек.

На голосование членов П.Б. по телефону.

И. Ст.

БЮРО С... Р.К.П.(б)
Дата 16/IX-22
Вх. № 12048/с

Секретарю Ц.К.
т. Сталину

В виду того, что т. Рыков получил отпуск с приезда Цюрупы (приезд ожидается 20.IX), а мне врачи обещают (конечно, лишь на случай, что ничего худого не будет) возвращение на работу (в начале очень умеренную) к 1.X, я думаю, что на одного т. Цюрупу взвалить всю текущую работу невозможно, и предлагаю назначить еще двух замов (зампред СНК и зампред СТО), именно: т.т. Троцкого

DOCUMENT 109. Letter to Stalin, 11 September 1922

« Каменева. Распреде-
лить между нами
работу при участии
моем и, разумеется,
Политбюро, как вы-
шей инстанции.

11 сент. 1922

(Члены П.б.)
Голосование по телефону (........... Ленин)

1) „за" (Сталин)

2) „Категорически отказываюсь"
                                    (Троцкий).

3) „за" (Рыков)   6) „воздерживаюсь"
                                       (Каменев)
4) „воздерживаюсь" (Томский)
5) „не возражаю" (Калинин)

4. The votes of Stalin and Trotsky are handwritten; the votes of the remaining Polit-buro members were recorded by the secretary.

R eference here is to Lenin's order to deport several hundred socialist intellectuals (see above, Document 107).

Document 110
Note to Unshlikht

17 September 1922

17 September
Comrade Unshlikht!

Be so good as to see to it that **all** the attached papers are returned to me **with notations** of **who** is exiled, who is in prison, who has been spared from deportation (and why). Make very brief notes **on this same sheet.**

Yours, Lenin

T he following private letter to Radek indicates that as late as October 1922 Lenin still believed in the imminence of a revolution in England. It also indicates that Moscow was financing Communist electoral activities in England in support of the Labour Party. The election to which Lenin refers was occasioned by the withdrawal on 19 October 1922 of the Unionists (Conservatives) from Lloyd George's cabinet. In the elections held in mid-November 1922, the Unionists won a majority, but the Labour Party secured enough seats to constitute for the first time His Majesty's Opposition.

Document 111
Letter to Radek

[28 October 1922]

Comrade Radek!

Truly, you are misbehaving. You write satirical articles of monstrous size (about Lloyd George). No one reads them. They belong in journals; newspapers need short ones. You know how [to do it] in fifty lines.

Why today's editorial "About Martov and Dan"?[1] Horrors! Horrors! This belonged on the third page and in **small print.** All would have read and smiled. And you have **unintentionally** extolled [the two]—to the point of absurdity.

For the editorial you should have used one of the adjoining **articles.**

Now about something else. In England, in my opinion, there is a decisive battle—**elections.**

In my view, one should as **quickly as possible** turn back all Englishmen who are en route to here.

Arrange it so: twelve hours in Russia and **fly** back.

It is inanely stupid to stay here even one extra hour when elections are under way there.

During those twelve hours agree on tactics: 1) for the Labour Party; 2) full freedom of agitation; 3) full freedom of speech (the candidate is a **super-scoundrel; for this reason I am** for him; the masses will learn); 4) leaflets **for the masses** in such a spirit—**brief, merry, very cheap;** 5) how much will **our** help cost? 6) mobilize **all** members of our party: go from house to house, **all day** on the streets, **etc., etc.**

Please send me all the arriving Englishmen.

Call.

Yours, Lenin

1. The article by Radek actually appeared in *Pravda*, 10 October 1922, pp. 2–3.

Document 112
Note to Zinoviev[1]

[Between October and December 1922]

In **Petrograd** there is a Central Committee of Mensheviks (it is apparent from *Sotsialisticheskii vestnik*[2]).

Is Rozhkov in Petrograd?

He should be deported.

[Unsigned]

1. See Lenin's letter to Stalin of 13 December 1922 (Document 113).
2. *Sotsialisticheskii vestnik* [Socialist herald], the leading Menshevik émigré periodical, published consecutively in Berlin, in Paris, and in New York.

Document 113
Letter to Stalin for the Central Committee Plenum

13 December 1922

To Comrade Stalin

Letter for Members of the Central Committee

For a correct evaluation of our disagreement on the matter of Rozhkov it must be borne in mind that we have already raised this question several times in the Politburo. The first time, Trotsky came out in favor of postponing Rozhkov's exile. The second time—when, under the influence of pressure from Messing, Rozhkov reformulated his views—Trotsky advocated exiling him, finding that this formulation not only was entirely useless but clearly demonstrated the insincerity of Rozhkov's views. I fully concur with Zinoviev that Rozhkov is a person of firm and stubborn convictions, but he is yielding to us in the bargaining with Messing and makes every kind of statement against the Mensheviks, exclusively for the same reasons we in our day swore oaths of loyalty to the tsar upon taking our seats in the State Duma. For this reason, if Steklov[1] or anyone else is assigned to use Rozhkov's statement (for example, to "challenge" the Mensheviks), first of all, this will not achieve its purpose, and second, it will put us to shame, since the Mensheviks will answer straightaway that like us, they were always in favor of signing any sworn oath if under coercion. In such a "duel" with the Mensheviks we will be the only losers.

I propose:

First—deport Rozhkov abroad.

Second—if that will not pass (for example, on the grounds that Rozhkov deserves leniency on account of old age), then Rozhkov's statements obtained under duress ought not to be subjected to any public discussion. Then we must wait until Rozhkov, even a few years from now, makes a sincere statement in our favor. And until that time I would propose sending him to Pskov, for example, creating tolerable living conditions for him and providing him with material support and work. But he must be kept under strict surveillance, because this man is our enemy and is likely to remain one until the end.

Lenin

13 December '22

Dictation taken over the telephone.

L. Fotieva

1. Yury M. Steklov (1873–1941): Old Bolshevik; publicist. From 1917 to 1925, editor of *Izvestiia* and author of several books on socialist history.

Appendix

This report from Moscow's chief negotiator with the Polish government at the height of the Russian civil war reveals that Marshal Pilsudski of Poland promised to help the Red Army defeat the White army commanded by General Anton Denikin.[1]

1. See Document 47.

Document 1A
Memorandum from Julian Marchlewski to the Politburo

26 October 1919

26 October 1919

Boerner returned from Warsaw and came to me in the evening to talk. [. . .] [A] political discussion ensued: he stated that he had no written authorizations; the situation in Warsaw is such that they do not wish to put anything in writing. I said that this was not necessary: we would not exchange authorizations but would show them to one another and then hide them in our pockets or burn them; for me it was enough if he informed me verbally that there is a definite and clear decision by the Polish command: Polish troops **will not go farther, will definitely not go [farther].** [Boerner said]: "It is important to us that you beat Denikin; take your regiments, send them against Denikin, or against Yudenich, we will not touch you." I replied that this statement would be very important at this time if it were made by an authorized person, for surely it was impossible for us to move our units from the front on the basis of private conversations. He once again pointed out that the Polish command had already proved its intentions in deed and that the political situation was entirely clear: Poland cannot desire the victory of Denikin, it does not want to prevent us from beating Denikin, and it is simply helping Petliura to beat him. I insisted on a clear answer: Would this be stated to me by an authorized person? and he replied, "Yes, in a few days." Then I began to ask ["What] about the agreement[?"]: it had to be made concrete, we had to come to an understanding, and then ratify an agreement, if not in writing, then verbally. He stated that it could be done as follows: Pilsudski would send his representative to Moscow, who would give Lenin such a guarantee, but a [Soviet] delegate could not be received in Warsaw, because it would be impossible to hide such a fact under the conditions prevailing there, and receiving a delegate would be tantamount to signing an agreement, and consequently to recognizing the Soviet government, which was something Poland could not do now. I said: ["]In that case the entire agreement carries no weight. If Poland depends on the Entente to such an extent, then there is no guarantee that tomorrow the Entente won't order you to attack and [that] you [won't] do it.["] He said: "No, we will not do that; it is one thing to enter into political deals that are not advantageous to us and another thing to attack. It is not advantageous for us to attack; we have already gone against the will of the Entente a number of times, and we will not go along with it in this case. The guarantee is the person of Pilsudski."

I said: ["]All right, we will look for a way to formalize the agreement.["] The question is essentially clear regarding Lithuania and Belorussia, but complicated regarding Petliura. [Boerner] proposed to clarify this in a future conversation. But it had to be postponed because on 27 October Boerner went to the front to meet our courier.

The Red Army under Frunze's command began offensive operations against Bukhara on 29 August 1920. The principality fell on 2 September, following which the conquerors declared Bukhara a People's Soviet Republic. Four months later Lenin ordered the conquest of the neighboring principality of Khorezm (Khiva—see Document 65). It is surprising to learn from the following document that Kemal Atatürk, the head of the Turkish Republic, advised the Soviet government to conquer the Muslim principality of Bukhara, traditionally a semi-sovereign state under a Russian protectorate.

Document 2A
Telegram from Frunze to Trotsky

[24 August 1920]

To Comrade Trotsky (the ending is No. 161)

. . . Yesterday I had a lengthy discussion with Cemal Pasha[1] on the question of Bukhara. His opinion, outlined meanwhile in a dispatch from Mustafa Kemal Pasha,[2] is as follows: either Bukhara is finished off with a decisive strike if there is an opportunity to do this, or else one must yield to it all along the line, but one way or another it must be fully secured for us. Major complications with Afghanistan can hardly be expected if the matter is resolved quickly. Thus, at the moment of receiving the directive, everything was ready for a strike, [but] everything was delayed until the arrival of the new Turkestan Commission. Delay is most harmful under the given circumstances. I and the Revolutionary-Military Council of the front consider it a duty of conscience to bring this to the attention of the highest organs of the republic.

Commander of the Turkish Front,
Frunze
Revolutionary Council of the Front,
Ibragimov[3]

Resolution of Lenin
To Krestinsky, Stalin, and Bukharin[4]

Proposal from Krestinsky
[This was] adopted the twenty-first, today is the twenty-fourth. It is quite likely that Safarov[5] and Sokolnikov, who left on the thirteenth, have already arrived, and the matter is likely to have been resolved on the spot. I propose not sending a new directive.

N. Krestinsky
Approve[.] Lenin
Approve[.] N. Bukharin

Proposal from Stalin
I propose conducting an inquiry about Sokolnikov, and if he has not yet arrived, acting without delay according to Comrade Frunze's formula.
Stalin

1. Ahmet Cemal Pasha (1872–1922): Turkish officer who belonged to a triumvirate that governed the Ottoman Empire during World War I. Later fled Turkey, first to Germany and then to Afghanistan, where he helped organize the Afghan army. While there, maintained treasonous relations with Soviet Russia, as is evident from this document.

2. Mustafa Kemal Pasha (1881–1938): better known as Kemal Atatürk.

3. Yu. I. Ibragimov (1895–1951): Muslim operative active in Bolshevik causes. In 1920, member of the Military-Revolutionary Committee of the Turkestan front.

4. This line was written by Lenin. Lenin forwarded the resolution to Krestinsky, who later reported to him on what had happened to it.

5. G. I. Safarov (1891–1942): Old Bolshevik; specialist on Eastern questions. Perished in Stalin's terror.

Document 3A
Telegram from Artuzov to the Chairman of the Yekaterinburg Province Cheka

[November 1920]

Copy

Coded Telegram
To the Chairman, Yekaterinburg Province Cheka

Reports received of an abnormal regimen of confinement for former White officers transported from Moscow. For example guards take bribes for kettle of hot water stop Urgently conduct investigation report results after taking measures to eliminate above stop No. 38667 24 November Necessary to soften regimen.

Artuzov,[1] Head of Operations Department

Directorate of Cheka Special Department

Signatures: Artuzov, Head of Operations Department

Directorate of Cheka Special Department, Deputy Secretary
[signature illegible]

True copy: Meier,[2] Head of Operations Department
Cheka Special Department

1. A. Kh. Artuzov (1891–1943): Cheka official.
2. This individual cannot be identified.

Document 4A
Telegrams from Trotsky to Kerzhentsev and Krasin[1]

4 October 1921

Top Secret

Telegram (Coded)

To Comrade Kerzhentsev
Copy to: Comrade Krasin

A purchase within the limit of ten million [rubles] in gold is acceptable to us if the terms are indeed favorable—that is, with a discount from the prices indicated and with real guarantees of delivery to the designated place. Get in touch immediately with Comrade Krasin, to whom we are sending a copy of this telegram, regarding the exact determination of the price, the terms for delivery, and the guarantees of actual delivery.

Regarding the purchase itself, the basic decision is as follows: about three-fifths of the allocated sum is to be spent on rifles with ammunition; about two-fifths on automatic weapons with 7.6-millimeter ammunition and on Maxim machine guns. In any event, report to Moscow all the possible variations on the deal before it is finally concluded.

Of course, the strictest technical control is required for the receipt of the delivery. Are there absolutely competent employees for that, and who are they, specifically? Or is it necessary to send them from here, which involves certain delay? Is it possible to move the formal receipt of the delivery and the technical control to Petrograd, with the participation of a representative of the firm selling [the weapons]?

4 October

Trotsky

Top Secret

Telegram (Coded)

To Comrade Krasin
Copy: to Comrade Kerzhentsev

Comrade Kerzhentsev proposes acquiring a substantial number of rifles and Russian-system machine guns of American manufacture. It has been decided here to allocate ten million rubles for this. The most important points are to secure:

a. Strict technical control of receipt of the delivery.
b. Guarantees against excessive losses in the event of confiscation, sinking, etc., during shipment.

    c. Maximum reduction of price.

    d. Maximum speed for the whole operation, and speed of delivery.

In addition, Comrade Kerzhentsev will provide you with more specific information. We urge you to treat this very important matter most attentively and energetically and make all efforts to achieve the complete success of the deal.

4 October

Trotsky

1. See Document 78.

Document 5A
Message from Chicherin to Lenin

30 January 1922

Ultrasecret   30 January 1922

To Comrade Lenin. Copies: Comrades Trotsky, Stalin, Kamenev,
Zinoviev, and Molotov

My dear Vladimir Ilich,

               If it has been decided to adhere to the directives which will lead to an unquestionable disruption of the [Genoa] conference, [then] it is better not to leave [for Genoa] at all and to announce immediately that we do not accept the Cannes Resolution, thereby disrupting the conference. To leave *in corpore* and denounce everything there and then go back would mean to make a recurrence of this [gathering] impossible for a long time to come.

France is issuing an ultimatum, demanding the acceptance of the Cannes Resolution by all participants, prior to any debates. We are saying neither yes nor no for now. When the Genoa Conference opens we will be faced with this ultimatum. The Central Committee anyway passed a directive "in no event" to go further (this is reminiscent of the famous *jamais*)— Lloyd George by that time will undoubtedly be bound by an agreement about this with France, and anyway, this was always essentially the demand of England as well. We will be up against a wall, and Lloyd George will be unable to make a concession to us. His brainchild—the conference—will turn into a scandal: we come and immediately leave. This will be a resounding slap in the face to Lloyd George. After such a vivid, dramatic, instant break-off, of course, a loan will not be possible, economic prospects will be ruined for a long time to come, a furious onslaught of intervention will erupt—grandiose raids by French airplanes on Moscow from Poland and on Petrograd from Finland, and so on.

If we announce now that we do not accept the [Cannes] Resolution, there will be no conference, there will be no dramatic rupture and scandal, there will be no trip [undertaken] with the deliberate intention of immediately and demonstratively departing. We will be refused a large loan, but Lloyd George will not be bound yet, and further economic ties with England within the current framework will be possible.

Personally, I am against this policy. Not only France but England will not accept a comprehensive peace and [offer] large loans without a complete acknowledgment of all debts. At issue is only nationalized property—here debate would still be possible if it were not for the ultimatum. I am speaking on the basis of the whole course of previous negotiations with England. I propose: 1) under the influence of their ultimatum at the conference, to accept the Cannes Resolution; 2) in complete accord with it, to put forth counterclaims that will cover everything (that is possible), but in the further course of the negotiations, if necessary, to purchase a large loan by lowering our counterclaims, and if there is no loan without that, to reduce our counterclaims even **lower** than their claims, haggling about the difference and "converting" it into a new loan for us.

Incidentally, the radio station of the American Vigand[1] from Berlin reported that Radek had announced in *Die Rote Fahne* that if we are given thirty billion gold marks and recognition de jure, we will adhere to the Versailles treaty and acknowledge all our debts . . . (!!)

With communist greetings,
Chicherin

1. Reference unclear.

Document 6A
Chicherin's First Telegram from Genoa

15 April 1922

Top Secret
Incoming No. 2895/s

From Genoa
Received 16 April, decoded 17 April '22
Moscow to the People's Commissariat of Foreign Affairs

We spent the whole day today in negotiations with Lloyd George, Barthou, Schanzer[1] and Henri Jaspar[2]—but in fact we are marking time for the third day now, and our proposal about the commission has also been rejected.

The Allies are absolutely unwilling to give up their ultimatum, insisting that we unconditionally [acknowledge] all private claims in the future, regardless of a settlement between governments. They are likely to agree to continue the moratorium on [our] debts with them for up to ten years and make other concessions, but only on the unalterable condition that we acknowledge in principle our obligations to [compensate] private persons. For our counterclaims, they will write off our war debts. But they are going no further than that. They are renouncing restitution, demanding the return of industrial plants to their previous owners on long-term lease. With the maximum of pressure they will agree [word illegible] to compensation for the nationalized enterprises with the inclusion in a total sum, subject to payment within ten years, or within a period in the more or less near future to be set by a joint commission. Lloyd George is pressing for a reply, unwilling to drag out the conference in the event that an agreement with us is impossible. Further negotiations with us will lead nowhere. All that remains is to state the impossibility of an agreement and attempt to draft an appropriate declaration by the political commission during the meeting. We request immediate instructions.

[One word missing] the financiers and industrialists have come here but are not entering into negotiations with us until there is an intergovernmental accord. In relation to us, the Allies have formed a united front and [one word missing]. The English do not deviate much from the tactic of the French.

15 April 1922

Chicherin

1. Carlo Schanzer (1865–1953): Italian foreign minister.
2. Henri Jaspar (1870–?): Belgian foreign minister, who along with Lloyd George, Barthou, and Schanzer, met the Russians on 14 April. See Fink, *Genoa Conference*, 160–61. The Russian code clerk misspelled his name "Jas Paul."

Document 7A
Chicherin's Second Telegram from Genoa

15 April 1922

From Genoa   Top Secret
Received and decoded 17 April '22   Incoming No. 2906/s
Moscow, to the People's Commissariat of Foreign Affairs

For the Politburo. Today, 15 April, the Allies told us their final terms. We must renounce counterclaims for the intervention, in exchange for which they will write off [our] war debts as well as the interest on prewar debts until the end of the moratorium, the duration of which is to be established by mutual agreement as approximately eight to ten years. Nationalized property is to be returned to the owners on the basis of long-term lease, or [of] restitution in individual cases where concessions are not possible for technical reasons, about which there may still be negotiations. Russian property located abroad, such as ships and so on, is to be returned to us. Lloyd George, and then Schanzer through a messenger especially sent to us, advise that they will not go beyond these terms. We ask you to provide the most urgent instructions, whether you are authorizing us to break off or to make further concessions. We have not yet made any concessions on the matter of the debts and have not bound ourselves to anything. Still, much as Lloyd George, and to some extent the Italians, are interested in a successful outcome of the conference, we are certain that they will not back down under any conditions from the two above-mentioned basic principles—i.e., that they will not pay us anything for the intervention, because it would look like a contribution for a war they lost, and that they will not release us from the claims of private persons, in particular the owners of nationalized property. They consider the substitution of concessions for property [restitution] a very great compromise, in accordance with the first point of the Cannes Resolution. Various minor concessions may still be obtained, and we may dictate our terms in the matter of guarantees for the future work of foreigners in Russia. A reply is required no later than Monday. Indicate in the reply that it refers to the proposal of 15 April. In the event that we break off, we will probably depart no later than Wednesday. Confirm receipt of the telegram immediately upon decoding.

Chicherin

In December 1922, when Lenin was virtually incapacitated, some of his associates wanted to relax the state's monopoly on foreign trade. Lenin vehemently opposed such a change and requested Trotsky to fight it on his behalf, which Trotsky did, successfully. Frightened by the prospect of a Lenin-Trotsky coalition, the triumvirate voted to keep Lenin in the dark about Politburo proceedings, allegedly to safeguard his health. Stalin had himself formally empowered by the Central Committee to "isolate" Lenin.[1]

1. See *RUBR*, 468–69.

Document 8A
Resolution of the Central Committee Plenum Concerning Lenin

18 December 1922

Proletarians of the world, unite!

RUSSIAN COMMUNIST PARTY (BOLSHEVIK).

CENTRAL COMMITTEE DEPARTMENT: BUREAU OF THE SECRETARIAT

No. 20695/s   18 December 1922

To Comrades Stalin, Fotieva   Top Secret

Resolution of the Central Committee Plenum

18 December 1922, No. 9

In the event of an inquiry by Comrade Lenin concerning the plenum's decision on the issue of foreign trade, upon Comrade Stalin's agreement with the doctors, inform him of the text of the resolution, adding that both the resolution and the composition of the commission were approved unanimously.

The report of Comrade Yaroslavsky[1] must under no condition be given [to Lenin] now, but held back in order to hand it over to him when the doctors, upon agreement with Comrade Stalin, allow this.

Place personal responsibility on Comrade Stalin for the isolation of Vladimir Ilich regarding both personal relations with [party] workers and correspondence.

Secretary of the Central Committee,
Stalin

/ZAS/

1. It is not clear to what Ye. M. Yaroslavsky's "report" refers.

Document 9A
Dzerzhinsky's Instructions Following Lenin's Death

22 January 1924

In cipher. Top Priority

To All Organs of the GPU
To All Provincial Organs
To All Special Regional Organs

Yesterday, at seven o'clock in the evening, as announced by the government, Vladimir Ilich passed away. Our organs[1] must, first, mobilize and second, maintain complete calm and prevent panic, giving no cause for it with external manifestations and unjustified mass arrests. Third, clarify the mood of the masses and [people on] the street. Fourth, pay principal attention to the behavior of Black Hundreds, monarchists, White Guardists. Fifth, help in every way you can to raise the spirit of the army. Sixth, rally around the provincial party committee, adhering to its directives. Seventh, keep us informed of everything of importance.

F. Dzerzhinsky
22 January '24
14:00 hours

1. The GPU.

Document and Illustration Credits

Documents

All documents are in the Russian Center for the Preservation and Study of Documents of Recent History (RTsKhIDNI) in Moscow.

DOCUMENT 1. F. 2, op. 1, d. 22, l. 3 ob. Original certificate.

DOCUMENT 2. F. 2, op. 1, d. 27,094. Handwritten. Published in part in Dmitrii A. Volkogonov, *Lenin: Politicheskii portret* [Lenin: A political portrait], vol. 1 (Moscow, 1994), 107.

DOCUMENT 3. F. 2, op. 1, d. 27,056. Handwritten.

DOCUMENT 4. F. 2, op. 1, d. 27,097. Copy with the signature of A. I. Lyubimov. Published in Volkogonov, *Lenin*, vol. 1, p. 108.

DOCUMENT 5. F. 2, op. 1, d. 27,131. Handwritten in the Latin alphabet.

DOCUMENT 6. F. 2, op. 1, d. 3,281. Handwritten. The bulk of this letter was originally written in English, and Lenin's orthography has been preserved. Italics denote English; roman characters indicate that the phrase was originally in Russian.

DOCUMENT 7. F. 2, op. 1, d. 24,299, l. 4. Handwritten. Published in truncated form in *PSS*, vol. 48, pp. 299–300. The omitted passage is here restored. The bulk of this letter was originally written in English, and Lenin's orthography has been preserved. Italics are used where Lenin wrote in English; roman characters indicate that the phrase was originally in Russian.

DOCUMENT 8. F. 2, op. 1, d. 3,327. Handwritten. Published in truncated form in *PSS*, vol. 48, pp. 307–12. The omitted passage is here restored. It was originally written in English.

191

DOCUMENT 9. F. 2, op. 1, d. 3,341. Handwritten. Letter was originally written in English (shown in italics), and Lenin's original orthography is here preserved.

DOCUMENT 10. F. 2, op. 1, d. 27,136. Handwritten. Addresses on the postcard: "Herrn Roman **Malinowski,** Mannschaftsgefangenlager Gruppenübungsplatz (Batal'on 2, Rota 8, barak 43, Alten-Grabow, Deutschland," and "Wl. Ulianow, Seidenweg 4a III (bei Fr. Schneider), Bern (Schweiz)." "**21 September**" is marked in the hand of Malinovsky.

DOCUMENT 11. F. 2, op. 1, d. 27,137. Handwritten.

DOCUMENT 12. F. 2, op. 1, d. 27,139. Handwritten.

DOCUMENT 13. F. 2, op. 1, d. 4,303. Handwritten. Published in truncated form in *PSS*, vol. 49, p. 327. The excised passages are here restored. The address on the postcard is "Mme Armand, Kurhotel Mariental, Sorenberg (Kt. Luzern)."

DOCUMENT 14. F. 2, op. 1, d. 4,365. Handwritten. Published in truncated form in *PSS*, vol. 49, pp. 362–63. The omitted passage is here restored.

DOCUMENT 15. F. 2, op. 1, d. 4,389. Handwritten. Published in truncated form in *PSS*, vol. 49, pp. 368–71. The omitted passages are here restored.

DOCUMENT 16. F. 2, op. 1, d. 4,401. Handwritten. Published in truncated form in *PSS*, vol. 49, pp. 374–76. The omitted passage is here restored.

DOCUMENT 17. F. 2, op. 1, d. 4,578, ll. 1–6, 9. Handwritten by Lenin and Kolokolov. Only excerpts of this testimony were published in *PSS*, vol. 32, pp. 511–12. The text first appeared in *Vestnik vremennogo pravitel'stva* [Herald of the Provisional Government], 16 June 1917, p. 3.

DOCUMENT 18. F. 2. op. 1, d. 4,629. Handwritten.

DOCUMENT 19. F. 2, op. 1, d. 24,615, l. 4. Handwritten by the telegraph operator.

DOCUMENT 20. F. 2, op. 1, d. 25,617. Copy.

DOCUMENT 21. F. 2, op. 1, d. 27,142. Handwritten.

DOCUMENT 22. F. 2, op. 1, d. 6,601. Handwritten on a telegraphic blank. Published in *Rodina*, 1 (1993): 184. In English.

DOCUMENT 23. F. 2, op. 1, d. 26,258, ll. 11–12. Wire tape.

DOCUMENT 24. F. 2, op. 1, d. 6,898. Handwritten. Published in full in *Komsomol'skaia Pravda*, 12 February 1992, p. 2. E. B. Bosh referred to this in general in *Proletarskaia revoliutsiia* [Proletarian revolution], 3 (1924): 155–73, esp. 169, saying that Lenin offered "comradely advice." Repeated in *LS*, vol. 18 (Moscow, 1931), 205–6. The editors of *LS*, citing excerpts from this letter, wrote that it was "apparently lost."

DOCUMENT 25. F. 2, op. 1, d. 24,310. Handwritten. Annotation on the envelope: "To the Russian Ambassador in **Bern, Ya. Berzin** (from Lenin)."

DOCUMENT 26. F. 2, op. 1, d. 6,787. Handwritten.

DOCUMENT 27. F. 2, op. 1, d. 27,143. Handwritten.

DOCUMENT 28. F. 2, op. 2, d. 492. Handwritten. Published in *Komsomol'skaia Pravda* [Komsomol Pravda], 12 February 1992, p. 2.

DOCUMENT 29. F. 2, op. 1, d. 25,671. Handwritten. Published in truncated form in *PSS*, vol. 50, p. 194. Annotation on the envelope: "**To Comrade Berzin,** Russian ambassador to Switzerland (from Lenin)."

DOCUMENT 30. F. 2, op. 1, d. 27,149. Handwritten.

DOCUMENT 31. F. 2, op. 1, d. 7,310. Handwritten.

DOCUMENT 32. F. 2, op. 1, d. 8,196. Handwritten.

DOCUMENT 33. F. 2, op. 1, d. 8,492. Manuscript copy. Published in *Rodina,* 3 (1994): 49.

DOCUMENT 34. F. 41, op. 1, d. 9, ll. 79–80. Corrected stenographic record.

DOCUMENT 35. F. 2, op. 1, d. 24,327. Handwritten. Points 1 and 2 written by Kamenev, point 3 by Lenin.

DOCUMENT 36. F. 2, op. 1, d. 27,051, ll. 1, 5. Handwritten with Lenin's annotation.

DOCUMENT 37. F. 2, op. 1, d. 10,874. Handwritten by Lenin and Krestinsky.

DOCUMENT 38. F. 2, op. 1, d. 11,049. Handwritten. A fragment of this telegram was published in *Pravda,* 24 July 1928, p. 4.

DOCUMENT 39. F. 2, op. 1, d. 24,348. Handwritten; annotated by Lenin. Trotsky's note is summarized in *Voenno-istoricheskii zhurnal* [Military-historical journal], 2 (1963): 29; Lenin's annotation on this document was published in *BKh,* vol. 7, p. 537.

DOCUMENT 40. F. 2, op. 2, d. 202. Handwritten.

DOCUMENT 41. F. 2, op. 1, d. 11,430. Original telegram.

DOCUMENT 42. F. 2, op. 1, d. 11,800. Handwritten. Partially published in *Pravda,* 11 July 1956, p. 2.

DOCUMENT 43. F. 2, op. 1, d. 24,364, l. 1. Handwritten. Cf. *BKh,* vol. 8, p. 294. The portions that were sent in code are printed in boldface.

DOCUMENT 44. F. 2, op. 1, d. 8,924. Handwritten by Ye. M. Skliansky. Partially published in *BKh,* vol. 8, p. 402.

DOCUMENT 45. F. 2, op. 2, d. 270. The letter from Chicherin, draft resolution, and note from Lenin are handwritten; the corrections and additions are typewritten.

DOCUMENT 46. F. 2, op. 1, d. 13,639. Original telegram.

DOCUMENT 47. F. 2, op. 1, d. 13,885. Handwritten.

DOCUMENT 48. F. 2, op. 2, d. 1,299. Handwritten.

DOCUMENT 49. F. 2, op. 1, d. 24,424. Handwritten.

DOCUMENT 50. F. 2, op. 1, d. 14,490. Original telegram.

DOCUMENT 51. F. 2, op. 2, d. 334. Handwritten.

DOCUMENT 52. F. 2, op. 1, d. 15,834. Copy (handwriting of L. A. Fotieva).

DOCUMENT 53. F. 2, op. 1, d. 14,706. Handwritten.

DOCUMENT 54. F. 2, op. 2, d. 348, l. 1. Handwritten. Published in *RUBR,* p. 177.

DOCUMENT 55. F. 2, op. 2, d. 363. Handwritten.

DOCUMENT 56. F. 2, op. 2, d. 375, l. 1. Handwritten.

DOCUMENT 57. F. 2, op. 2, d. 390. Handwritten.

DOCUMENT 58. F. 2, op. 2, d. 391. Handwritten.

DOCUMENT 59. F. 2, op. 1, d. 25,482, ll. 1–28. Typewritten transcript (from shorthand). The translation follows the manuscript form deposited in f. 2, op. 1, d. 25,482. Lenin personally edited only the first page.

DOCUMENT 60. F. 2, op. 2, d. 429, l. 1. Handwritten.

DOCUMENT 61. F. 2, op. 2, d. 454. Original telegram with Lenin's annotation.

DOCUMENT 62. F. 2, op. 1, d. 24,472. Handwritten. Coded words are in boldface.

DOCUMENT 63. F. 2, op. 2, d. 463. Original typescript with Lenin's annotation.

DOCUMENT 64. F. 2, op. 2, d. 459. Handwritten.

DOCUMENT 65. F. 2, op. 2, d. 1,292. Handwritten.

DOCUMENT 66. F. 2, op. 1, d. 24,510. Handwritten. This record was privately transcribed by a delegate named I. Barakhov. There is no official transcript, and the speech is not recorded in the protocols of the Tenth Party Congress.

DOCUMENT 67. F. 2, op. 1, d. 17,811. Original telegram.

DOCUMENT 68. F. 2, op. 2, d. 607. Original telegram with Lenin's annotation.

DOCUMENT 69. F. 2, op. 2, d. 708. Handwritten.

DOCUMENT 70. F. 2, op. 1, d. 19,580, l. 1. Original telegram.

DOCUMENT 71. F. 2, op. 2, d. 717. Original telegram with Lenin's annotation.

DOCUMENT 72. F. 2, op. 2, d, 773. Handwritten.

DOCUMENT 73. F. 2, op. 1, d. 26,847. Copy.

DOCUMENT 74. F. 2, op. 2, d. 1,328. Handwritten.

DOCUMENT 75. F. 2, op. 2, d. 830. Handwritten.

DOCUMENT 76. F. 2, op. 1, d. 24,694. Handwritten.

DOCUMENT 77. F. 2, op. 1, d. 25,609, ll. 10–11. Copy. Except for one sentence, this has not previously been published. See *BKh*, vol. 11, p. 370.

DOCUMENT 78. F. 2, op. 2, d. 914. Original text with Lenin's annotation.

DOCUMENT 79. F. 2, op. 1, d. 21,196, l. 1. Original telegram.

DOCUMENT 80. F. 2, op. 1, d. 21,514. Handwritten by Trotsky, with signature and additions by Lenin.

DOCUMENT 81. F. 2, op. 1, d. 22,300. Handwritten.

DOCUMENT 82. F. 2, op. 1, d. 24,747, ll. 1–1 v. Handwritten.

DOCUMENT 83. F. 2, op. 2, d. 1,105. Handwritten by L. A. Fotieva.

DOCUMENT 84. F. 2, op. 2, d. 1,106, l. 1. Handwritten.

DOCUMENT 85. F. 2, op. 1, d. 22,737. Handwritten by L. A. Fotieva.

DOCUMENT 86. F. 2, op. 1, d. 25,985. Handwritten.

DOCUMENT 87. F. 2, op. 1, d. 23,536. Handwritten.

DOCUMENT 88. F. 2, op. 2, d. 1,119. Handwritten.

DOCUMENT 89. F. 2, op. 1, d. 22,768. Handwritten.

DOCUMENT 90. F. 2, op. 1, d. 27,071. Handwritten.

DOCUMENT 91. F. 2, op. 1, d. 22,905, l. 1 ob. Typewritten text.

DOCUMENT 92. F. 2, op. 2, d. 1,164. Typewritten text with Lenin's marginalia.

DOCUMENT 93. F. 2, op. 2, d. 1,166. Handwritten.

DOCUMENT 94. F. 2, op. 1, d. 22,947. Typewritten text. First published in *Vestnik russkogo studencheskogo dvizheniia* [Herald of the Russian student movement], no. 98 (1970): 54–57.

DOCUMENT 95. F. 2, op. 1, d. 22,960, l. 2. Handwritten by L. A. Fotieva.

DOCUMENT 96. F. 2, op. 1, d. 23,018. Handwritten.

DOCUMENT 97. F. 2, op. 1, d. 23,036. Handwritten.

DOCUMENT 98. F. 2, op. 1, d. 24,788, ll. 3–5. Original telegram.

DOCUMENT 99. F. 2, op. 1, d. 25,669, ll. 1–2. Handwritten by Zinoviev.

DOCUMENT 100. F. 2, op. 1, d. 23,098, l. 3. Copy.

DOCUMENT 101. F. 2, op. 1, d. 23,114. Trotsky's letter is an original typescript. The record of the voting is handwritten. The draft of the resolution is typewritten.

DOCUMENT 102. F. 2, op. 1, d. 25,989. Handwritten.

DOCUMENT 103. F. 2, op. 1, d. 23,226. Handwritten.

DOCUMENT 104. F. 2, op. 1, d. 25,992. Handwritten by M. I. Ulianova.

DOCUMENT 105. F. 2, op. 1, d. 25,995. Handwritten.

DOCUMENT 106. F. 2, op. 2, d. 1,239. Handwritten.

DOCUMENT 107. F. 2, op. 2, d. 1,338, l. 1. Handwritten. Published in part in the *New York Times,* 15 June 1992, p. A11.

DOCUMENT 108. F. 2, op. 1, d. 26,000. Handwritten.

DOCUMENT 109. F. 2, op. 1, d. 26,002. Handwritten.

DOCUMENT 110. F. 2, op. 2, d. 1,245, l. 1. Handwritten. The list, annotated by Unshlikht, is stored at RTsKhIDNI, attached to Lenin's letter.

DOCUMENT 111. F. 2, op. 2, d. 1,255. Handwritten. Published in *Istoricheskii Arkhiv,* 1 (1995): 4–5.

DOCUMENT 112. F. 2, op. 1, d. 26,003. Handwritten.

DOCUMENT 113. F. 2, op. 2, d. 1,344. Typewritten text.

DOCUMENT 1A. F. 2, op. 2, d. 206. Typewritten text.

DOCUMENT 2A. F. 2, op. 2, d. 395. The telegram exists as a copy; Lenin's resolution and the various proposals are handwritten.

DOCUMENT 3A. F. 2, op. 2, d. 463, l. 6. Typewritten text. See Document 63.

DOCUMENT 4A. F. 2, op. 1, d. 914, l. 2. Original telegram. See Document 78.

DOCUMENT 5A. F. 2, op. 2, d. 1,106, ll. 2–3. Copy. See Document 83.

DOCUMENT 6A. F. 5, op. 1, d. 1,968, l. 4. Certified typewritten copy. See Document 98.

DOCUMENT 7A. F. 5, op. 1, d. 1,968, l. 6. Certified typewritten copy. See Document 98.

DOCUMENT 8A. F. 5, op. 2, d. 27, l. 88. Original typewritten memorandum. Published in part in *RUBR,* p. 468.

DOCUMENT 9A. F. 76, op. 3, d. 287. Handwritten.

Photographs

1. Photo by E. Balois. F. 393, op. 1, d. 17.
2. Photo in the public domain.
3. Photo by G. Volkov. RTsKhIDNI.
4. Photo in the public domain.
5. Photo by V. K. Bulla. F. 393, op. 1, d. 264.
6. Photo by M. I. Ulianova. F. 393, op. 1, d. 352.
7. RTsKhIDNI.
8. Courtesy of the David King Collection, London.

Index

Afanasiev, 61
Afghanistan, 4, 181
Akselrod, Pavel, 59
Aleksandrovsk, 109
Alekseev, M. V., 55
Aleksinsky, G. A., 113, 115n39
Allies, 42, 185, 186
All-Russian Central Executive Committee,
   154
All-Russian Congress of Producers, 124
All-Russian Extraordinary Commission, 129
Alsky, A. O., 126, 127n1
American Relief Administration, 13, 133
Antonov-Ovseenko, Vladimir Alek-
   sandrovich, 54
APRF, 3
Arkhangelsk region, 113
Armand, Inessa, 11, 25–26
Armenia, 46n2, 92–93, 122
Artuzov, A. Kh., 182
Artyom, Fyodor Andreevich, 64, 66n18
Atatürk, Kemal, 121, 180, 181, 182n2
Atkarsk District Land Department, 81
Austria, 30; support from, 15
Avanesov, Varlaam Aleksandrovich, 75
Azef, Yevno Fishelevich, 25n2, 38, 40n10
Azerbaijan, 122, 136; Red Army in, 119

Badaev, Aleksei Yegorovich, 25, 36, 38
Baku, 10, 46, 53, 122, 136, 170
Balabanoff (Balabanova), Angelica,
   12n20, 55, 69
Baranovka, 117
Barter. See Food taxes
Barthou, Jean-Louis, 160, 185
Belavin, Vasily Ivanovich, 155n2
Beloborodov, Aleksandr Georgievich, 63,
   65n7
Belorussia, 95, 128, 180
Berlin, 47, 49, 54, 79
Berzin, Ya. A., 31n3, 53, 58, 58n3, 59,
   116, 133
Bialystok, 96, 108
Black Hundreds, 101, 103, 114n12, 152,
   153, 154, 189
Boerner, Ignacy, 82–83, 179, 180
Bogdatiev, S. Ya., 136, 137n2
Bolshevik Center, 20–21, 22n1, 23
Bolshevik Party: growth of, 15, 16, 20, 41;
   name, 15
Bolsheviks, Old, 22n1
Bonds, 126
Borotbists, 76, 76n1
Bosh, Yevgenia B., 49
Brest-Litovsk, 96, 111

Brest-Litovsk peace treaty, 42, 47. *See also* Supplementary Treaty
Briansk, 72
British Trade Union delegation, 4, 12, 79–81
Briukhanov, Nikolai Pavlovich, 130, 131*n*1, 157
Brussels conference, 30, 139
Bubnov, Andrei Sergeevich, 64, 65*n*15
Budenny, 73
Bufferite, 93
Bukhara, 122, 180, 181
Bukharin, N. I., 2, 2*n*1, 34*n*2, 63, 90, 93*n*2, 137, 138, 160
Burtsev, Vladimir, 25

Cannes Conference, 139–40
Cannes Resolution, 139, 184, 187
Carpathian Rus, 107
Caucasus, 119, 122
Cemal Pasha, Ahmet, 181
Central Committee Commission, 136
Central Committee members, 63–64
Central Party Archive, 2–3; Lenin Deposit (*Fond*), 3
Cheka (secret police), 10, 12, 57*n*4, 61, 66, 120, 135
Cheliabinsk, 109
Cherniakhov, 117
Chernykh, A. S., 59, 60
Chicherin, Georgy Vasilievich, 49*n*1; and American Relief Administration, 133; on British Trade Union delegation, 79; on Cannes Conference, 140, 184; to Curzon, 88; on debt, 158–59, 161, 184–87; on diplomatic loans, 93; on France, 129; and Genoa Conference, 7, 141, 144, 155–56, 158, 162, 163, 184–87; on Ioffe, 49; on Lithuania, 85–87; medical assessment and, 8, 156–57; on Nansen, 83; on slogans for English, 94; on Supplementary Treaty, 54; on Turkey, 120
Chirkin, Vasily Gavrilovich, 35, 40*n*3
Chudnov, 117
Churches and clergy, 10–11, 150, 151, 152–54
Codes, deciphering of, 93
Comintern. *See* Communist International
Commissariat. *See* People's Commissariat, *under individual listings*
Commission of Nine, 160

Committee to Aid the Hungry (Pomgol), 134, 134*n*1
Communist International (Comintern), 11, 22*n*2, 99, 111, 113, 134; Congress, 99, 103, 104
Communist Party, Russian: minutes of Eighth Congress of, 63–65; Ninth Party Conference of, 94–95; and participation in economy, 148–49. *See also* Bolshevik Party
Concessions, foreign: Lenin on, 112–13
Constitutional Democratic Party, 155*n*4. *See also* Kadets
Cossacks, 69, 70–72, 84, 120
Council of Action, 100, 104, 105, 107, 113
Council of Labor and Defense, 157, 171
Council of People's Commissars (Sovnarkom, SNK), 22*n*6, 43, 45, 56, 61, 65; Lenin's deputy to, 157, 171
Crimea, 78, 90, 119
Curzon, Lord, 88, 89, 96, 102, 104, 107, 122
Curzon Line, 88–89*n*2, 96, 111
Czechia, 4, 90
Czechoslovakia, 7, 110

d'Abernon, Viscount, 7
Dan, Fyodor I., 105, 115*n*25, 175
Danishevsky, Karl Kristianovich, 64, 65*n*14
Danish newspaper: cable about tsar to, 47
Daszyński, Ignacy, 37, 40*n*6
Dating (of documents), 19*n*1
Debts, 158–59, 160, 161, 185, 186, 187. *See also* Loans
Democratic Centralists, 93*n*2, 123
Denikin, Anton Ivanovich, 67*n*1, 87; campaign against, 68*n*1, 70–72, 82*n*2, 97, 100, 106, 179–80; defeat of, 67*n*1, 70, 75, 102, 108, 110; Trotsky on, 65
Department of Forced Labor, 120–21
Deportations, 12, 168–69, 174, 175, 176
Dom literatorov, 169
Donetsk (region), 70, 72, 76, 107, 112
Dubrovinsky, Iosif Fyodorovich, 23*n*1
Duma, 38, 39
Dzerzhinsky, Feliks Edmundovich, 10, 56, 147; on Central Committee, 63; on Lenin's death, 188; on prisoners of war, 10, 119–20; about Tikhon, 154; in Zubalovo, 164

Egypt, 144
Eighth Congress of the Communist Party; minutes, 63
Ekonomist, 168
Eliava, Sh. Z., 74
England: actions concerning, 4, 73; Communists in, 134; Council of Action, 100, 104, 105; elections, 174, 175; at Genoa Conference, 186; Kamenev in, 89, 94, 100, 105, 107, 113; Lenin on, 6, 7, 94, 97, 99, 100, 104, 105, 106, 108, 134, 170, 174; policy on, 122; and Polish-Soviet mediation, 89–90, 96, 97, 104; propaganda for, 57, 94; timber concessions, 113; trade union delegation, 4, 12, 79–81, 99
Entente: on debts, 160; Poland and, 89, 90, 96–97, 98, 102, 103, 109, 110–11, 180; relations with, 49, 102, 113, 131
Erfurt program, 40
Estonia, 34, 98, 103

Fabergé, Peter Carl, 150
Fainberg, I. I., 80, 81n2
Famine (of 1920–22), 5, 11, 13, 129, 130–31, 133, 134n1, 139, 151
February Revolution, 15, 105
Finland, 7, 45n2, 86, 103, 184; Kamenev in, 30; Lenin in, 15; Murmansk and, 42, 43, 44
Finnish Communists, 4, 12, 45n2, 83, 99
Finnish Social Democrats, 39
Finnish Socialist Party, 83
Foerster, Otfrid, 164–65
Food taxes, 127, 130, 131
Foreign trade, 187–88
Fotieva, Lidia Aleksandrovna, 141, 142, 147, 157, 176
Fraina, Louis C., 134, 135n6
France, 58; Cannes Resolution and, 184; Chicherin on, 129; at Genoa Conference, 186; Lenin on, 96, 97, 101, 102, 104, 105, 109, 110, 170
Frank, S. L., 168, 169n11
French Communists, 12, 68, 160
Frumkin, M. I., 93
Frunze, Mikhail Vasilievich, 10, 69, 180, 181

Galicia, 6, 77–78, 95, 96, 107, 110, 111
Ganetsky (Fürstenberg), Yakov Stanislavovich, 26n4, 37, 40n8

Genoa Conference, 6, 7, 139, 140, 143n2, 144–45, 152, 155, 158, 161, 162, 184, 185, 186; on debts and loans, 141, 156, 158, 160, 184; delegates to, 143n2; on Georgia, 144; Lenin's intent concerning, 6, 7, 140, 144–45, 161, 162, 184; origins of, 139
Georgia, 92, 98, 102, 103, 114n4, 119, 144
German Independents, 99
German Social Democratic Party, 41n13, 114n5
Germany, 42; advance on, 6, 94; border with, 107; civil war in, 79; Communists in, 90, 100, 101–3; deportations to, 168; and Genoa Conference, 7; and intervention in Russia, 53, 54; Lenin in, 15; Lenin on, 11, 62, 100, 101, 102, 103, 146, 170; and Petrograd, 132; support from, 12, 15, 53, 56; treaty with, 6, 161; weapons from, 125–26, 131, 135, 137
Gerson, V. L., 147
Glavki, 124
Gliasser, M. I., 147
Gokhran, 164
Gomel Province, 129
Gorbunov, Nikolai Petrovich, 146, 156
Gorbunov, Pavel Petrovich, 139
Gorky, Maksim, 10, 11; Shmit and, 20
Gornfeld, Arkady Georgievich, 168, 169n3
Goroshki, 117
Gorter, Herman, 53, 58
Gots, A. R., 105, 115n24
GPU, 12, 154, 168
Grain, 112; confiscation of, 130; exchange of, 127; quotas, 112
Great Britain: and anti-propaganda agreement, 121–22. *See also* England
Grigory, 21, 22n2, 23
Grishin-Almazov, General, 73n3
Grodno, 106, 109
Groman, Vladimir Gustavovich, 75
Guilbeaux, André, 53, 58, 59
Gukovsky, I. E., 125, 126n2
Guriev: oil in, 10, 69
Gusev, Sergei Ivanovich, 136

Hauschild, Herbert, 54
Helsinki, 39, 45n2
Henderson, Arthur, 144
Hertzog, Jacob, 58

Hitler: Stalin and, 40*n*12, 95
Hoover, Herbert, 12, 133, 134*n*1
Hungary, 4, 7, 90, 107, 110, 134*n*1

Ibragimov, Yu. I., 181, 182*n*3
Ilin, M. V., 58
IMEL (Marx-Engels-Lenin Institute), 2, 4
India, 4, 144, 145
Innokenty, 23
Internationale, L' (newspaper), 69
Internationals (conferences), 159
International Socialist Bureau, 30*n*1
Ioffe, Adolf, 47*n*1; and Lithuania, 86, 87,
    88*n*8; and Poland, 115–16; and Supple-
    mentary Treaty, 47, 49, 54
Ireland, 144
Iskra, 15
Istochnik, 3
Istoricheskii arkhiv, 3
Italy, 7, 91, 187
Itchner, Hans, 53
Ivnitsa, 117
Izgoev, A. S., 168, 169*n*5
Izvestiia, 94

Jasper, Henri, 185, 186*n*2
Jews: pogroms against, 4, 10, 76, 77,
    87*n*4, 114, 116, 117, 128–29; Lenin
    on, 77, 77*n*10; in Ukraine, 75, 77

Kadets (Constitutional Democrats), 168
Kalinin, Mikhail Ivanovich, 63, 65*n*9, 68,
    141, 147, 153, 155, 157, 158, 171
Kamenev, Lev Borisovich, 22*n*6, 31*n*6,
    170; on codes, 93; as deputy, 171; in
    England, 88, 94, 100, 105, 107, 113;
    Lenin on, 9, 26*n*3, 138; on Lenin, 41;
    medical assessment of, 157; as member
    of Central Committee, 63; as member of
    triumvirate, 9, 10, 16, 22*n*6; on
    printers' strike, 66; on Rykov, 157;
    Trotsky and, 9, 68, 166; work leaves
    for, 8, 147; in Zubalovo, 164
Kamenev, S. S., 67, 79*n*2, 119
Kapp, Wolfgang, 114*n*14
Kappists, 79*n*3, 101, 114*n*14
Karakhan, Lev Mikhailovich, 162, 170
Karelia, 4
Kascher, Leonie, 59
Kashirin, Nikolai Dmitrievich, 119
Kautsky, Karl, 41*n*13
Kazan, 38

Kemal, Mustafa, 181. *See also* Atatürk,
    Kemal
Kemalists, 121
Kerensky, Aleksandr Fyodorovich,
    114*n*15, 145, 145*n*1
Kerzhentsev, Platon Mikhailovich, 137,
    183, 184
Kesküla, Alexander, 34*n*2
Khalatov, A. B., 66
Kharkov, 70, 76, 78, 120, 169
Khiva, 122, 180
Khodorkov, 117
Khorassan, 122. *See also* Khiva
Khorezm, 122, 180
Kiental conference, 25, 55*n*1
Kiev, 96
Kirghizia, 127
Klemperer, Georg, 164–65
Klinger, G. K., 69
Kolchak, Aleksandr Vasilievich, 71, 73*n*2,
    78*n*1, 99, 102, 107, 108, 110; Denikin
    and, 72; Entente and, 97
Kolokolov, 35
Komsomol, 142*n*2
KOPE, 117
Kopp, Viktor Leontievich, 132, 132*n*2,
    135
Korenev, Vladimir A., 22*n*5
Kormilitsyn, 61
Kornienko, Ignat, 81
Kornilov, Lavr, 67*n*1, 101, 103, 114*n*15
Kotelno, 117
Kozhevnikov, A. M., 164
Kraków, 30, 36, 37, 38, 39
Kramer, V. V., 164
Krasin, Leonid Borisovich, 47, 48–49, 75,
    122, 125, 137, 145, 150, 183
Kremlin Pharmacy, 146, 158
Krestinsky, Nikolai Nikolaevich, 56*n*1; on
    Armenia, 92–93; on Bukharin, 138–39;
    for Finnish Communist Party, 83; and
    medical assessments, 156; as member of
    Central Committee, 10, 56, 63, 73;
    about Red Terror, 56; on Ukraine, 75–
    76
Kronshtadt, 124
Krupskaia, Nadezhda Konstantinovna, 25,
    32*n*1, 33*n*1
Kulaks, 10, 49, 72, 76, 97, 110
Kuraev, V. V., 50
Kursk, 72
Kursky, D. I., 58–59, 64, 120, 156

Lansbury, George, 89
Larin, Yuri, 56
Latvia, 30, 39, 86, 87, 98, 103
Latvian Social Democratic Party, 36
League of Nations, 83, 90, 102, 104, 107
Leiteizen, G. D. (G. Lindov), 58, 59
Lenin Deposit (Fond), 3
Lepeshinskaia, E. S., 147, 148n3
Letuvos Tariba, 92
Lezhnev, I. G., 169, 169n.15
Lippman, Walter, 115n30
Liquidatorism, 36, 37
Lithuania, 4, 8, 85–87, 89, 92, 98, 180
Litvinov, Maksim Maksimovich, 83–84,
    125–27, 150, 162
Lloyd George, David, 107, 115n28, 144,
    158, 160, 161, 174, 184, 185, 186, 187
Loans, 5, 7, 140, 141, 156, 159, 161. See
    also Debts
Łódź, 100
Lomov, Georgy Ippolitovich, 86, 87n3
Longuet, Jean, 69
Lossky, N. O., 170n18
Ludendorff, Erich, 54
Lunacharsky, Anatoly V., 61, 61n1, 64

Maksimov, K. G., 21, 22n4
Malinovsky, Roman V., 3, 24–25, 26, 28,
    31–32; Lenin's deposition on, 35–40
Mannerheim, Karl, 45n2
Mantsev, V. N., 169
Manuchariants, Shushanika M., 149
Marat, 21
Marchlewski, Julian, 82, 85, 86, 96, 179
Martov, L., 103, 114n18, 175
Marx-Engels-Lenin Institute (IMEL), 2, 4
Marz, Charles, 115n30
Mdivani, P. G., 121, 121n1
Medical assessments, 8, 156–57, 163
Medical facilities, 165
Melnichansky, Grigory Natanovich, 80,
    81n1
Mensheviks, 15, 20, 104, 105, 106, 175
Messing, S. A., 169, 176
Metalworkers, Union of, 35
Miakotin, V. A., 168, 169n2
Middle East, military actions in, 73–74
Mikhailov, Vasily Mikhailovich, 137,
    138n2
Miliukov, Pavel Nikolaevich, 154n4
Miliukovites, 153
Miliutin, Vasily Pavlovich, 56

Minesweepers, 45
Minkin, A. E., 50
Minsk Province, 128, 129
"Miracle on the Vistula," 7
Mitskevich, Vikenty Semyonovich, 64,
    65n13
Mobilizations of civilian labor, 124–25
Molotov, Vyacheslav Mikhailovich,
    128n1, 147; and churches, 151–55; on
    commission for American Relief Admin-
    istration, 133; on food taxes, 127, 130–
    31; on Lenin, 11; on party and econ-
    omy, 148; on work leaves, 147
Mongolia, 4
Moscow, 20, 124, 135
Muranov, Matvei Konstantinovich, 36,
    38, 40n4, 63
Murmansk, 6, 42, 43, 45, 53–55
Mysl' (Petrograd), 169, 170n18

Naglovsky, Aleksandr Dmitrievich, 75,
    75n1
Nansen, Fridtjof, 83–84
Nazis, 131
Neumann (Oskar, Ritter von Nieder-
    mayer), 132, 132n1
New Economic Policy, 127, 149
Nicholas II, Tsar: cable on death of, 47
NKVD (People's Commissariat of Internal
    Affairs), 120
Nogin, Viktor Pavlovich, 41, 42n1
Noulens, Joseph, 134, 135n2
Novitsky, A. A., 143
Novocherkassk, 72

Obolensky, Prince V. V. See Osinsky, N.
Odessa, 135
Okhrana (Okhranka), 12, 38, 39, 40n11
Ordzhonikidze, Grigory Konstantinovich,
    119, 120, 121n1, 136
Orel, 72, 108, 120
Orgburo (Organizational Bureau), 67–68,
    77, 122, 134
Orthodox Church, 5, 10, 150–51. See also
    Churches and clergy
Osinsky, N., 157, 157n1, 163
Ozerov, I. Kh., 168, 169n7

Parsky, D. P., 54
Paul, Cedar and Eden, 134, 135n3
Peluso, E. P., 59
Penza, 10, 49–50

People's Commissariat of Internal Affairs
(NKVD), 120
People's Commissariat of Justice, 154
People's Commissariat of War, 66
People's Will, 14, 15, 22*n*3
Péricat, Raymond, 69
Peshekhonov, A. V., 168, 169*n*1
Petliura, Semyon Vasilievich, 87, 87*n*4,
180
Petrishchev, 168
Petrograd (St. Petersburg), 25, 30, 31*n*4,
79, 135, 184; Cheka, 61, 135; churches,
152; and deportations, 169; evacuation
of, 74, 75; Finnish Communist Party in,
83; Lenin in, 15, 103; press on, 108; re-
construction of, 131–32; relief for, 135;
and weapons delivery, 183
Petroleum, 112
Petrovsky, Grigory Ivanovich, 25*n*3, 36, 38
Piatakov, Grigory Leonidovich, 63, 65*n*12
Piliavsky, Stanislav Stanislavovich, 141*n*2
Piliavsky commission, 140
Pilsudski, Joseph, 6, 82, 88, 94, 109, 179,
180
Platform of Ten, 123
Platinum, 126
Platten, Friedrich, 53, 59
Plekhanov, Georgy Valentinovich, 14, 30,
30*n*2, 105
Podvoisky, Nikolai Ilich, 44, 45, 45*n*1
Pogroms. *See* Jews: pogroms
Poincaré, Raymond, 160
Poland: Britain and, 94; and Brussels con-
ference, 30; campaign in, 77, 88, 94–
98; against Denikin, 82*n*2, 179–80;
Galicia, 6, 77–78, 95, 96, 107, 110,
111; and invasion of the Ukraine, 6, 89;
Lenin's report on, 95–102, 106, 108,
109, 110, 111–12; and Lithuania, 86,
87, 92; peace negotiations, 115–16;
policy on, 89–90; Red Army in, 5, 6,
10, 85, 94, 116, 179; and truce with So-
viet Russia, 82
Poletaev, Nikolai Gorevich, 37, 40*n*7
Polish Social Democrats, 37
Polish Socialist Party. *See* PPS
Pomgol. *See* Committee to Aid the Hungry
Popov-Dubovsky, V. S., 114*n*3
Popular Socialists, 168
Potresov, A. N., 168
PPS (Polish Socialist Party), 110, 115*n*35
Prague, 35

Pravda, 23, 24, 35, 36, 37, 38, 39, 40*n*7,
94, 144
Preobrazhensky, Yevgeny Alekseevich, 143
Presidential Archive (APRF), 3
Price, M. Phillipps, 134, 135*n*4
Printers' strike (Moscow), 66
Prisoners of war, 83–84, 119–20, 182
Private ownership, 60
Proletarii, 20, 21, 22*n*1, 23–24
Provisional Government, 15, 24
Prussia, 101
Pskov, 176
PSL (Polish Peasants' Party), 110, 115*n*35

Rabochii, 27*n*5
Radchenko, Lyubov Nikolaevna, 168,
169*n*10
Radek, Karl Berngardovich, 63, 65*n*11,
79, 80, 135, 159, 160, 170, 174, 185
Radlov, E. L., 170*n*18
Rakovsky, Khristian G., 63, 65*n*2, 141
Rapallo, Treaty of, 7, 144, 161, 162*n*2
Raskolnikov, F. F., 42
Red Army, 78, 180; in Azerbaijan, 119; in
Bukhara, 180; Denikin and, 67*n*1; lead-
ership, 66–67; and pogroms, 4, 10,
117; in Poland, 5, 6, 10, 85, 94, 116,
179; Trotsky and, 69
Red Cross, German, 146
Red Guards, 15, 43
Red Terror, 55, 56*n*4. *See also* Terror
Reed, John, 134, 135*n*5
Revolutionary-Military Council, 67, 68,
73, 129, 181
Revolutionary Tribunal, 154
Riga, 86, 109
Rogachev, 117
Romania, 4, 7, 90
Romanov (town), 117
Rote Fahne, Die, 99, 185
Rozanov, N. S., 168, 169*n*8
Rozhkov, Nikolai Aleksandrovich, 12, 62,
168, 175–76
RSDLP. *See* Russian Social Democratic La-
bor Party
RTsKhIDNI (Russian Center for the Pre-
servation and Study of Documents of
Recent History), 2
Rudzutak, Ian Ernestovich, 74, 74*n*2
Russian Center for the Preservation and
Study of Documents of Recent History
(RTsKhIDNI), 2

Russian Social Democratic Labor Party
(RSDLP), 14, 15, 22*n*1, 38; Central
Committee, 22, 23, 41; Prague Confer-
ence, 35, 36
Russo-Finnish Commission, 45
Rykov, Aleksei Ivanovich, 9, 56, 139,
157–58, 171

Sabanin, 93
Safarov, G. I., 181, 182*n*5
St. Petersburg. *See* Petrograd
Samara, 108
Saratov, 72, 73*n*3, 80
Sbornik "Sotsial-Demokrata," 32
Schanzer, Carlo, 185, 186*n*1
Scheidemannites, 103, 114*n*19
Second Congress (Russian Social Demo-
cratic Labor Party), 15
Secret police, 40*n*11. *See also* Cheka;
GPU; Okhrana
Semashko, N. A., 146
Serbia, 30
Serebriakov, Leonid Petrovich, 63, 65*n*4
Sereda, Semyon Pafnutevich, 85
Sergeev, V. 21, 22*n*5
Shantser, Virgily Leonovich, 22*n*3
Sher, Vasily V., 40*n*2
Shliapnikov, Aleksandr, 123
Shmidt, Vasily Vladimirovich, 64, 66*n*16
Shmit, Nikolai Pavlovich, 12, 20, 24
Shmit, Yelizaveta Pavlovna, 20–21
Shorin, Vasily Ivanovich, 72, 73*n*4
Shuia, 151, 152, 154
Siberia, 127; Lenin in, 14
Simbirsk nobility: certificate from, 19
Skliansky, Yefraim Markovich, 54, 120
Smilga, I. T., 63, 65*n*8, 92
Smirnov, G. L., 4, 5, 64
Smirnov, Ivan Nikolaevich, 65, 66*n*19,
109, 115*n*31
Smirnov, Vladimir Mikhailovich, 64,
66*n*22
Smolianinov, V. A., 143
SNK. *See* Council of People's Commissars
Social Democratic Party, 20, 37. *See also*
Russian Social Democratic Labor Party
Socialist Internationals, 159
Socialist-Revolutionary Party (SRs), 41,
42, 104, 105, 153, 159–60, 168, 169.
See also Borotbists
Sokolnikov, Grigory Yakovlevich, 122,
122*n*1, 142, 144, 156, 181

Sotsial-Demokrat, 32, 35
Southern front, 70–73
Sovnarkom. *See* Council of People's Commissars
Spargo, John, 113, 115*n*38
Spartacists, 79
Speerd. *See* Spargo, John
SR Combat Organization, 25*n*2, 40*n*10
SRs. *See* Socialist-Revolutionary Party
Stalin, Iosif Vissarionovich, 1, 39, 40*n*12;
appointment as general secretary, 9–10;
about budget, 142; and Central Com-
mittee, 63, 166, 187; correspondence, 3;
about deportations, 168; and Galicia,
78; and Georgia, 119; Lenin and, 8, 9,
187–88; on Lenin editions, 2; medical
assessment of, 157; as member of trium-
virate, 9, 16, 22*n*6; on Rakovsky, 141;
on satellite regimes, 85; on Sokolnikov,
144, 181; with southern army, 7; and
Trotsky, 187; on Trotsky, 148, 166; on
Turkey, 121; work leaves for, 8, 147;
Yuriev and, 43–45
Stasova, Yelena Dmitrievna, 63, 65*n*3
State and Revolution (Lenin), 58
Steklov, Yury M., 176
Stomoniakov, Boris Spiridonovich, 132,
133*n*3
Struve, Pyotr Berngardovich, 14
Stuchka, Pyotr Ivanovich, 63, 65*n*5
Supplementary Treaty (Soviet-German),
47, 49, 53, 54
Supreme Allied Council, 139
Switzerland, 12, 56, 58

Taratuta, Viktor Konstantinovich, 23*n*2
Tashkent, 122
Teodorovich, I. A., 163, 164*n*3
Terek Regional Revolutionary Committee,
84
Ter-Gabrielian, Saak Mirzoevich, 46
Terror, 10, 14, 16, 55, 153; and kulaks,
50
Tikhon, Patriarch, 152, 154, 155*n*2
Tomsky, Mikhail Petrovich, 63, 65*n*6,
171
Trade unions, 113, 129, 149
Transcaucasia, 4, 92
Treaty of Brest-Litovsk, 42, 47
Triumvirate (troika), 8–9, 16, 22*nn*2, 6;
187
Troianovsky, A. A., 31*n*5

Trotsky, Lev Davidovich, 23n3, 170; on budget, 142–43; on churches, 150, 153–54, 155, 155n5; on deputy position, 171; on foreign trade, 187; on Genoa Conference, 162; on Gokhran, 164; Ioffe and, 47n1; Kamenev on, 166; Lenin on, 9–10, 70, 124, 166; medical assessment of, 157; on Murmansk, 42; offer to resign, 67–68, 69; opposition to, 22n6, 166, 187; on party economic management, 148–49; Red Army and, 69–70; on Rozhkov, 176; on slogans for Britain, 94; on Smirnov, V. M., 64; on southern front deployments, 70–73; on Stalin, 7, 148, 166; on weapons purchase, 136, 137, 183–84

Trotsky Papers, 2, 5

Tsaritsyn Province: Fuel Directorate, 136; Labor Committee, 125

Tseirei-Tsion, 128, 129n4

Tsiurupa, Aleksandr Dmitrievich, 171

Tsivtsivadze, I. B., 64, 66n21

Tukhachevsky, Mikhail Nikolaevich, 78, 129, 129n1

Tula, 70, 72, 73

Turkestan, 10, 74, 181

Turkey, 4, 8, 121, 180

Ufa, 108

Ukraine: communist policy in, 76–77; Denikin in, 70–72, 76; famine in, 11, 13, 133, 151; invasion of, 6, 89; Jews in, 76, 77; pogroms in, 117; reoccupation of, 75; timber in, 113; Trotsky on, 71

Ukrainian Soviet Socialist Republic, 76

Ulianov, Aleksandr, 14

Ulianova, Maria Ilinichna, 19, 165

Union of Metalworkers, 35

Unshlikht, Iosif Stanislavovich, 88, 133, 135, 154, 174

Vandervelde, Emile, 58

Vatsetis, I. I., 66

Versailles treaty, 7, 95, 101, 102, 103, 104, 111, 132, 170, 185

Vienna, 26; *Pravda* in, 23

Vigand, 185

Vigdorchik, N. A., 168

Viktor, 23, 23n2

Vilna, 86, 87, 92

Vladimirsky, Mikhail Fyodorovich, 56, 64, 66n20

Volga region, 72

Volkogonov, Dmitri A., 3, 151

Volksrecht, 59

Volodicheva, Maria Akimovna, 155

von Niedermayer, Oskar (Ritter). *See* Neumann

Vorovsky, V. V., 54–55

War Communism, 7, 124, 150

Warsaw, 7, 38, 100, 101, 104, 111, 179, 180

Weapons, purchase of, 125–26, 131–32, 135, 136, 137, 183–84

White armies, 7, 10, 44, 53, 67n1, 70, 74, 84, 98, 120, 179, 189; and Jews, 76

Wilhelm II, Kaiser, 101, 103, 114n16

Workers' Opposition, 93n2, 123

Working class: Lenin on, 10, 15, 123

Work leaves, 8, 147

Wrangel, Pyotr Nikolaevich, 89, 90, 94, 109, 111, 120

Yakovenko, V. G., 163, 164n2

Yaroslavsky, Yemelian, 64, 66n17, 188

Yegorov, A. I., 7, 68, 68n1

Yekaterinburg, 46, 119, 120, 182

Yekaterinodar, 70

Yekaterinoslav, 108

Yeltsin, Boris, 2

Yevdokimov, Georgy Yereemevich, 63, 65n10

Yudenich, Nikolai Nikolaevich, 74, 97, 99, 102, 106, 180

Yuriev, Aleksei Mikhailovich, 42, 43–45

Zemstvos, 84n1

Zhitomir, 117

Zilist, 117

Zimmerwald conference, 25, 55n1

Zinoviev, Grigory Yevseevich, 22n2; on Italy, 90; on Lenin, 41; Malinovsky and, 26n4, 37, 38–39; medical assessment of, 156; as member of Central Committee, 63, 165; as member of triumvirate, 16, 22n6; on Rozhkov, 176

Zubalovo, 164, 164n5

Zurich, 32, 59